THE
ALAMO CHAIN
OF MISSIONS

The sculptured exterior frame of the sacristy window of Mission San José, which is known the world over as San José's "Rose Window."

THE
ALAMO CHAIN
OF MISSIONS

A History of San Antonio's
Five Old Missions

By

Marion A. Habig

Revised Edition

FRANCISCAN HERALD PRESS
Publishers of Franciscan Literature
Chicago, Illinois 60609

Reprinted by
Pioneer Enterprises
Publishers of Specialized History Books

Library of Congress Cataloging-in-Publication Data
compiled by publisher:
Habig, Marion Alphonse
The Alamo Chain of Missions : a history of San Antonio's Five
Old Missions / Marion A. Habig
     p.   cm.
Includes bibliographic references, index, illustrations
and photographs

1. Title
2. Author
3. Missions — San Antonio
4. History — San Antonio (Tex.)
5. Spanish Colonial history
6. Texas — history — to 1846

F394.S2 1968   266.2764'351   68-54397

ISBN 0-9659012-1-1

First Edition 1968
Revised Edition 1976
Second Printing Revised Edition 1997
Third Printing Revised Edition 2004

Imprimi Potest: Germain Schwab O.F.M., *Minister Provinical*; Nihil
Obstat: Mark Hegener O.F.M., *Censor Deputatus*; Imprimatur: Rt. Rev.
Francis W. Byrne, Vicar General, Archdiocese of Chicago, June 24, 1968.
"The Nihil Obstat and Imprimatur are official declarations that a book
or pamphlet is free of doctrinal or moral error. No implication is contained
therein that those who have granted the Nihil Obstat and Imprimatur
agree with the contents, opinions, or statements expressed."

Pioneer Enterprises is dedicated to reprinting books which contribute to greater understanding of this nation's important cultural and natural touchstones which are preserved for future generations.

It is with great satisfaction that we are able to reprint *The Alamo Chain of Missions*. Our thanks to the Franciscan Press for this opportunity.

Pioneer Enterprises
13220-172 Houston Ave.
Hudson, Florida 34667-6149

PREFACE

San Antonio, Texas, which is celebrating its two hundred and fiftieth birthday in 1968, is the only city in the Americas that can say, it has five old Spanish missions—four of them within the city limits and one just outside its southern boundary. They are only two, or two and a half, miles apart. The distance from the first to the fifth is nine miles.

The first is the world-famous Alamo, in the heart of downtown San Antonio. Though it is better known as the cradle of Texas liberty, it was Mission San Antonio de Valero for seventy-five years in the eighteenth century, 1718-1793.

The second is Mission Nuestra Señora de la Purísima Concepción de Acuña, originally founded in eastern Texas in 1716 and moved to its present location in 1731. Its church is the oldest unrestored and unchanged edifice of its kind in the United States. It is still substantially the same as it was when it was completed in 1755. Situated on the east bank of the San Antonio River, it is two and a half miles south of the Alamo.

The third, two miles farther south on the west bank, is Mission San José y San Miguel de Aguayo, the Queen of the Missions, now a State and National Historic Site. Founded by Fr. Antonio Margil in 1720, the year of 1968 marks the two hundredth anniversary of the inception of its beautiful (restored) stone church.

The fourth, San Juan Capistrano, is two and a half miles farther on the east bank of the river. Like Mission Concepción, it was founded in eastern Texas in 1716 as Mission San José de los Nazonis, and moved to its present site in 1731. Although restored several times, its present little church is as old as that of Mission Concepción.

The fifth is Mission San Francisco de la Espada, two miles farther south on the west bank. It too was founded in 1716, as Mission San Francisco de los Neches, the second Mission of San Francisco in eastern Texas (the first having been San Francisco de los Tejas, 1690-1693); and it was moved to the San Antonio River in 1731. Its small, restored church was under construction in 1745 and completed before 1756; and its aqueduct across Piedra Creek, part of the mission's irrigation system, was likewise built in the 1740's.

In 1794, the year after the suppression of Mission San Antonio de Valero, the other four were partially secularized; but they continued to be missions for another three decades until 1824, when the final secularization took place.

The entire chain of five missions, therefore, was in existence for sixty-two years in the eighteenth century, 1731 to 1793; and the time from the founding of the first in 1718 to the secularization of the other four in 1824 covers a span of one hundred and six years.

During this period of more than a century, at least ninety-three Franciscan missionaries devoted themselves patiently and valiantly to the task of serving and developing these missions and through them to train the numerous tribes of the nomadic Coahuiltecan Indians in the ways of civilized life and the practice of the Christian religion.

Though the principal facts, events, and achievements of the five San Antonio missions are known, they have not always been presented with historical accuracy; and a satisfactory history of these missions has not been written so far. Even today their complete story cannot be told.

However, while engaged in research on Mission San José, the writer found much concerning this and the other four missions that has not hitherto been related in an orderly fashion. While the history of each of the five missions is similar to that of the others, it is not the same. It is not correct to say that if one has narrated the story of one of them, he has told all.

We have, therefore, assembled all we could find in available documentary sources concerning the five San Antonio missions and present a separate narrative of each of them. Some day in the uncertain future, it may be possible to write a more complete history of these missions; but at the present time, on the occasion of the two hundred and fiftieth anniversary of the founding of San Antonio and its observance by HemisFair '68, it is surely worth while to offer an authentic account of the San Antonio missions in as far as this can be done.

Since this book is published for the general reader as well as the historian, we have not encumbered the text with an array of references and footnotes; but the bibliography at the end is an exhaustive one. The scholar will thus be able to identify the primary sources from which all the facts and events related in this book have been taken.

In its five old missions, San Antonio possesses a treasure of inestimable value. They are not merely relics of a glorious past, but also an inspiration for the present and the future. An accurate and detailed account of their history cannot but elicit our admiration of what was accomplished and increase our appreciation of what still remains as invaluable historical monuments.

To the many friends who have aided the writer by their encouragement, advice, suggestions, and information, he wishes to express his sincere and heartfelt gratitude. This is their book as well as his.

M.A.H.

CONTENTS

Contents 13

ILLUSTRATIONS

PLANS AND DIAGRAMS

I

The Spanish Mission

"One of the marvels in the history of the modern world is the way in which that little Iberian nation, Spain, . . . by rapid yet steady advance, spread her culture, her religion, her law, and her language over more than half of the two American continents, where they still are dominant."

These words were written by Professor Herbert E. Bolton in 1917, in his brilliant essay on the Spanish Mission as a frontier institution. He went on to say, that "whoever undertakes to interpret the forces by which Spain extended her rule, her language, her law, and her traditions over the frontiers of her vast American possessions, must give close attention to the missions; for, in that work they constituted a primary agency."

What Was a Mission?

A Spanish mission was not merely a church and priest's house. Besides a church with a sacristy and an adjoining residence for one or two missionaries and guests, a mission comprised a granary, various workshops, dwellings for the Indian neophytes, and quarters for a few soldiers. These were built around a square or rectangular plaza; and where it was necessary, as was the case in the San Antonio missions, the entire complex was enclosed by a protecting and fortified wall. Often the buildings or some of them formed a part of the wall.

Outside the compound or square, there was a large farm and, at some distance, a big cattle ranch.

The first and principal task of the missionary was that of converting the pagan natives into good Christians. But it was his aim also to raise the aborigines from their primitive state, often characterized by a very low degree of culture, to that of civilized and responsible citizens of the Spanish empire. Lacking a sufficient number of colonists, the Spanish crown made use of the missions, together with the presidios which were established at strategic points, as frontier agencies to occupy and hold and settle its vast domains.

This was made possible by the union of church and state which existed in Spain. There were disagreements between the two, but there was also cooperation. For the establishment of a mission, the government bore the initial expense, providing church goods, tools, and some cattle, sheep, and horses. It also gave the missionary an annual allowance for his personal needs, usually the equivalent, more or less, of a private soldier's pay. Under the guidance of the missionary, the mission, if it was successful which was not always the case, developed into a communal, cooperative enterprise and a self-supporting and self-sufficient community and frontier settlement.

While the Indian policy of the government reflected a genuine interest in the welfare of the natives and sought to better their way of life, the Spanish crown and its representatives were more willing to assist and promote the work of the missions when they were needed to hold and expand the colonial territory of Spain. The missionaries, on the other hand, made all other ends subordinate to the one great objective of propagating the Christian Faith. Prompted by spiritual motives, they sought no earthly gain for themselves. Ultimately, that was the secret of their remarkable success and achievements and their amazing perseverance in the face of almost insuperable obstacles.

Far from being a hindrance, the all-absorbing religious motives of the missionaries enabled them to devote themselves unselfishly, with all the energies of mind and heart, to the work of introducing the natives to a way of civilized and dignified human existence no less than to teaching them the doctrine and practices of Christianity. They were as much interested in improving the Indians' temporal status as they were in promoting their eternal salvation. Thus the missions became, not only religious centers, but also training schools, in which the illiterate aborigines learned agriculture, animal husbandry, various crafts and trades, the Spanish language, the arts of singing, dancing, and playing musical instruments, and sometimes also reading and writing.

The mission was also a school of self-government and political science. When a mission pueblo was established, its civil as well as military officers were selected from the ranks of the Indians. Though the first officials were appointed, their successors were elected by the Indians for a one-year term. They were a *gobernador* (governor or mayor), the *alcaldes* (judges), and an *alguacil* (policeman). The military head was the *teniente* (captain), and he had his subalterns. Minor penalties for infringements of the mission rules were meted out by the officials under the watchful fatherly eye of the missionary. Eventually there were also Indian overseers in the workshops, on the farm, and at the ranch.

The missionary, however, remained completely in charge of the mission; and he ruled it with kindness and patience. He did not own anything that the mission had or produced. The mission Indians were the common owners, and the missionary administered everything for them, until the mission was secularized and its Indians became private landowners. The missionary was the mission Indians' superintendent, working for them without remuneration. Though the Indians rarely manifested sentiments of gratitude, they must have realized in the course of time that the missionary was a true friend of theirs. He was not only their spiritual shepherd, but also their teacher, doctor, counsellor, and protector.

Ordinarily the missionary was protected and aided by a guard of a few Spanish soldiers who also served as mayor-domos and teachers. The ultimate restraining force, if neces-sary, and the protection of the missionary and his charges, was the nearby presidio. There were instances, for example at Mission San José during its later years, when no Spanish soldiers were stationed at the mission; and reliable Indian soldiers then took their place. When there were two missionar-ies at a mission, an ideal arrangement which could not always be carried out, the superior devoted himself principally to spiritual affairs, and his assistant gave his attention particularly to temporal matters. The latter taught the Indians by his own example, working with them in the shops and on the farm.

In this way the missionaries were able to control a large number of natives who were persuaded to settle down and live in a mission. They were not forced to do this. However, discipline was absolutely necessary to maintain order, just as in any other school. Sometimes, especially in springtime, when the lure of the wild was a strong temptation for them, some of the Indians would run away. Accompanied by a protecting escort of soldiers from the presidio, and sometimes without such an escort, the missionary would go in search of his wayward and truant children; and finding them, he would induce the runaways to go back to the mission with him. More often than not, the fugitives would welcome their padre with joy and willingly return with him.

In a successful mission the natives of different tribes, who may have been hostile to each other, lived a peaceful, contented, carefree, and even idyllic life. The mission took care of all their needs. They had sufficient food, clothing, and lodging; attended divine services daily; were kept busy with moderate and rewarding work; enjoyed their recreational games, dances, and music. They got up with the sun; worked about four hours after breakfast until noon; took a siesta after dinner; worked about three hours in the afternoon from two to five; received instructions in Christian doctrine in the morning and evening; had their amusements and entertainment at the close of work days and on all Sundays and a great many feastdays.

Who Were the Missionaries?

Throughout the Spanish borderlands of the United States, the missionaries were Friars Minor, popularly known as Franciscans. The only exception was the Pimería Alta of northern Mexico which extended into what is now southern Arizona. This was a Jesuit mission field until the expulsion of the Jesuits from Spanish America in 1767; and then it too was entrusted to the care of the Franciscans.

In the sixteenth and seventeenth centuries the Spanish Franciscans were doing missionary work in Florida and Georgia, and in New Mexico and northern Arizona. In both regions they established about forty missions, some of which continued into the eighteenth and nineteenth centuries. The first nine missions in the present state of Texas were begun toward the end of the seventeenth century; and in the course of the eighteenth century no less than thirty additional missions, not counting the different sites of some of them as separate missions, were founded within the present confines of the state. The missionary conquest of Upper California, the present state, by Fr. Junípero Serra and his companions was started in 1769, when the Texas missions had begun to decline. The Franciscan chain of missions in Pimería Alta, including southern Arizona, was contemporary with that of California. Its outstanding mission, built by the Franciscans, was that of San Francisco Xavier del Bac near Tucson.

"Conspicuous in North America," wrote Professor Bolton, "were the great Franciscan establishments in Alta California, the last of Spain's conquests. Not here alone, however, but everywhere on the northern frontier they played their part—in Sinaloa, Sonora, and Lower California [where they succeeded the Jesuits and were followed by the Dominicans]; in Chihuahua, Coahuila, Nuevo León, and Nuevo Santander; in Florida, New Mexico, Texas, and Arizona. If there were twenty-one missions in California, there were as many in Texas, more in Florida, and twice as many in New Mexico. At one time the California missions had over thirty thousand Indians under instruction; but a century and a half earlier, the missions of Florida and New Mexico had an equal number."

Not only on the northern frontier, however, but throughout Latin America and the Far East the Franciscans played a leading role in the missionary conquest of the new lands. In 1700, the Franciscans of Spain and Portugal counted a total of 27,939 friars and 1,771 friaries; and of these, 10,802 friars and 927 friaries were in the colonies. They belonged to 57 regional units called provinces, of which 23 were in the New World and the Far East.

Toward the end of the seventeenth century and during the two following centuries, while the provinces continued to do missionary work, so-called Franciscan apostolic colleges were founded in Spain and America. They were smaller units, similar to the provinces, and drawing their membership largely from the provinces; and they were established for a twofold specialized purpose. Their members were missionaries who devoted themselves exclusively to the preaching of parish missions or renewals in Christian towns and cities, lasting usually a week or two, and to missionary work among the as yet unconverted pagan natives on the frontiers. To the work of converting and civilizing the Indians, these colleges gave a new impetus.

The number of Jesuits in Spanish America, when they were banished in 1767, was 2,260; and at that time they had 191 colleges, residences, and missions. In many instances, the

Franciscans had to take over the former Jesuits missions and care for them in addition to those which they had. Some two decades later, in 1786, the total number of Franciscans in Spanish America was 4,838. They belonged to 17 apostolic colleges and 17 provinces. The colleges were in charge of 227 missions, and the provinces had 221 missions, a total of 438.

Who Are the Franciscans?

The Franciscans were, and are today, the followers of St. Francis of Assisi, the medieval saint who is still admired and loved by many in our modern age. St. Francis founded his First Order of Friars Minor or Franciscans in 1209. He also founded a Second Order, the contemplative Poor Ladies or Poor Clares, and a Third Order for people living in their homes and following secular avocations. From the latter, after the death of St. Francis, developed another religious order of friars and numerous congregations of brothers and especially sisters engaged in works of mercy.

The Franciscans are not monks, though they are often called that. They are friars, who are not attached to a monastery or abbey but go wherever they are sent. They devote themselves to an active apostolate among the people, especially the poor and needy. However, like St. Francis, a friar tries to combine his work with a life of prayer; and hence the Friars Minor have not inappropriately been called "contemplatives in the market-place." They commit themselves to a literal observance of the Gospel and bind themselves to a life of celibacy, obedience, and poverty. They renounce the ownership of everything they have and use, and accept what is given them for their needs as an alms. Since the time of St. Francis, who was Christian Europe's first foreign missionary since apostolic times, the Franciscans have been particularly active in the missionary countries of the world.

Since 1517, the Friars Minor are divided into two autonomous branches, namely the Franciscans simply so called, and formerly known as Observants, and the Conventuals. A third branch, the Capuchins, came into existence in 1528. Subsequently several stricter groups, such as the Alcantarines or Discalced Friars of Spain and Portugal, were founded within the ranks of the Observants or Franciscans; but they never became independent groups. They were merged with the Franciscans in 1897, when the minor existing differences were abolished.

At one time (in 1768), the Franciscans had 167 provinces in the world and a total membership of 77,000. Today (1967) they have 2,748 friaries in the world and 26,666 members. That is less than there were in Spain and Portugal in 1700. But the Franciscans are still the second largest religious order of men, being outnumbered only by the Jesuits. However, if the separate orders of Conventuals and Capuchins are added, the First Order of St. Francis is the most numerous.

As in the past, the Franciscans of today regard missionary work as one of their main activities. The latest statistics (1967) show that they have charge of 115 mission fields in all parts of the world — Europe, Africa, Asia, the Americas, and Oceania. A total of 3,932 friars, priests and brothers, have the care of 2,042 individual missions and additional mission stations, in which there are 690 churches and 2,691 chapels. In these missions, 61,418 catechumens are under instruction. The number of friaries in the mission countries is 985.

The San Antonio Missions

While the San Antonio missions constituted only a small part of the Franciscans' missionary work in the eighteenth century, their story forms a glorious chapter, hitherto but little known, in the annals of the Franciscan Order, of Spain, and of our country.

Constantly harassed by marauding Apaches and Comanches, these missions were never able to congregate as many Indians as did the later California missions, where as many as two thousand natives were assembled in a single mission. In their best days, the San Antonio missions never had more than two hundred to three hundred and fifty Indians in each of the five.

The Indians of the San Antonio missions belonged to numerous small tribes of Coahuiltecan stock, each speaking a different dialect. Fr. Ortiz wrote in 1745 that more than two hundred tribes were represented in these missions, and they spoke twenty different languages. It was impossible for any missionary to learn all of them. However, the Indians were able to understand each other to some extent; and the missionaries succeeded in reducing their many dialects to a common Coahuiltecan language. One of them wrote a manual in this language for his confreres, and it was printed in Mexico in 1760.

Though the Coahuiltecan Indians were nomads of a very low degree of culture, the missionaries had more success with them than with the more advanced Tejas, a name given to a large number of tribes in central and eastern Texas. Within a generation, especially at Mission San José, they succeeded in making many of the natives devout Christians, good craftsmen, farmers, ranchers, and loyal citizens of Spain. The mission Indians were able to speak the Spanish language, manage their own affairs, and sing and dance as well as the Spaniards. This was indeed a remarkable achievement.

Not counting San José, which was in the care of the College of Zacatecas, the other four San Antonio missions, which were in the hands of missionaries from the College of Querétaro, in 1745 had a total of 5,115 head of cattle, 3,325 sheep and goats, about 257 horses, and 86 yokes of oxen. On their farms they raised annually 5,333 bushels of corn, 226 bushels of beans, 2,000 pounds of cotton. This record prompted Professor Bolton to declare that "the most conspicuous work of the period was that done by the missionaries."

By 1745, also, in the four Querétaran missions, 2,282 Indians had been baptized; and of the 885 Indians living in these missions, 141 were preparing for baptism.

It was in the 1740's that the five San Antonio missions entered upon their most flourishing period. A quarter of a century later they began to decline for reasons beyond the control of the missionaries. In 1773 the Querétaran missionaries left Texas to work in Pimería Alta, and turned over their four missions to the College of Zacatecas, which had the care of Mission San José from the beginning. Mission San Antonio was suppressed in 1793. In the other four, a modified form of secularization was carried out the following year; but they continued to be missions until their final secularization three decades later, in 1824.

It may be well to add that the Franciscan missionaries of the San Antonio missions did not wear a dark brown habit, that is a tunic with a white cord and a detachable capuch, as do those of today. The religious garb of the missionaries from the apostolic colleges had a grey color, that of undyed wool. The habit worn by the members of the Franciscan provinces of New Spain had a light blue color, with the exception of the Alcantarine Province of San Diego which had a light brown or coffee-colored garment. The dark brown habit was introduced for all Franciscans in 1897. At that time the greater number of Franciscans already wore a garment of that color.

It should be kept in mind also that the San Antonio missions were situated at the western end of the Spanish Province of Texas. The territory lying between San Antonio and the Rio Grande belonged in colonial times to the Province of Coahuila. When the Province of Nuevo Santander, the present State of Tamaulipas, was established in 1746, it extended across the lower Rio Grande all the way along the

Gulf coast to the lower San Antonio and Guadalupe rivers; but in 1775 its boundary was moved west to the Nueces.

The Province of Texas comprised what lay north and east as far as the Sabine River and beyond. The Presidio of Los Adaes, founded near present Robeline, Louisiana, in 1721, was the capital of the province until 1773, when San Antonio de Béxar was officially made the capital and the residence of the governor. However, the Governor's Palace in San Antonio, which was restored in 1929-1930, was built in 1749. In the same year or the following the first parish church of Villa de San Fernando was likewise completed.

The church of Mission San Antonio, or the Alamo, as completed by the U. S. Army in 1848. (H. L. Summerville photo; courtesy of San José Mission Friary.)

II

Mission San Antonio de Valero
1718-1793

Two and a half centuries ago San Antonio, Texas, was founded on the west bank of the San Antonio River near San Pedro Springs. On May 1, 1718, the Mission of San Antonio de Valero was formally founded, and four days later the Presidio and Villa of San Antonio de Béxar were established. Officially the founder was Don Martín de Alarcón, Governor of Coahuila and "Governor of Texas and such other lands as might be conquered." But he merely carried out the instructions he received from the viceroy of New Spain; and he did so only after a delay of an entire year.

The true founder, not only of the mission but also of the presidio and villa, was a Franciscan missionary of the College of Querétaro, Fr. Antonio de San Buenaventura y Olivares. Dr. Castañeda wrote of him that "he may justly be called the true father of the idea," that is, "of the founding of a mission and the establishment of the nucleus for a civil government on the San Antonio River. It was he and no other who conceived the plan, succeeded in winning the approval of the viceroy, and was instrumental in obtaining the final authorization of the project. Ever since 1709, he had longed for an opportunity to put his plan into execution." We may add that it was ever since 1700.

Fr. Antonio Olivares

Before he joined the College of Querétaro, which was founded in 1683, Fr. Olivares had been a missionary of the Franciscan Province of Zacatecas for many years. Although advanced in years, he was sent in 1699 to the Mission of San Juan Bautista, recently founded in Coahuila, north of present Sabinas, Mexico. For reasons beyond his control, he was forced to abandon the mission soon afterwards and to retire with his companion to Mission Nuestra Señora de los Dolores, near present Lampazos.

Nothing daunted, Fr. Olivares then undertook the establishment of another Mission San Juan Bautista on the west side of the Rio Grande, not far from Eagle Pass, Texas. With two companions he arrived at this place on January 1, 1700, and named it the Valle de Circuncisión. After founding the new mission with more than five hundred Indians of the same tribes as those who had been gathered on the Sabinas, Fr. Olivares left it in the care of his companions and made an expedition into the present state of Texas. Incidentally, this expedition is not mentioned by historians among those made into Texas in the early eighteenth century.

Accompanied by Captain José de Urrutia and a few soldiers, Fr. Olivares traveled some thirty leagues (75 miles) after crossing the Rio Grande and went as far as the Rio Frio. Here and on the way he found numerous friendly and docile Indians who were willing and anxious to settle down in one or more missions. Fr. Olivares would have liked to remain on the Rio Frio, but the distance from San Juan Bautista was too great. With the firm hope and intention of establishing new missions in this part of Texas later on, he returned to the Rio Grande.

At this time Bishop Felipe Chaves Galindo of Guadalajara was visiting the establishments in Coahuila; and Fr. Olivares personally made a report to him about his trip into Texas and the prospects of new missions in that area. On Easter Day, 1701, the bishop convoked a meeting of the missionaries and officials of Coahuila; and it was decided that a presidio and additional missions should be established near San Juan Bautista Mission as a stepping stone for new missions beyond the Rio Grande.

The bishop prepared a memorial in which he requested the viceroy, Don José Sarmiento de Valladares, Conde de Moctezuma to establish a presidio on the Rio Grande; and Fr. Olivares was chosen to go to Mexico City in order to present the matter to the viceroy. He succeeded in obtaining the necessary approval; and the Presidio of San Juan Bautista was established near the mission of the same name. In accordance with the viceroy's orders, the presidios of Nueva Vizcaya and Coahuila provided a total of thirty soldiers for the new presidio; and these were placed under the command of Captain Diego Ramón.

Returning from Mexico City, Fr. Olivares stopped at Querétaro, where Fr. Francisco Hidalgo was then the Fr. Guardian of the College. With two new missionaries, he went back to Mission San Juan Bautista and Mission San Francisco Solano nearby. A third mission, San Bernardo (of which the ruins are still standing) was founded in the vicinity early in 1702. For the latter the Duquesa de Sessa, wife of the viceroy, donated the church furnishings. For Mission San Francisco Solano Fr. Olivares had also brought along such furnishings from Mexico City.

Mission San Francisco Solano

With the founding of San Francisco Solano, which had taken place as early as March 1, 1700, Mission San Antonio de Valero may be said to have had its beginning. For it was this mission which was later transferred to the San Antonio River.

At San Francisco Solano and the other two missions, churches of adobe with adjoining residences for the padres, were constructed; irrigation ditches were dug; and farms were cultivated. In a short time, Fr. Olivares gathered at his mission more than three hundred Indians, not counting little children, namely Jarames, Siabanes, and Payoguanes. In the morning and in the evening, he instructed them in Christian doctrine; and soon he was able to baptize more than 150 of them.

All three missions prospered to such an extent that it was found they were too close together. In 1703, therefore, Fr. Olivares moved San Francisco Solano to the Valle de San Ildefonso, sixteen leagues (forty miles) west of San Juan Bautista. Only a few Jarames went along to the new site; but about four hundred Indians of various tribes were quickly assembled, and success crowned the efforts of Fr. Olivares during the next three years.

In 1706 Fr. Olivares was elected Fr. Guardian of the College for a term of three years. Two years later, young Fr. Isidro Félix de Espinosa reported to him that 140 Indian families (about 420 persons) were living at Mission San Juan Bautista, 200 families (about 600 persons) at San Bernardo, and about 400 Indians at San Francisco Solano. But later that year, all the mission Indians except a few Jarames fled into the mountains because of the nearness of the barbarous and cruel Tobosos. Not long afterwards eight Jarames were killed five miles from the mission.

The furnishings of the church were then taken to San Juan Bautista for safekeeping, but the mission was not abandoned entirely. A Franciscan brother of the Third Order of St. Francis remained with a few Jarames for an entire year, instructed them morning and evening, and helped them to maintain the farm. On feast days a missionary from San Juan Bautista traveled to San Francisco Solano to celebrate holy Mass and to baptize the sick and the children. He made the trip of eighty miles in twenty-four hours, because his services were needed on the Rio Grande, where the missionaries had the spiritual care also of the presidio.

A new missionary from Querétaro was then assigned to San Francisco Solano; but all his efforts to restore the mission to its former status failed, and it was moved once more back to the Rio Grande to a place called San José. This was three leagues (seven and a half miles) distant from the other two missions. An adobe church was built and some of the fugitive Indians came back, since they had the protection of the nearby presidio.

The Expedition of 1709

Ever since 1693, when the first two missions which had been founded in eastern Texas had to be abandoned, one of the missionaries who had taken part in the venture, Fr. Francisco Hidalgo, while continuing his work in Coahuila and serving as guardian of the College (1701-1703), had persistently advocated by every means at his disposal the reestablishment of missions among the friendly Tejas and the permanent occupation of the Province of Texas.

During the last year of his term as guardian at the College (1709), Fr. Olivares was informed by Fr. Espinosa about a report that the Tejas or some of them had moved to the Colorado River, which was much closer to the Rio Grande. Fr. Olivares not only agreed that it was worth while to investigate the correctness of the report but joined Fr. Espinosa and Captain Pedro de Aguirre of the San Juan Bautista Presidio in an expedition to the Colorado.

From the diary which Fr. Espinosa kept during this expedition we learn that the report rested only on the fact that the Tejas sometimes wandered as far as the Colorado on their buffalo hunts. On the way, however, the party crossed the San Antonio River near San Pedro Springs, and found it an ideal spot for a Spanish settlement and mission.

Unaware of the fact that in 1691 Fr. Damian Massanet and Domingo Terán de los Ríos had already given the name of San Antonio to the river and to an Indian village which they found on its banks, Frs. Olivares and Espinosa, by a happy coincidence, likewise named the river the Rio de San Antonio.

More important, however, was Fr. Olivares' decision that not only should the missions among the Tejas be re-established, but one or more missions should be founded also on the Rio San Antonio near the springs. This center would serve as a halfway station between San Juan Bautista and eastern Texas as well as the headquarters for missionary work among the other Indians of Texas, including those he had encountered near the Rio Frio in 1700.

After completing his term as guardian in 1709, Fr. Olivares was sent to Spain to recruit new missionaries for Texas. After his return, he resumed his work at Mission San Francisco Solano, and looked forward to the day when his plans for Texas could be realized.

Fr. Olivares in Mexico City

When six missions were finally established in eastern Texas in 1716 and 1717, with the cooperation of the College of Nuestra Señora de Guadalupe de Zacatecas, Fr. Olivares did not go along. Instead he was sent again to Mexico City to obtain from the viceroy fuller governmental support for the new missions in eastern Texas and to propose his own plan for a mission, presidio, and settlement on the Rio de San Antonio.

Fr. Olivares arrived in the capital late in September, 1716, and remained until December 28. He had a conference with the new viceroy, the Marqués de Valero, Don Baltazar de Zúñiga, and presented two written memorials. The first was concerning eastern Texas. In the second, dated November 20, he proposed to move his Mission of San Francisco Solano from the west side of the Rio Grande to the Rio de San Antonio. There were only a few Christian Jarame Indians at San

Francisco Solano, but these would be very helpful as teachers of the pagan Indians who would be congregated at the new site. He envisioned the latter as numbering from three to four thousand. He asked for a guard of ten soldiers until the Indians had been assembled on the San Antonio River; and he suggested that civilians of Mexico be induced to form a settlement near the mission by offering them free land and water rights.

After consulting his advisors, the viceroy gave his approval to all of Fr. Olivares' requests; and on December 7, he appointed Don Martín de Alarcón (who was already governor of Coahuila since August 5) governor also of Texas, for the purpose of bringing aid to the missions of eastern Texas and of helping Fr. Olivares to establish the mission on the San Antonio, near which he was to found a presidio and a settlement.

On December 28, Fr. Olivares presented a petition for supplies; and the same day he left for Querétaro, where he selected two companions, Fr. Francisco Ruiz and Brother Pedro Maleta, who were to assist him at the new Mission of San Antonio. Leaving Querétaro with them on February 9, 1717, he reached Saltillo on March 24; but Governor Alarcón was still in Mexico City and did not arrive at his capital until June. Fr. Olivares went on to Monterrey, and from there to San Juan Bautista, which he reached on May 3.

Waiting for Governor Alarcón

Governor Alarcón was taking his time; but there was no need for Fr. Olivares to wait for him as long as he received the escort and guard of ten soldiers, which the viceroy had granted him. He asked the captains of the presidios of San Juan Bautista and of Coahuila for ten soldiers, but both refused to supply the men.

Fr. Olivares' long disappointing wait had begun; and he did his waiting at Mission San Francisco Solano, which was to be transferred to the Rio de San Antonio. He had to wait almost a full year. Who could remain patient that long? And there were other disappointments besides that of waiting. It was a sore trial for Fr. Olivares, who was a veteran missionary, far advanced in age; and during this period of waiting, his companion Fr. Francisco Ruiz died. Only Brother Pedro Maleta remained to help him establish the new mission.

On June 5, 1717, Fr. Olivares wrote a letter to Alarcón. The governor found it waiting for him when he arrived in Saltillo. In it Fr. Olivares told him about the refusal of the presidio captains to supply ten soldiers; but Alarcón did not reply.

After the governor came to San Juan Bautista on August 3, he assigned eight soldiers to Fr. Olivares at Mission San Francisco Solano to guard the supplies the missionary had gathered; but they were careless guards and had instructions to take orders only from the governor, not the missionary.

As many as 150 Indians from the San Antonio area came to visit Fr. Olivares. Would a mission really be established on the Rio de San Antonio? Why the delay? They were anxious to settle down at the new mission.

About the middle of September, Fr. Olivares wrote a letter to Alarcón, and begged him to furnish the ten soldiers so he could go on alone. But the governor replied that he could not spare the men. It would have been foolhardy to try to make the transfer from Mission San Francisco Solano to the new mission on the San Antonio without the military escort; and so Fr. Olivares had to keep on waiting,—waiting until the spring of the following year.

Finally on February 16, 1718, Alarcón and his party of 72 persons, including three missionaries and the soldiers (of whom only six, according to Fr. Mezquía, were taking along their families), crossed the Rio Grande and then stopped there for another seven weeks. Fr. Olivares was not among the missionaries. The eight guards assigned to his mission would now have to serve as an escort anyway; and Fr. Olivares preferred to make the journey to the San Antonio River independently of Alarcón's expedition.

The missionaries with Alarcón were: Fr. Pedro de Mesquía, who had been a missionary in Coahuila and later (1724-1727) was the guardian of the College of Querétaro; Fr. Joseph Guerra, who had just completed his term of office as guardian of the College of Zacatecas (1713-1717) and was now once more a member of the College of Querétaro; and Fr. Francisco de Céliz, a missionary in Coahuila, of the Franciscan Province of Zacatecas, who served as the chaplain and diarist of Alarcón's expedition. Fr. Mesquía also kept a short diary.

On April 9 (the 7th, according to Fr. Mesquía) Alarcón's party finally got under way. Besides a herd of cattle, they were taking along 548 horses, of whom 300 as well as most of the cattle had been furnished by the Marqués de Aguayo from his huge ranch in Coahuila.

On April 15, special instructions from the viceroy were delivered to Alarcón. The latter misinterpreted them and changed the direction of his march toward Lavaca Bay until the 23rd, when he reversed his decision and headed for San Pedro Springs and the San Antonio River, arriving there on the 25th.

Fr. Mesquía says the water of the springs was sweet, and the place was very pleasant because of the trees that surrounded the springs. The volume of water at the point where the flow from the two springs met to form San Pedro Creek was five and a half feet wide and four feet deep; and though the stream had a swift current, the water could easily be led off to irrigate "good and sufficient lands."

On the basis of an ancient tradition, it has been claimed that some Spaniards from Mexico had settled at San Pedro Springs without authorization, long before Alarcón's arrival, as early as 1715 or 1716.

Founding of Mission San Antonio

For some reason or other, Fr. Olivares and Brother Maleta with their escort of soldiers and some Jarame Indians did not leave the former San Francisco Solano Mission until April 18; but they probably covered the distance to San Antonio in half the time that it took Alarcón and thus arrived about the same time as the governor's party.

Anyhow, Fr. Olivares immediately constructed a temporary mission chapel with the aid of three Jarame Indians. Fr. Mesquía says it was located about a mile south of San Pedro Springs, on high ground, near a small grove of oak trees, where they found Fr. Olivares building a hut for himself. Fr. Céliz writes that the site which Fr. Olivares picked for his mission was almost two miles south of the springs, along San Pedro Creek, on the west side of San Antonio River.

Dr. Castañeda remarks that, "since the mission stayed at its first location, the chronicler meant river where he says creek." However, we have the testimony of Fr. Isidro Félix de Espinosa that Frs. Mesquía and Céliz did not make a mistake; the first location of the mission, he writes, was on the west bank of the San Antonio River, and only after about a year did Fr. Olivares transfer it to the east side, where the land was better and it could more easily be irrigated.

The formal founding of Mission San Antonio de Valero by Governor Alarcón, with the usual ceremonies, did not take place until May 1; and four days later, the governor officially established the Presidio of San Antonio de Béxar and the Villa de Béxar near San Pedro Springs. According to the governor's own statement, the Villa comprised only ten families, and twenty more came to San Antonio later. In 1722 the Marqués de Aguayo moved the presidio and villa to the west side of the San Antonio River, 555½ feet from the bank, opposite the mission which was then on the east side.

Among those who were present at the founding of Mission San Antonio was Fr. Miguel Núñez de Haro, later one of the first two missionaries of Mission San José y San Miguel de Aguayo. Because of the dilatory ways of Alarcón, the missions in eastern Texas were in dire straits by the end of 1717. Only then was Fr. Núñez commissioned to take a train of supplies with an escort of soldiers to eastern Texas from San Juan Bautista. When they reached the Trinity, it had overflowed its banks and looked like the sea. It was impossible to cross the river. At the cost of great hardships, Fr. Núñez waited for two months, then hid the supplies, and gave a letter to a Tejas Indian for the missionaries in eastern Texas. On the return trip Fr. Núñez met Alarcón west of the Medina on April 21, and went along to San Antonio. He administered the first baptism at the new mission to a dying child on the day of its founding, May 1.

"Valero" was added to the name of the mission, because the Marquis de Valero was the viceroy of New Spain at the time; and "Béxar" honored the memory of the viceroy's brother, one of Spain's heroes, the Duke of Béxar, who died in the defense of Budapest against the Turks.

In June, 1718, says Fr. Olivares, there were six missionaries at the San Antonio Mission. They were, besides Fr. Olivares himself and Brother Maleta, Fr. Núñez and the three priests who had come with Alarcón, Frs. Mesquía, Guerra, and Céliz.

Another missionary passed through San Antonio during the first part of July. He was Fr. Pedro Múñoz, the president or superior of the missions at San Juan Bautista. He had left the latter place on June 27, and on July 21 arrived with a new train of supplies at the place where Fr. Núñez had hid his. Not only did he find the latter intact, but he also met Fr. Espinosa and Captain Ramón who had come to fetch them. The letter which Fr. Núñez had given to the Tejas Indian had finally been delivered.

Fr. Espinosa, who was the president of the three Querétaran missions in eastern Texas, and Captain Ramón, learning that Mission San Antonio and the Villa de Béxar had been established, went to the new foundation to welcome Governor Alarcón, and arrived August 27. With them came the chiefs of 23 tribes who had been in revolt, but now offered their allegiance to the new governor.

Beginning of the Mission

At Mission San Antonio, however, the Indians who had been so desirous to have a mission were slow in coming. In fact, they had suddenly become hostile. In a letter which he wrote to the viceroy on June 22, 1718, Fr. Olivares mentioned the fact that Alarcón had treated his Indian guide so badly that the latter ran away after they reached San Antonio and joined the Indians of the vicinity; and Alarcón had made the threat that if the Indians would not come to the mission, he would go in search of them and put them to the sword. That was no doubt one reason why the Indians did not come.

Accompanied by 29 persons, including Frs. Espinosa, Guerra, and Céliz, Alarcón made a side trip to Lavaca Bay in September, 1718. Returning to San Antonio, he finally set out for eastern Texas on September 28. Fr. Núñez may have gone along with the others. At any rate, Fr. Olivares was now the only priest in San Antonio. But, with the help of Brother Maleta and his Jarame friends, he was able to gather a large number of Payaya and Pamaya Indians at Mission San Antonio de Valero during the months that followed.

When Alarcón returned on January 12, 1719, to San Antonio from eastern Texas, without having accomplished anything worth while there to the missionaries' great disappointment, he found numerous Indians at Fr. Olivares' mission, gave them gifts, and appointed Indian officials for the pueblo. He was edified on seeing the Indians assemble for prayer when the mission bell was rung. He had brought along a bell that he had found on the site of the first mission of San Francisco which had been abandoned in 1693. It weighed about 150 pounds. The entire month of January was spent in digging irrigation ditches for the presidio-villa and the mission.

Although Mission San Antonio and a little presidio and villa were established, the Alarcón expedition, expensive though it was, had accomplished little; and not only Fr. Olivares but also the other missionaries were altogether dissatisfied with the governor. Returning to Saltillo, Alarcón asked the viceroy for more soldiers; and when his request was not granted he tendered his resignation early in 1719. The viceroy accepted it immediately, but Alarcón continued in office until the end of the year.

Accident of Fr. Olivares

It must have been in the spring of 1719 that Fr. Olivares had a serious accident. Fr. Espinosa tells us about it in his *Crónica,* which was printed in 1746-1747. "At the mission's first location," he writes, "Fr. Olivares maintained himself for more than a year; and in the beginning he did not have a priest companion, because the one who had been assigned to him died before his departure from the Rio Grande. During this time, he suffered an accident as he passed over a wooden bridge, covered with earth, which was near the mission. The beast on which he was riding broke through with one leg; and the blow that the father received as he fell was such that it broke one of his legs.

"This put him in the greatest danger, and it was necessary to send a messenger to the missions on the Rio Grande to get a confessor. Riding on a beast, Fr. Pedro Múñoz came immediately and with such speed that in forty continuous hours he covered the eighty leagues (200 miles) which, according to the soldiers, is the distance from the Rio Grande to San Antonio. The presence of a priest at his side gave much consolation to the sick man; and after he had made his confession he could give greater attention to the care of his leg.

"The Lord was kind to him and enabled one of the soldiers to promote the knitting of the broken bone by the application of home remedies. The father had to remain in bed for a long time, but in the end the leg was entirely healed. After he had fully recovered, the father moved the mission to the other side of the San Antonio River, because it offered greater advantages. There the mission has continued down to the present day and enjoyed much success."

Missionaries at San Antonio

The transfer of the mission to the east side of the river probably took place in June or July, 1719. At that time Fr. Pedro Múñoz paid another visit to Fr. Olivares, and brought along an assistant in the person of Father Joseph Andrés Rodríguez de Jesús María. These two, at any rate, made no less than twenty-one entries in San Antonio's register of baptisms at the end of June and the early part of July. There is also one entry by Fr. Olivares, for June 28, showing that he had recuperated by that time. There are thirty-six entries by Fr. Rodríguez also in 1720, indicating that this missionary remained with Fr. Olivares.

Mission San Antonio soon proved its worth as a halfway station. In October-November, 1719, the missionaries, soldiers, and settlers of eastern Texas came to San Antonio as refugees. France and Spain were at war, and the French in the colonies learned about it before the Spaniards. The French of Natchitoches had seized the Mission of San Miguel and were on the point of taking the other five as well.

The two Fr. Presidents, Espinosa and Margil, wanted to stay, but the others all thought it best to retreat; and so they too were forced to abandon the missions temporarily. The refugees remained in San Antonio until 1721, when the

Marqués de Aguayo and his army of 500 came and re-established the presidio and six missions in eastern Texas and added another presidio at San Miguel de los Adaes.

During the year 1720 there was no lack of assistants, Zacatecan as well as Querétaran, at Mission San Antonio; but the aged founder had now accomplished his great task — the establishment of this mission on a firm basis. The Fr. Guardian of the College of Querétaro decided that it was time for Fr. Olivares to retire to the College for a well deserved rest.

In the register of baptisms of Mission San Antonio we read that on September 8, 1720, by order of the Fr. Guardian Diego de Alcántara, Fr. Olivares turned over the mission to his successor, Fr. Francisco Hidalgo, one of the refugees from eastern Texas. Fr. Olivares went back to Querétaro; and two years later, on June 7, 1722, he died at the College.

Assisted by Fr. Joseph González, Fr. Hidalgo remained in charge of Mission San Antonio for about four years. He welcomed the Marqués de Aguayo when he arrived in San Antonio in 1721 and paid a visit to the mission on April 26. Aguayo found no less than 240 Indians, young and old, residing at the mission; and to all of them he distributed "clothing and other articles which they value highly."

Fr. Hidalgo went back to Mission San Juan Bautista on the Rio Grande in 1724; and there he died on November 6, 1726, at the age of 67 years. To him and to Fr. Olivares must be given the credit, in great measure, for the permanent occupation of the Spanish Province of Texas during the years from 1716 to 1722.

Second and Third Site of the Mission

When Fr. Olivares moved Mission San Antonio from the west bank of the river to its east bank in the summer of 1719, he did not establish it at its present site. The mission was moved once more some years later to the place it now occupies, namely Alamo Plaza. That much is certain. In his report of 1756, Fr. Ortiz tells us that in the time of Fr. Margil (who was at the mission in 1719-1721) Mission San Antonio was situated "a distancia de mas de una quadra de la Mision" (at a distance of more than a block from the mission's site in 1756).

Charles Ramsdell, who has identified the first site of Mission San Antonio as having been near the present-day Chapel of the Miracles (at the corner of Ruiz and Laredo streets), also tells us that "the second location was very near today's Alamo, about where the Alamo Ditch would cross East Commerce Street, where the Alameda, the avenue lined with cottonwoods, would be laid out in 1805, and where St. Joseph's Church stands."

The same writer assures us, there is documentary evidence that the second transfer of the mission to its final site in Alamo Plaza took place in 1724, after a hurricane had destroyed the mission, then consisting of huts and a small stone tower (*San Antonio, A Historical and Pictorial Guide*, pp. 16-17).

Others claim that the final location was the mission's fourth site and there was a third, "two gun-shots distance" from the second (Lon Tinkle in *Six Missions of Texas*, p. 9). This opinion cannot be correct, since the later reports of 1745, 1762, and 1777, speaking of the third and final site of Mission San Antonio, all use the same expression, "a distance of two gun shots," to indicate how far the mission was from the church of Villa de San Fernando.

Successors of Fr. Hidalgo

Fr. Joseph González, who had been Father Hidalgo's assistant, remained at Mission San Antonio until 1726. Because of his eagerness to begin missionary work among the Apaches, he became involved in a disagreement with Captain Flores of the presidio. According to Fr. Miguel Sevillano de Paredes, who resided at Mission San Antonio in 1726 as *presidente* and was elected guardian of the College of Querétaro the following year, Fr. González "perished on the road from Texas to the Rio Grande" before August of 1728.

When Brigadier General Rivera visited San Antonio in 1727, he found conditions at the presidio to be in good order; and at the mission, where Fr. Benito Sánchez was in charge, there were 273 resident Indians. While the building of a friary of stone had been commenced, the church was still a temporary structure. Much work had been done on an irrigation ditch two and a half miles long.

During the years 1728 to 1733, the missionary who made most of the entries in the baptismal register at Mission San Antonio was Fr. Juan Salvador de Amaya. As a Franciscan priest of the Province of Jalisco, he joined the College of Querétaro in 1728, and in the same year was assigned to the Mission of San Antonio. He served as a missionary in Texas for 24 years, until his death which occurred on November 17, 1752.

Fr. Benito de Santa Ana Fernández, who was the Fr. President of the Querétaran missions in Texas from 1733 to 1750, also resided at Mission San Antonio for three years before he became president and established his headquarters at Mission Nuestra Señora de la Purísima Concepción.

Both Fr. Amaya and Fr. Fernández had encounters with the Apaches who frequently attacked travelers and made raids on the missions and the presidio and settlement. On January 9, 1731, Fr. Amaya and Brother Francisco Bustamente were going with a small party from San Antonio to the Rio Grande when they were suddenly attacked by about fifty Apaches near the Medina River. The savages killed a woman and carried off a child. The others escaped with their lives, but lost their baggage and many of their horses and pack animals.

On June 25 of the same year, Fr. Fernández and Brother Estevan Sáenz Monge, were making the same trip with an escort of five soldiers when a band of Apaches swooped down upon them, killed two of the soldiers, and ran off with the

Copyrighted 1900

The church of Mission San Antonio de Valero, or the Alamo, about 1847. (Painting by Theodore Gentilz in the Daughters of the Republic of Texas Library at the Alamo.)

baggage and all the horses. If Brother Estevan had not been wearing a leather shield he too would have been killed or wounded.

Another missionary of the San Antonio mission, Fr. Francisco de Frias, going to the Rio Grande, on September 20, 1736, with an escort of ten soldiers, met a large group of Apaches at Atascoso, about 35 miles south of San Antonio. They were able to hold off the enemy, although the captain of the soldiers and a friendly Indian were wounded. Fearful of another assault, they retraced their steps to San Antonio. Despite the persistent hostility of the Apaches, the missionaries were opposed to military campaigns against them. They hoped to establish friendly relations with them and to make Christians of them.

While Frs. Amaya and Fernández were at Mission San Antonio, in 1731, the Villa de Béxar at the presidio became the town of San Fernando. This development took place on March 9, when fifteen families from the Canary Islands, comprising a total of 55 persons, joined those who had already settled near the presidio.

In the same month and year, the three Querétaran missions of eastern Texas were moved to the San Antonio River, one between the San Antonio and San José missions, and the other two below the latter. Thus, within a distance of nine miles, there were now five missions.

Governor Franquis de Lugo

When General Rivera's recommendations were approved in 1729, the soldiers who were serving as guards at the missions in Texas were removed; but, at the request of the missionaries, these were restored the following year. In 1731 there were two soldiers at San Antonio, two at San José, and three at each of the other three on the San Antonio River.

The tempestuous Governor Carlos Franquis Benites de Lugo, who arrived in San Antonio in September, 1736, once more removed the guards at missions San Antonio and San José, and reduced the soldiers at the other three to one in each. After his short but stormy rule came to an end, Governor Orobio y Basterra sent the guards back to the missions.

In 1733 Fr. Mariano de los Dolores y Viana began his great missionary career of thirty-six years in Texas, principally at Mission San Antonio. Also after he was appointed the Fr. President of the Querétaran missions in 1750, he continued to reside at Mission San Antonio. In May, 1736, he built a bridge across the San Antonio River, using for this purpose six large beams which he had procured for repairs in the mission chapel. But the bridge was abused by the soldiers and settlers, who frequently came to the mission only to cause trouble.

On October 16, with the permission and orders of the Fr. President Fernández, Fr. Mariano had the bridge dismantled. That aroused the ire of Governor Franquis, who had the bridge rebuilt by forced Indian labor and threatened to pack Fr. Mariano on a mule and send him back to the College. Fr. Mariano retired to Mission Concepción and then to Mission San Juan Capistrano, but after Governor Franquis was removed from office he went back to Mission San Antonio. In the mission's baptismal register there are numerous entries for the years 1739-1757 that were signed by Fr. Mariano.

The Epidemic of 1739

A virulent epidemic swept through the San Antonio area in 1739. Many of the mission Indians died and many others fled to the woods. The number of Indians at Mission San Antonio, which had been 300 before the plague, was reduced in 1739 to 184. But the missions recovered quickly. By the end of 1740, Mission San Antonio once more had 238 Indians.

Some of these Indians belonged to the Tacame tribe. Originally they had belonged to San José Mission, but they abandoned it in a group. Later, in 1736, they joined the Indians at the Espada Mission; but the following year they

San Antonio Mission   49

wanted to move to San Antonio. Not obtaining permission,
they deserted once more. The missionaries tried in vain to
bring them back. However, in the winter of 1739 and the
spring of 1740, the missionaries of San José, by making
repeated trips, were able to conduct 77 Tacames to Mission
San Antonio.

In the spring of 1740 Fr. President Fernández reported
that the missions in the San Antonio area were all faring well,
but San Antonio de Valero, the oldest of them, had the largest
and best organized pueblo of Indians.

At the end of the same year, in a letter to the viceroy,
Captain Toribio de Urrutia praised the work of the mission-
aries, but noted that the mission buildings, including those of
Mission San Antonio, were still only of a temporary nature.
The churches had only thatched roofs of straw. A note in the
baptismal register of Mission San Antonio records the fact that
the first stone of the mission's first stone church was laid on
May 8, 1744.

Visit of Fr. Ortiz, 1745

The very next year Fr. Francisco Xavier Ortiz came from
Querétaro to inspect the missions of this college in Texas. For
more than a month he lived in San Antonio, made a thorough
investigation of the status of the four Querétaran missions, and
prepared a detailed report.

He mentions the fact that a new church of stone and mortar was being built at a distance of two gun shots east of the
church of San Fernando. The earlier church, probably an
adobe structure, had fallen down; and while the new church
was under construction, a large (adobe) hall was being used
as a church. In this temporary church, there were two
confessionals, two benches, and an altar with a carved statue
of St. Anthony about 33 inches high and above it a crucifix
that was twice as large.

In an adjoining room, used as a sacristy, there was another
altar with a statue of the Immaculate Conception of the same

size as that of St. Anthony. In the sacristy were kept twelve large pictures or paintings which were to be placed in the new church and four large bells for its tower.

The friary or residence of the missionaries was a two-story structure of stone and mortar. On the ground floor were offices and other rooms (kitchen and dining room), and on the second floor three private rooms.

Adjoining the friary, was the textile shop, with three looms, six pairs of cards, eight combs, six shuttles, and twenty spinning wheels. It had an open gallery. Here the Indian women and others who could not work on the farm manufactured excellent sackcloth, coarse cotton weaves, and brown domestic fabrics. The wool was provided by the mission's flock of sheep and the cotton came from its fields.

There was also a carpenter shop, a blacksmith shop, and chisels and hammers for the stone masons. Next to the textile shop stood the granary, where the corn harvest and other grain was stored, and beyond it several office rooms.

The mission Indians, who numbered 311 (275 baptized and 36 under instruction), lived in two long rows of huts, built of adobe bricks and roofed with straw. They stood on both sides of the irrigation ditch which ran through the mission compound; and along each row there was a sort of street.

The mission had 23 yokes of oxen for cultivating the fields of the mission farm. It was irrigated by a large *acequia* or ditch which led the water from the river to the fields. The annual corn crop in good years, grown from $12\frac{4}{5}$ to $14\frac{1}{3}$ bushels of seed, was 1,600 to 1,920 bushels. Three and a half bushels of beans yielded 96 bushels. Two fields of cotton produced about a thousand pounds. Two or three patches were used to grow watermelons, melons, and pumpkins.

The pasture land which lay east and north of the mission was a big ranch with about 2,300 head of cattle, 1,317 sheep, and 304 goats. While Fr. Ortiz was at the mission, an actual count of the cattle was made; 2,002 head were counted, but

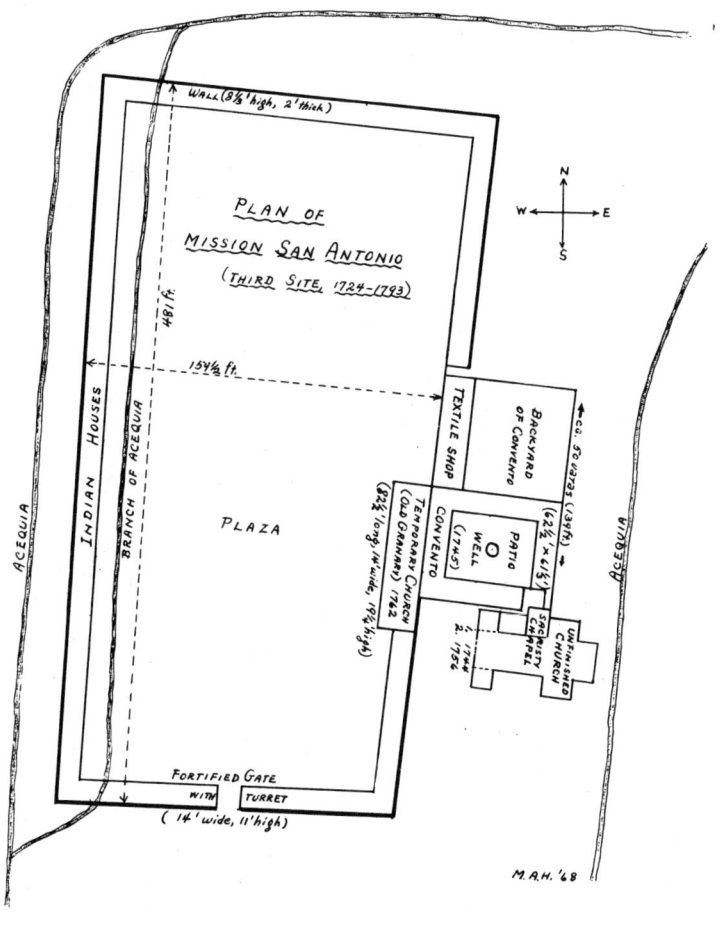

PLAN OF
MISSION SAN ANTONIO
(THIRD SITE, 1724-1793)

N
W — E
S

WALL (5¾' high, 2' thick)

481 ft.

154½ ft.

ACEQUIA

INDIAN HOUSES

BRANCH OF ACEQUIA

PLAZA

TEXTILE SHOP

BACKYARD OF CONVENTO

ca. 59 varas (139 ft.)

CONVENTO

PATIO

WELL

(62½' x 61½')

TEMPORARY CHURCH (OLD GRANARY) 1742

(82½' long, 14' wide, 19½' high)

SACRISTY CHAPEL

UNFINISHED CHURCH

4, 1744
2, 1756

ACEQUIA

FORTIFIED GATE
WITH   TURRET
(14' wide, 11' high)

M.A.H. '68

Author's diagram of the mission square of San Antonio de Valero.

the rest could not be counted because of the nearness of Apaches. The Indian cowboys of the mission did their work with the aid of forty horses. San Antonio Mission had its own branding iron, and the branding took place once a year.

Since its founding, Mission San Antonio had made a large number of Indian converts. Its registers showed that the missionaries had baptized a total of 981 Indians and had given Christian burial to 685.

Not satisfied with seeing the remarkable achievements of the mission with his own eyes, and to provide an answer to the false accusations which were lodged at times against the missionaries, Fr. Ortiz submitted a questionnaire on the conduct of the missionaries to a representative group of officials and settlers in San Antonio on June 25, 1745.

All testified that the missionaries had been and were toiling selflessly and indefatigably for the temporal and spiritual welfare of the natives but the missions were by no means ready for secularization. With much kindness and patience, the missionaries gradually induced the Indians to overcome their natural laziness and to work for a living.

Besides devoting themselves faithfully to the sacred ministry, the missionaries often performed the most menial tasks in order to encourage the Indians by their example. The inborn repugnance of the Indians to systematic labor was the reason why some of them, even after they had become Christians, sometimes ran off to the freedom of the wilds. To bring new Indian converts into the missions, the missionaries made journeys to points that were more than 200 leagues (500 miles) distant. This distance no doubt included the return trip.

The Apache Indians

Fr. Ortiz was probably still in San Antonio five days later (June 30, 1745), when a force of 350 Ypandi and Natage

Apaches (including women and children) made an attack on the presidio and the town of San Fernando. It happened during the night. While some of the Indians remained in ambush outside the town, others went up to the presidio to set fire to it.

Fortunately a boy discovered them and gave the alarm. The citizens and soldiers were able to hold the enemy at bay for a time; but then the Indians divided into separate groups and made attacks at different places at the same time. The Spaniards would surely have succumbed, if at the critical moment one hundred Indians from Mission San Antonio de Valero had not come to their rescue. The Apaches were not only repelled but routed; and the Spaniards and mission Indians pursued them as far as a place called Buenavista, where the victors were ordered back.

Concerning this attack on San Antonio, Dr. Castañeda wrote: "The fate of Fort St. Louis (the French settlement of Lavaca Bay which was destroyed by the Karankawas in 1689) might have been the fate of San Antonio de Béjar, had it not been for the timely aid of the mission Indians of Valero and the friendly policy of Fr. Benito Fernández de Santa Ana. The cackling of geese saved Rome; the loyalty of the recently converted Indians of today's Alamo saved San Antonio in 1745. No more eloquent proof of the success of the missionaries in Christianizing and civilizing the wild children of the plains can be found."

On November 28, 1749, a peace treaty between the Spaniards and Apaches was ratified in San Antonio amid elaborate ceremonies; but it was a treaty which many of the Apaches did not keep. They continued to be a menace and a danger to the end of the Spanish period, and even into the Mexican and American periods. But the missionaries of the College of Querétaro were not daunted. They did everything they possibly could to make them Christians, friends, and civilized, law-abiding citizens.

They began by establishing a short-lived mission for the Apaches of Texas in Coahuila, 1754-1755. In the latter year almost a thousand Apaches joined the two Querétaran missions on the San Marcos River. These missions, plus a third mission, had been founded originally in 1748-1749 on the San Gabriel River for various tribes of the Tejas Indians. Two of these missions were moved in 1755 to the San Marcos; and the following year one of them, San Francisco Xavier, the only one that remained, was continued on the Guadalupe near New Braunfels. But it too came to an end in 1758.

In the meantime, in 1757, the Apache mission of San Sabá was established near Menard with the cooperation of the College of San Fernando in Mexico City. It was destroyed the very next year by the Comanches; and two missionaries died as martyrs.

Another attempt was made in 1762, when two Apache missions were founded on the Nueces. Two years later each of them had over 400 neophytes; but after seven years, these also had to be given up.

In these endeavors Fr. Mariano de los Dolores of Mission San Antonio, who was named the Fr. President of the Querétaran missions of Texas in 1750, played an important role. If the missionaries did not succeed in making Christians of the Apaches, it was not due to any failure on their part to do their level best and that with an amazing preseverance.

Second Visit of Fr. Ortiz, 1756

In 1756 the same Fr. Ortiz who had visited the missions in 1745 returned to make another inspection. At Mission San Antonio he found that the stone church which was begun in 1744 had been completed, but it had been poorly constructed and had fallen down completely. It was now being rebuilt, and in the meantime an adobe hall was being used as a church.

The friary was a two-story structure, with four rooms on the second floor and on the ground floor a guest room and various offices. On the second floor there was a door leading to the choir loft of the church.

At the place where the mission had stood in 1719-1724, the mission still had a chapel, 30½ feet long and 11 feet wide, in which there was a stone cross that was greatly venerated. The chapel was fitted out for divine services, and holy Mass was offered up in it sometimes.

In the mission square there were 30 Indian houses of adobe, of which 20 had open galleries with stone arches. Additional Indian quarters were still *jacales*, huts of brush; but new ones like the others were being built. No less than 328 Indians were living in the mission, the largest number in its history. An *acequia* ran through the square. The textile shop had four looms.

For work on the farm there were 24 yokes of oxen. On the ranch were 1,000 head of cattle, 2,050 sheep, 50 swine, 100 horses, and 50 mares. The horses were used by the cowboys and shepherds.

Since 1703, when the mission was first established on the other side of the Rio Grande, the records showed that 1,279 had been baptized, 944 had received Christian burial, and 308 had entered Christian marriages.

Although the second stone church of Mission San Antonio, which was under construction in 1756, was never completed while the mission was in existence, this was done in the nineteenth century. The date on the façade, 1757, can still be seen. Already in 1758 Governor Jacinto Barrios reported that considerable progress had been made. It was to be a large church of cut stone, with a transept and two towers.

Concerning this the second stone church of Mission San Antonio Fr. Mariano de los Dolores wrote in 1762: "Although the church of this mission (the one which was begun in 1744) had been completely finished, including a tower and sacristy, it fell to the ground because of the poor skill of the architect; and another of harmonious design is now being built with quarried stone which is found almost on the spot. It has the solidity and perfection that is required for beauty and for the support of the vaults."

Fr. Mariano de los Dolores wrote the above words in an important report that he compiled concerning all the Querétaran missions in Texas and sent on March 6, 1762, to Fr. Francisco Xavier Ortiz who had visited the missions in 1745 and 1756 and was now the Fr. Guardian of the College of Querétaro.

A graphic picture of Mission San Antonio is presented in Fr. Mariano's description of his own mission as it was in 1762; and it indicates the improvements that had been made, despite the fact that the newly built church collapsed shortly after it was completed.

A new stone granary had been built. It was a large building, in which the annual harvest of 1,440 bushels of corn and over a hundred bushels of beans was stored.

The old granary, which was 35 *varas* (97½ feet) long, had been converted into a temporary church. It had two altars, one with a crucifix, 4⅔ feet in length, and a carved statue of St. Anthony, 2¾ feet high, standing in a niche. The second altar had an artistically clothed statue of Our Lady of Sorrows, which was taken down once a week and carried in an outdoor procession during which the Indians recited the Rosary. In the choir of the church there was a third altar with a statue of Jesus of Nazareth and benches along the sides.

In the church were two benches, two confessionals, a holy water font, and a copper baptismal font with a cover. There were also four large church bells. A separate room, adjoining the church, served as a sacristy. Among its furnishings were fourteen complete sets of vestments and four copes.

The little stone chapel at the second site of the mission was still there and equipped with all that was needed for the celebration of holy Mass.

The new granary and the temporary church, together with the houses of the Indians and various workshops formed a large rectangular walled enclosure. On the south side there was a fortified gate, and above it a turret in which three cannons were installed. The Indian houses, built of stone against the walls, had arched porticoes and were arranged in seven rows or tiers; and on the west side of the plaza there was flowing water, connected with the irrigation canal and shaded by willows and fruit trees.

The Indian quarters were all provided with doors and windows, with beds raised above the ground, with chests having drawers, and with the necessary household utensils. The latter included a *metate* (a stone for grinding corn), a *comal* (a flat iron to make corn bread), and pots and pans. Inside the enclosure a good well had been dug to provide drinking water.

The friary and textile shop formed a separate little square on the east side of the large rectangular enclosure. This smaller square was about 50 *varas* (137½ feet) long on two sides.

"Back of the friary," there was a large hall in which there were four looms, and adjoining it two store rooms where the wool, cotton, combs, cards, and spools were kept. In this workshop the Indian women manufactured cotton and woolen cloth and blankets of various kinds.

The friary was a two-story stone building, with private rooms, a dining room, a kitchen, and offices, all of which were flanked by open archways facing the patio. Outside the friary square, the new church was being built, with its main entrance facing west.

Irrigation canals, with stone trenches, ran along both the west and the east sides outside the two enclosures and

supplied water for the fenced mission farm, on which corn,
beans, chile, cotton, and some vegetables were raised. The
mission had forty yokes of oxen, thirty plows, and other
implements for cultivating the soil, and also twelve carts for
transporting stone, timber, and other supplies.

On the mission ranch there were 115 saddle horses, 1,015
head of cattle, 2,300 sheep and goats, 200 mares, 15 donkeys,
and 18 mules. Since the ranch was at some distance from the
mission compound, a stone house and a stone chapel had been
constructed on the site for the cowboys and shepherds and
their families. The ranch house, which was 25 *varas* (about 69
feet) long, had three rooms and an arcade. Its chapel was 11
varas (about 30 feet) long; it had an altar with a stone cross
5½ feet high and two sets of vestments for the celebration of
holy Mass.

The total number of mission Indians in 1762 was 275 or 76
families. All were Christians except 32 who were still receiving
instructions and preparing for baptism. The various tribes
represented among them were the Jarames, Payayas, Zanas,
Apaches (Yprandes), Cocos, Tops, and Karankawas.

Since the founding of the mission near the Rio Grande the
number of Indians baptized was 1,572. Those who had
received Christian burial numbered 1,247; and the total of
Christian marriages was 454. The Bureau of American Ethnology's *Handbook of American Indians* is mistaken when it
says that Fr. Mariano indulged in an "obvious exaggeration"
of the number of converted Indians. The register of baptisms
of Mission San Antonio, which is in the Archives of San
Fernando Cathedral in San Antonio, is proof that Fr. Mariano
reported the exact number of entries that he found in the
mission's registers; but they included those that had been
made since 1703, not 1718.

Carefully recorded in the baptismal register of Mission San
Antonio is the name of every Indian who was baptized, the
day on which this was done, and the signature of the

missionary who administered the sacrament. It is interesting to note that the first three baptisms were those of dying children, the first by Fr. Miguel Núñez de Haro, the second by Fr. Olivares, and the third by Brother Pedro Maleta. The record of baptisms ends with the year 1783; and so, the entries for the last ten years of the mission's existence are missing.

Fr. Mariano Viana concluded his account of Mission San Antonio by mentioning that, besides himself, its missionaries in 1762 were Fr. José López and Brother Juan de los Angeles. Fr. José López of the College of Querétaro must be distinguished from Fr. José Francisco López of the College of Zacatecas, who was in charge of Mission San Antonio later on and, like his namesake, held the office of *presidente*.

Fr. José López seems to have succeeded Fr. Mariano Viana as Fr. President in 1763. We find him at Mission Concepción in 1764. He may also have substituted for the Fr. President in 1760, when Fr. Mariano Viana traveled all the way to Mexico City in a vain attempt to prevent the return of Felipe de Rábago y Terán to Texas as the captain of the Presidio de San Luís de las Amarillas.

The successor of Fr. José López, probably in 1766, and the last Fr. President of the Querétaran missions on the San Antonio River was Fr. Asisclos Valverde. He took up his residence at Mission Concepción in 1766; and his signature appears in the baptismal register of Mission San Antonio in 1773.

Fr. Mariano Viana, however, was still at Mission San Antonio in 1769. Early that year, the governors of Coahuila and Texas met with Colonel Ortiz Parilla to plan a campaign against the hostile northern tribes. Authorized no doubt to do so by the College, Fr. Mariano took the occasion to present to the governors a formal offer to surrender to them the temporal administration of the four Querétaran missions on the Rio de San Antonio and the two on the Rio Grande.

It was a challenging proposal and a demolishing reply to the false charges repeatedly made against the missionaries that they were more interested in accumulating wealth than in saving the souls of Indians. If they accepted the offer, Fr. Mariano warned them, it would henceforth be their responsibility to protect and increase the possessions of the missions, which belonged to the Indians. In their reply, the governors praised the efficient administration of the missionaries and said they could not consider the offer without first consulting the viceroy.

Zacatecan Friars at San Antonio

The Querétaran friars left the Texas mission field in 1773; and their four missions on the San Antonio River passed into the care of the missionaries of the College of Zacatecas. Those of Querétaro departed regretfully, in order to devote themselves to missionary work in the former Jesuit missions of Pimería Alta (northern Mexico and southern Arizona); and there they developed a flourishing chain of missions similar to the contemporary missions of the College of San Fernando in Alta California. Their missions of San Juan Bautista and San Bernardo on the Rio Grande were entrusted at this time to the Franciscan Province of Guadalajara.

When the transfer was made, the missionary in charge of San Antonio was Fr. Manuel Carrasco. In July, 1772, Fr. Carrasco, with only two Christian companions, had made a journey to the Lipan-Apaches in search of runaway Indians and had brought back eight apostates. Captain Rafael Martínez Pacheco declared that "he might have returned with all the runaways, if he had been given an adequate (military) escort, as had been done in the past."

The Fr. President at the time of the transfer of the missions, writes Dr. Castañeda, was Fr. Diego Jiménez, who was then the superior of the missions on the Rio Grande as well as those on the Rio de San Antonio. However, it seems that, while his jurisdiction extended to the two Texas missions for the Apaches which existed on the Nueces and hence in the Province of Coahuila, 1762-1769, it did not include those on the San Antonio.

The Zacatecan missionaries, in 1773, already had the care of Mission San José and the two at La Bahía; and in that same year they were forced to abandon their three missions in eastern Texas. Thus they were able to take over Mission San Antonio and the other three missions without difficulty.

The first Zacatecan friar to be placed in charge of Mission San Antonio was Fr. Joseph Francisco Mariano de la Garza. He was followed in 1777 by Fr. José Maria Salas, who was transferred to Mission San José in 1783. The next missionary of San Antonio was Father José Francisco López, who became Fr. President of the Texas missions a few years later and remained at San Antonio until 1793.

The rapid decline of Mission San Antonio had already begun when it became a Zacatecan mission. Its decline was not due to the fact that another College was placed in charge, as some have thought. The true reasons were pointed out by Fr. López in his report of 1789. But before we give our attention to that report, we must mention Teodoro de Croix' visit to San Antonio in 1777-1778.

Fr. Morfi's Account of San Antonio

During his tour of inspection of the entire frontier of New Spain, De Croix was accompanied by Fr. Juan Agustín Morfi; and after he returned to Mexico, the latter wrote the first *History of Texas, 1673-1779*. In this work he gives an account of Mission San Antonio as he found it at the time of his visit. It agrees for the most part with Fr. Mariano Viana's description written in 1762.

We learn, however, that the sacristy of the new church had been completed and was being used as a church while the church itself was still under construction. "The church," he writes, "was ruined through the ignorance of the builder; but a new one, simple, roomy, and well planned, is being erected on the same spot, though it is not finished. In the meantime services are held in the sacristy, which is a small room, but very tidy and neat, with a small new golden altar, where a handsome image of the patron St. Anthony is venerated."

Fr. Morfi also throws some light on the location of the textile shop and indicates that when Fr. Mariano said the friary was 50 *varas* square he included not only the friary proper (which was only half as large) but also its "backyard," that is, a second patio of the same size, on the north side of the friary.

The mission, says Fr. Morfi, "has a small friary, 50 *varas* square, with an arched gallery around the patio, on the first and the second floors, around which have been built the necessary rooms for the missionaries with the usual porter's lodge, refectory, offices, and kitchen; and in the second patio, there is a large room with four looms and the necessary spinning wheels to weave cotton cloth for shawls and ordinary coarse cotton and woolen cloth for the Indians. Two other rooms, in which the raw materials and the tools are kept, adjoin the workshop." Actually, therefore, each of the two smaller squares or patios must have been about 25 *varas* square.

"At the entrance to the friary," Fr. Morfi adds, "a small watchtower was built, with three loopholes for three swivel guns, which, with other firearms and their ammunition, are carefully guarded."

Fr. Morfi also supplies the information that since 1762 the number of mission Indians "has been greatly reduced, and today (1778) the mission has scarcely enough of them to cultivate the fields; and the looms have been abandoned" because of the lack of workers. According to a census made in 1777, only 44 Indians were living at Mission San Antonio, far less than in any of the other missions. Little wonder, then, that the new church could not be completed.

The mission farm was being cultivated, at least to some extent with the aid of Spanish labor; and the missionary was able to give these farmhands only relatively low wages. However, the missionary of San Antonio continued his efforts to bring in new Indian converts to the very end, and he did succeed in assembling a few of them.

In the course of the following decade, too, a fairly large settlement of families grew up just southeast of the mission compound. They were called *agregados* or squatters; and many of the mission Indians intermarried with these settlers. This settlement was called La Villita, at least later on; and eventually it formed an important part of the town of San Fernando and the city of San Antonio.

Report of Fr. López, 1789

In 1789 Mission San Antonio had more resident Indians than in 1777. This we learn from the carefully prepared and illuminating report which Fr. José Francisco López wrote at Mission San Antonio and signed on March 5, 1789. After presenting a detailed account of the seven missions of Texas which were then still in the care of the missionaries of the Zacatecas College, he frankly and clearly points out the true reasons for their sharp decline.

The principal reason, he declares, was the decree which Teodoro de Croix issued after his visit in 1777-1778. This decree appropriated all unbranded cattle, making them government property; and it required everyone, the missions included, who took or slaughtered any such cattle to pay a fee of four *reales* (one half a peso) per head. The wealth of the missions had consisted principally in their cattle. The Apaches had stolen all but a few of their horses, and hence they had been unable to round up the cattle and brand them.

As a result, the missions were impoverished overnight. To feed the Indians they had to buy their own cattle from the government with the corn they raised. Thus several vicious circles ensued; and the missions were unable to assemble and take care of a large number of Indians within their walls. There were other contributing causes, enumerated by Fr. López, but the principal one was the loss of the mission cattle. His report is one last urgent plea that the situation be remedied and the missions saved from extinction, but it failed to achieve its purpose.

The account of Mission San Antonio shows that this mission was still in a fairly good condition. All it needed was more mission Indians, but it was now impotent to gather them. The mission, writes Father López, "is built to form almost a square [an irregular rectangle], surrounded by a single stone and mud wall that stands about 300 paces from the center. The same rampart serves as a wall for most of the fifteen or sixteen houses, with ample capacity for lodging the Indians. Nearly all the houses are covered with wood and mortar, as a protection against the rain; and they have hand-carved, wooden doors with locks and iron keys. Within the square is the granary, made of stone and lime, which has enough room to hold 3,200 bushels of corn, 320 or more bushels of beans, etc.

"Next [outside the square, adjoining it on the east side] is the house or living quarters, adequate for the missionary and the officers of the community, made of stone and lime, with good roofs, doors, windows, and locks.

"Adjoining this building, is the sacristy which serves today as the church [that is, the sacristy of the new church, on its north side], while another room [next to the sacristy, on its west side] now serves as the sacristy. Both structures are of stone and mortar, and are built with arched roofs.

"This mission has under construction a church with a very large nave [and a transept]; the walls of the nave are built as high as the cornices, but the latter have been built only in the dome of the sanctuary. In the front, its beautiful façade of sculptured stone has been completed to the same height as the walls. . . . [Because of the lack of mission Indians and for other reasons] it cannot now be carried on to completion.

"The lowest evaluation that may be placed upon the church and sacristy is 20,000 pesos, with an additional 8,000 for the furnishings and ornaments . . .

"The population of this mission consists of:

Married couples, 12 in number, from 20 to 50 years of age	24
Widowers and bachelors, from 25 to 40 years of age	8
Boys, from 1 to 10 years, and one girl	20
Total number of persons	52

"This mission was founded with Indians of various tribes, such as the Hierbipiames, Pataguas, Scipxames, Xaranames, Samas, Payatas [Payayas], Yutas, Kiowas, Tovs, and Tamiques. The Samas and Payatas were the principal ones. But all these may be considered as Samas and Payas, whose language is in general use.

"Spanish is now more commonly used, the Indians having married mulattoes and meztizoes, who are called Coyotes in this country.

"It should also be noted that, although this mission was founded in the year 1716 [the year was 1718], most of the Indians in it, and there are more than fifty, are sons of uncivilized tribes; and, further, they were baptized as adults when some were as much as forty years of age." In other words, they were brought to the mission as pagans and converted to Christianity.

Extant census figures show that the population of Mission San Antonio fluctuated considerably during the last decade of its existence: in 1783 the mission had 144 Indians; in 1786, 126; in 1788, 45; in May of 1789, 52 (as above); but in December of the same year, 121; in 1790, 48; and in 1793, 57.

Suppression of the Mission

In 1790, the year after Fr. López made his report, the College of Zacatecas sent its commissary and prefect of missions, Fr. Manuel Silva, to Texas, to see what could be done to improve the missionary situation. Since there were still many unconverted Indians in Texas, he suggested that Mission San Antonio be secularized, that its four neighbors be reduced to two missions, and that new missions be founded elsewhere in the province. The result was that one, and only one, new mission, namely Nuestra Señora del Refugio, was founded in 1793; Mission San Antonio was suppressed the same year; and the other four San Antonio missions were partially secularized the following year.

After the viceroy's decree of January 9, 1793, for the suppression of Mission San Antonio was received, Governor Manuel Múñoz of Texas, who was at La Bahía at the time, issued a proclamation to that effect on February 23; and on April 11, after the governor had arrived in San Antonio, Fr. José Francisco Lozano, who was then the missionary of San Antonio, according to directions received from Fr. President José Francisco López, distributed among 39 mission Indians a supply of corn which was to take care of their needs until the new crop was harvested. This was given to ten heads of families, one of them a widow, and to four other unmarried adults. Each of these fourteen persons also received a pair of oxen, a plow, a harrow, a hoe, and a cow with a calf. Additional corn and other supplies, including ten horses, were given to them two days later.

The other 18 mission Indians who were Lipan Apaches, were to be moved to Mission San José; but they preferred to stay at San Antonio, and were permitted to remain. They, no doubt, also received both supplies and land.

Pedro Huizar surveyed and subdivided the lower mission farm *(Labor de Abajo);* and on April 12, Governor Múñoz gave to each of the fourteen heads of families and unmarried adults a tract of land large enough for the planting of one and three-fifths bushels of seed. A similar plat was given to Pedro Huizar, and another to Vicente Amador, his assistant. Some of San Antonio's cattle, horses, corn, beans, and salt were assigned to the new Mission of Refugio.

Inventory of the Mission

An inventory of the church furnishings was made on April 23 and 24 by Governor Múñoz, Fr. President López, and Fr. José Mariano de la Garza, the companion of Fr. Silva. On the 24th the governor also appointed Pedro Huizar and three others to prepare a report on the mission buildings. The latter contains some interesting information and exact measurements. We shall translate the *vara* measurement (33⅓ inches) into feet.

The incomplete church, built in the Tuscan style of architecture, had a transept and a domed roof resting on groups of columns. One group of columns in the sanctuary had been completed, and three others were almost completed. The baptistry lacked only the doors. The façade was impressive; and two sculptured statues, one of St. Francis and the other of St. Dominic, stood in their niches. (Two other niches were still empty.)

The sacristy, on the north side of the church, which faced west, was a room, 33⅓ feet long, about 14 feet wide, and 14 feet high. Though its walls were not plastered, they were neatly white-washed. It had a domed roof, and two doors with frames of carved stone.

One of the doors of the sacristy led into an adjoining room on the west side, measuring 24 feet by 20¼ feet. Besides the connecting door, it had another; and both had iron hooks and eyes. It also had two windows, facing west and north. The roof was of wood, with cedar rafters; but it was in need of repair.

Next door, on the north side of the church, was the friary, a solidly built stone house, 62½ feet by 61⅓ feet. It formed a square with a patio in the middle; and in the center of the patio there was a well with an arched stone superstructure and a bucket.

The north and south wings, which were "divided by a hall," and the west wing, which had a corridor, were two stories high. The upper floors of the north and south wings each had five private rooms, each of which was about 14 feet by 11 feet; but these ten rooms were in need of repair, because the flat roofs were full of holes.

On the first floor of the west wing there were four rooms, larger than the other rooms, an office, and a small room at the bottom of the stairway; upstairs were three private rooms. Here too the roof was partly rotted and in need of repair. Near the entrance of the friary stood a small rampart with a one-pound gun.

Nothing is said of an east wing, but there must have been a wall at least. The former "backyard" of the friary with its textile shop is not mentioned either.

The church and friary were outside and just east of the large walled mission square which was an irregular rectangle. The wall, on the east and south side, was made of stone, adobe, and mud; and it was $8\frac{1}{3}$ feet high and 2 feet thick. The length of the wall on the east side, running north and south, was 481 feet; and the south wall, running east and west, was 159½ feet long. The main gate was placed in the south wall and was about 14 feet wide and 11 feet high. The north wall was half in ruins.

Within the enclosure were the Indian houses, most of which were built against the west wall and faced an archway running along this side. But only 12 of the houses were habitable. The others were in ruins.

On the east side of the rectangular enclosure stood the granary, and just beyond it the friary. The granary was 82½ feet long, about 14 feet wide, and 19¼ feet high. The floor was of adobe. The roof was in poor condition, only the beams being sound.

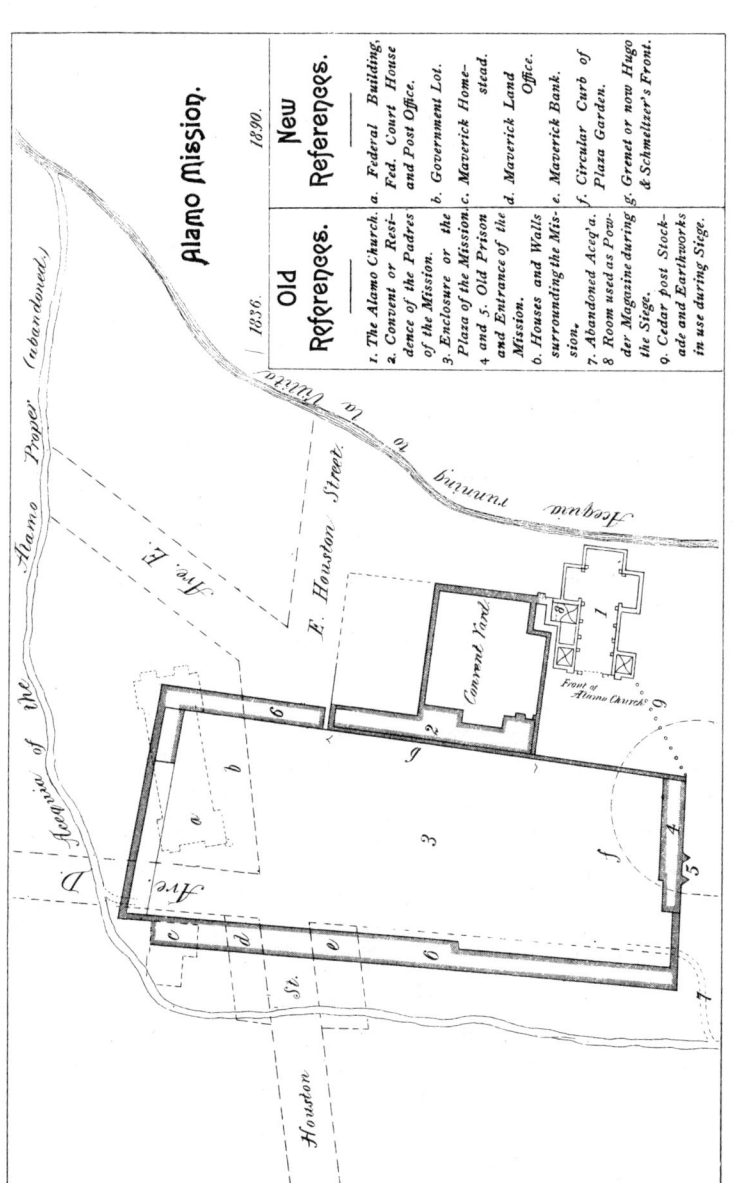

Alamo Mission.

Old References.	New References.
1836.	1890.
1. The Alamo Church.	a. Federal Building, Fed. Court House and Post Office.
2. Convent or Residence of the Padres of the Mission.	
3. Enclosure or the Plaza of the Mission.	b. Government Lot.
4 and 5. Old Prison and Entrance of the Mission.	c. Maverick Homestead.
	d. Maverick Land Office.
6. Houses and Walls surrounding the Mission.	e. Maverick Bank.
7. Abandoned Aceq'a.	f. Circular Curb of Plaza Garden.
8. Room used as Powder Magazine during the Siege.	g. Grenet or now Hugo & Schmelizer's Front.
9. Cedar post Stockade and Earthworks in use during Siege.	

William Corner's plan of Mission San Antonio de Valero,
1890.

The mission Indians who had become landowners continued to use the square and to live there. The church and friary with their furnishings were turned over to the pastor of San Fernando. The baptism, marriage, and burial records of the former mission were likewise entrusted to his care. The last pages of the baptismal register of Mission San Antonio, containing entries for the years from 1783 to 1793, must have been lost; for, Sidney Lanier in 1872 found on the last page of this register the following note:

"On the 22nd day of August, 1793, I placed this book of the Records of the pueblo of San Antonio de Valero in the archives of the parish of the town of San Fernando and presidio of San Antonio de Béxar, by order of the most illustrious Señor Dr. Don Andrés de Llanos y Valdez, most worthy bishop of this diocese, dated January 2, of the same year, for the reason that the said pueblo had been aggregated to the parish of Béxar; and that it may be so known, I sign my name. Fr. José Francisco López, *Parroco*."

The fact that Fr. López, the president of the Texas missions, added the title of *parroco* to his name indicates that at this time he was temporarily serving as the pastor of the San Fernando parish. Not long after the secularization and suppression of Mission San Antonio, Fr. López was succeeded by a new Fr. President, Fr. José Mariano Cárdenas; and Fr. López seems to have returned to Zacatecas after the pastor for whom he substituted returned to San Fernando.

Subsequent History of the Mission

Mission San Antonio thus ceased to exist after it had been in existence for 75 years, and it was absorbed into the parish of San Fernando. However, in 1801 a new parish was established at the former mission, namely the parish and Pueblo de San Josef y Santiago del Alamo; and its pastor used the church or sacristy of the former mission for divine services from that year until 1825. The members of this parish were the soldiers and families of the Segunda Companía Volante de San Carlos de Parras, a mobile cavalry unit, which established its headquarters on the east bank of the San Antonio River in 1801. They had their own pastor or a substitute until August 22, 1825.

All this we learn from their baptismal register which they brought along from Mexico and continued to use in San Antonio; and hence it has entries from 1788 to 1825. The last entries, those for 1822 to 1825 were made by Fr. José Antonio Díaz de León, the last of the Zacatecan friars in Texas, and by the Military Chaplain of the Presidio of San Antonio de Béxar, Francisco Maynes, who were substituting for the absent pastor of San Fernando. The baptismal register of the Alamo pueblo is in the Archives of San Fernando Cathedral.

It was probably this pueblo that gave the name of El Alamo to the former mission. El Alamo was the name of a town near Parras in Mexico, where the "flying company" had been recruited in 1788. The meaning of Alamo is poplar or cottonwood tree.

The former friary of Mission San Antonio was used as San Antonio's first hospital from 1806 to 1814 and perhaps also after that year. The hospital was founded by Simón Herrera. Dr. Jaime Guerra was in charge in the spring of 1814. At that time he was succeeded by his assistant, Dr. Francisco Favina; and when the latter took sick some months later, it seems that the patients were unofficially attended by Baron de Bastrop. The hospital took care of both soldiers and civilians.

The subsequent history of the Alamo as a fort and as a prison and the stirring story of the siege and battle of the Alamo, February 23 to March 6, 1836, are well known; and it is beyond the scope of this account of the Mission of San Antonio de Valero to relate these events.

In 1841, the Republic of Texas restored the ownership of the old mission to the Catholic Church; but after Texas joined the Union in 1845, the bishop leased the Alamo to the United

States Government as a military quartermaster depot. Two years later the Quartermaster Corps capped the façade of the mission church, raised the side and back walls, and built the roof. Thus San Antonio Mission's second stone church was finally completed, but not as a church.

In 1856 the German parish of St. Joseph wanted to make the old mission church its parish church; but at the time there was no other place to which the Army could move, and old St. Joseph Church was built two blocks south of the Alamo, on or near the second site of the mission.

The United States Army used the Alamo until 1861, when the Confederates took over. After the Civil War the U. S. Army resumed possession until 1876, when the quartermaster depot was moved to the new Fort Sam Houston. The following year Bishop Anthony D. Pellicer sold the mission property, including what was left of the friary, but not the former church and some surrounding land, to a commercial firm for $20,000. The former church was purchased for the same sum in 1883, and placed in the care of the City of San Antonio.

To remove the unsightly business houses adjoining the Alamo church, the Daughters of the Republic of Texas acquired the ownership of some of the former mission property early in the twentieth century; and about the same time, in 1905, the governor of Texas was empowered to do the same. The Daughters of the Republic of Texas sold what they had bought to the State; and the State assigned the custody of the Alamo to the Daughters of the Republic of Texas, who agreed to provide the necessary funds for its maintenance and upkeep. However, in 1909, because of some difficulties which had arisen over the question of what should be restored or torn down, the society asked the State to take charge. However, the care of the Alamo remained in the hands of the society; and in the end, the old friary wall, which some wanted removed, remained standing.

In 1936, on the occasion of the centennial of Texas independence, the Alamo Park and present enclosure of seven or eight acres was made possible by the allocation of funds from the City and the State. The Alamo Museum was built north of the church, so that the latter would have that sense of space and quiet that a church should have; and the Daughters of the Republic of Texas Library, with an adjoining meeting hall was built on the grounds. The society twice repaired the roof of the church, which was constructed in 1849-1850; and it continues to maintain the Alamo with the loving care that it deserves.

The Alamo is now a worthy and priceless historical monument, honoring the memory, not only of the heroes of 1836, but also of the Franciscan padres who during three quarters of the eighteenth century founded, developed, built, and served Mission San Antonio de Valero.

Legend of the Margil Vine

To the history of San Antonio de Valero Mission, it will not be out of place to add a legend about its early days when Fr. Antonio Margil was staying at the mission (1719-1721). Though his sojourn in San Antonio lasted only a year and a half, Fr. Margil was long remembered and his name was woven into local folklore. At Mission San Antonio—so the legend relates — there was at this time a little Indian Jarame Indian boy whose name was Shavano. He and his parents had come with Fr. Antonio Olivares from the Jarame Mission of San Francisco Solano in the Valle de San José on the other side of the Rio Grande, when Mission San Antonio was founded in 1718.

Shavano was a bright and precocious lad, not boisterous like the rest of the Indian children at the mission, but frequently given to deep thought and musings. Although he was only five years old, he could speak Spanish quite well besides his native Coahuiltecan dialect. He had learned to recite the Latin Mass prayers distinctly and fluently. He loved to serve Mass for Fr. Margil, who always offered up the Holy Sacrifice with great devotion. From the great missionary he had learned to love God with all his heart.

Even as a baby at the mission near the Rio Grande, Shavano was a quiet and well-behaved child. For this reason he had been chosen to act the part of the Christ Child lying in the Crib, when the Christmas play *Los Pastores* (the Shepherds) was presented by the mission Indians.

Los Pastores is an allegorical dramatization of the Biblical account of the Birth of Christ in Bethlehem, similar to the medieval mystery or miracle plays. It portrays the message of the angels to the shepherds and the latter's journey to the cave of Bethlehem. Enroute the Devil tries to hinder them in every way he can, while the angels urge them onward. They overcome the wiles of Satan and reach the manger of the Christ Child, and there offer him their homage and love and gifts.

It is a long play. The text, which has been printed in Spanish and in English at San Antonio, consists of thirty-five pages. Its cast of characters includes twenty-four performers. At the present day it is still presented annually in San Antonio, not just once but many times from December 24 to about February 2, and sometimes even up to the feast of St. Joseph on March 19.

According to the legend of the Margil vine, the mission Indians were wont to bring their gifts to the empty Crib in the chapel on the days before Christmas. Little Shavano was distressed because he had nothing worth while that he could give to the Infant Jesus.

He was sitting in the lower branches of an *alamo*, a poplar or cottonwood tree, on the banks of the river on the vigil of Christmas, when smiling Fr. Margil — he was always in a cheerful mood — happened to pass by. Looking up, he saw the sad and tearful face of Shavano.

"Come down, my boy, and tell me what is troubling you," said the padre kindly.

"I tried so hard," said Shavano sobbingly, "to find something I could give to the Child Jesus. But I have nothing, nothing at all, except a few colored feathers."

"That's no reason to be unhappy, child. The Infant Jesus came to give himself to you; and he wants you to give him your own heart in return. That is what counts. Any little gift you find will be enough to be a sign of your love. You will see. Do not worry!"

Shavano felt much better now and wiped the tears from his face with the palm of his hand. But he was not quite satisfied. He must find something better to offer than his three colored feathers.

After the padre had gone on, Shavano noticed a tiny plant with bright green leaves sprouting from the ground near the trunk of the *alamo*. His face lit up with joy. Here is something — not much, but something he could take to the Crib in the chapel.

With a stick he carefully dug up the plant with its roots and a handful of ground. He hurried to his mother and obtained from her one of her small earthen jars and potted the plant. Taking this to the chapel, he placed it in a corner beside the Crib.

When it got dark, the presentation of *Los Pastores* was begun at some distance from the mission chapel, and gradually the actors came nearer, accompanied by their audience. When the shepherds reached the entrance to the chapel, they were so astounded at what they saw that they forgot their lines and exclaimed: "*Un milagro! Un milagro!*" "A miracle! A miracle!"

An exuberant vine of rich green leaves and scarlet berries, such as they had never seen before, had entwined itself around and over the Crib, decorating it as nothing else could. Where could it have come from?

Finally little Shavano was able to push his way through the crowd and saw the miracle. It was his own tiny vine which had grown miraculously to become the most beautiful and precious gift of all. Now he understood what Fr. Margil had told him. He knew that the Infant Jesus had accepted his humble gift and was more than pleased with it.

When the Indians learned that Shavano had found the little plant, now suddenly grown into a big and beautiful vine, after Fr. Margil had spoken those consoling words to him, they named it Fr. Margil's Vine.

After the Christmas season, the Indians made cuttings of the vine and planted them beside their huts. All of them developed into luxuriant vines that made their poor abodes look like festive arbors. Since that time Fr. Margil's Vine was found thriving throughout the San Antonio River region.

Such is the legendary story of the origin of Fr. Margil's Vine, as it was handed down from father to son. Whether it rests on some actual occurrence, we do not know. It would not be surprising if it did; for, the life-story of Fr. Margil is full of proved events which cannot be explained in a natural manner.

The fact is that there is a vine in the Southwest that is called Fr. Margil's Vine. It is a member of the Moonseed Family (*Menispermaceae*), otherwise known as the Carolina Snailseed Vine (*Cocculus carolinus* (L.) DC.). In his book *The Trees, Shrubs, and Woody Vines of the Southwest* (p. 275), Robert A. Vines offers the following remarks concerning the Margil Vine:

"The genus name, *Cocculus*, refers to the curled, snail-like seed, and the species name, *carolinus*, is the Carolina. The author has been unable to ascertain whether the reference refers to North Carolina or South Carolina, or both. Vernacular names are Coral-bead, Coral-seed, Coral-vine, Moon seed, Red-berry Moonseed, Carolina Moonseed, Red Moonseed, Wild-sarsaparilla, Margil, and Hierba del Ojo.

"This climbing vine could be more extensively cultivated for ornament because of the brilliant red fruit. It is consumed by a number of species of birds. The vine is sometimes mistaken for a kind of Smilax-vine, but most of the species of Smilax have much more leathery and stiff foliage, and thorny stems. The red fruit also distinguishes it from closely related species of the Moonseed Family."

Important Dates

1718, May 1: Mission San Antonio de Valero was founded on the west bank of the San Antonio River.

1719, June: The mission was moved to its second site on the east bank of the river, near present old St. Joseph Church.

1724: Mission San Antonio moved to its third site, the present Alamo Plaza.

1744, May 8: First stones were laid for the first stone church, which collapsed before 1756.

1745, June 30: The mission Indians of San Antonio de Valero saved the villa and presidio of Béxar from attacking Apaches.

1756: The second stone church, the present Alamo, was begun at Mission San Antonio, but never completed during mission days. At the mission were 328 Indians, the largest recorded number.

1773: The Querétaran missionaries leave Texas, and San Antonio becomes a Zacatecan mission.

1793, April 12: Mission San Antonio is completely secularized and suppressed.

1801: The Second Flying Company of San Carlos de Parras is stationed at the former mission, and it becomes the Pueblo de San José y Santiago del Alamo.

1806-1814: The convento of the former mission is used as a hospital.

1836, Mar. 6: The fall of the Alamo.

1850: The Quartermaster Corps of the U.S. Army completes the building of the stone church of the former mission and uses it as a warehouse.

1905: The Daughters of the Republic of Texas assume the care of the Alamo as a Texas State Park or Historic Site.

III

Mission San Francisco
Xavier de Nájera
1722-1726

During the four years, 1722-1726, Mission San Antonio had a short-lived sub-mission, named San Francisco Xavier de Nájera, which never got beyond the founding stage. It owed its origin to an extraordinary Indian chief of the Sana tribe, who bore the Spanish name of Juan Rodríguez. His followers lived with others of the same tribe and the Yerbipiames in a settlement near the Trinity River, known as Ranchería Grande.

While the Marqués de Aguayo was still in Coahuila, getting ready for his expedition into Texas, Chief Rodríguez paid him a visit and asked him to establish a separate mission near San Antonio for his tribesmen who numbered about 600. He then returned to San Antonio and waited there with some of his followers for the arrival of Aguayo.

Chief Juan Rodríguez

When the latter and his imposing army reached San Antonio on April 4, 1721, he suggested to Rodríguez that he and his people join the Indians at Mission San Antonio; but the chief replied that this was not possible, because they were too numerous, and besides they were not on friendly terms with the mission Indians. The Marqués de Aguayo promised to found a mission for them later.

Chief Rodríguez then served as guide for Aguayo's march to eastern Texas; and after Aguayo had returned to San Antonio in January, 1722, the chief went to the Ranchería Grande and brought back fifty families of the Sanas for the new mission. On March 12 Aguayo founded a mission for them on a beautiful plain, midway between Missions San Antonio and San José on the east side of the San Antonio River, the same site that was later occupied by Mission Concepción.

Fr. Joseph González, the assistant of Fr. Hidalgo at Mission San Antonio, was present on this occasion, and promised to take care of the Indians from San Antonio until another father could be sent from the College of Querétaro. Fr. Espinosa, then guardian of the College, had promised to do that.

Aguayo sent a report of what he had done to the new Viceroy Casafuerte, who had just arrived in Mexico City with instructions to curtail expenses; and the viceroy informed Fr. Espinosa, that he could not disburse the customary aid for the founding of another new mission, nor the annual allowance of 450 pesos for another missionary. Neither could the College bear these expenses, replied Fr. Espinosa; the Sanas would be welcome at one of the other two missions.

In the meantime, at Mission San Antonio, Fr. González had begun a separate record book for the new mission; and he visited the Sanas regularly at their camp on the mission site. No doubt, the Indians erected a temporary chapel; and here Fr. González offered up holy Mass for them and instructed them.

Aguayo's Offer of Supplies

As governor, Aguayo had supplied the new mission community with necessities at his own expense; and he asked his successor to do the same till the mission was established on a firm footing. In 1725 the Marqués generously offered to supply everything needful, if one of the two missionaries stationed at Mission San Antonio would assume the care of the new mission. Both the viceroy and the guardian of the College accepted his offer; and Fr. Miguel Sevillano de Paredes, newly appointed Fr. President of the Querétaran missions in Texas, was sent to San Antonio with instructions to proceed with the establishment of the mission.

A few days after he arrived in January, 1726, Fr. Sevillano called Chief Rodríguez and his Indians to San Antonio to inform them that a mission would be built for them and they could have as their missionary either himself or his assistant Fr. Joseph Hurtado. Fr. González left San Antonio later that year.

Fr. Sevillano was surprised when only twelve Indians came. Many of the Sanas had gone back to the Ranchería Grande. The Fr. President was still more amazed, when Chief Rodríguez told him that he and his few remaining followers now preferred to stay at Mission San Antonio. They would be safer there against attacks of the Apaches, their enemies.

Attempts to Establish the Mission

Although a messenger was hastily sent to Saltillo to prevent the supplies from being sent, at least for the present, Fr. Sevillano made every possible effort to make Mission San Francisco Xavier a sub-mission of San Antonio. He invited the seven chiefs of the Sanas who were at Ranchería Grande to San Antonio, where they were feasted for three days; but they absolutely refused to settle down in a mission. Brother Juan de los Angeles was at the mission at this time. He knew the language of the Sanas, which was the same as that of the Tejas; but even he could not persuade them to change their mind.

If the Sanas would not come, perhaps the Yerbipiames would; and so Chief Rodríguez went with Governor Pérez de Almazán to the Ranchería Grande to see the Yerbipiames, among whom there were many apostates from the missions in eastern Texas, to persuade some of them to come to San Francisco Xavier. This attempt likewise failed.

Fr. Sevillano made one last effort, or intended to do so, by going in person to the Paquaches on the upper Nueces. The Apaches had recently made two severe attacks upon them. Nothing came of that plan either; and Fr. Sevillano was elected guardian of the College of Querétaro in 1727.

After 1726, a separate register for San Francisco was no longer kept at San Antonio. The sub-mission was merged with Mission San Antonio and absorbed by it; and Aguayo's generous offer could not be accepted. Some five years later, the three Querétaran missions in eastern Texas were moved to the San Antonio River; and one of them, Concepción, was established at or near the site which had been chosen for San Francisco Xavier.

Important Dates

1721, Apr. 4: Aguayo's army arrived at San Antonio de Béxar. Chief Rodríguez served as its guide to eastern Texas.

1722, Mar. 12: Returning from eastern Texas, Aguayo founded Mission San Francisco Xavier de Nájera as a sub mission of San Antonio de Valero, between it and San José.

1725: Aguayo offered to supply all that was needed for the establishment of the mission.

1726, Jan.: Chief Rodríguez told Fr. President Sevillano that he and his few remaining followers preferred to join the Indians at San Antonio de Valero. Thus the new mission was merged with San Antonio.

1731, Mar. 5: Concepción Mission was transferred from eastern Texas to the San Antonio River and established at or near the site of the short-lived San Francisco de Nájera.

Mission San José y San Miguel de Aguayo, after the dome had crashed in 1874. (From the Archives of San José Mission Friary.)

IV

Mission San José y San Miguel de Aguayo
1720-1824

San Antonio proved to be a haven of refuge to the missionaries of eastern Texas who were compelled by the French to leave their missions temporarily. They waited there for the arrival of the Marqués de Aguayo who was to reestablish the missions in eastern Texas.

Among these missionaries was Fr. Antonio Margil, the *presidente* of the Zacatecan missionaries who had been placed in charge of the three missions at present Nacogdoches and San Augustine, Texas, and Robeline, Louisiana, in 1716 and 1717. In the vicinity of Mission San Antonio, Fr. Margil found three Indian tribes, the Pampopas, the Suliajames, and the Pastías, who were desirous of having a mission of their own because they were not friendly with those who had been gathered in Mission San Antonio.

Fr. Margil Plans Another Mission

Why could not a second mission, one in the care of the College of Zacatecas, be founded on the San Antonio River, which was such a suitable place for missions? Mission San Antonio was a Querétaran mission, it is true; but in eastern Texas the two colleges had worked together in harmony, and the same could be done here. Like Mission San Antonio, the new Zacatecan mission would serve as a halfway station between Coahuila and eastern Texas; and from here the Zacatecan missionaries could extend their work towards the south, while the Querétaran friars would do the same towards the north. In fact, the two colleges had already agreed to do this in eastern Texas.

On December 26, 1719, Fr. Margil wrote a letter to the Marqués de Aguayo, newly appointed governor of Coahuila and Texas, who was gathering an army for his expedition, and told him how desirable it was to establish another mission near Mission San Antonio, one that would be named Mission San José y San Miguel de Aguayo. This could be done at once, because he had brought the necessary church goods from eastern Texas and some of these could be used for the present. He even had a statue of St. Joseph, which had been given to him for a mission which was to be named San José. All that was needed was the governor's consent and authorization.

The Marqués, who was personally acquainted with Fr. Margil, responded at once and on January 22, 1720, issued a decree delegating Captain Juan Valdez of the Presidio of San Antonio de Béxar to act in his name, and instructing him to select a suitable site for the new mission and to proceed with its establishment. Fr. Olivares expressed the fear that there would be trouble if another mission for Indians who were no friends of those at Mission San Antonio would be founded nearby; but Captain Valdez assured him that it would be at least three leagues distant, as required by the laws of the Indies.

Founding of San José

Without further delay, Fr. Margil sent two of his missionaries, Fr. Agustín Patrón and Fr. Miguel Núñez de Haro to look for a good site. Along the winding San Antonio River they went south for about three leagues, and on the east bank they found "an elevated, spacious, and very level plain" which could be easily irrigated; and here they built a straw hut.

On February 23, 1720, Captain Valdez with some companions including Lorenzo García who served as interpreter, the Zacatecan *presidente* Fr. Margil, and Fr. Joseph Guerra of the College of Querétaro proceeded to the place that had been selected. They were welcomed by the two missionaries who had established themselves there, as well as the Indian chiefs of the three interested tribes. After the captain had made sure that the spot was "more than three leagues," about seven miles, distant from Mission San Antonio (not in a straight line, but by the roundabout way along the bank of the river), the formal founding of Mission San José was carried out with the usual ceremonies.

A sufficiently large tract of land was assigned to the Indians and turned over to the Fr. President, who in turn entrusted it to the care of Fr. Patrón and Fr. Núñez de Haro. The course of an irrigation ditch, two miles long was traced; and the limits of the mission square, 120 *varas* (363⅓ feet) on each side, was marked. Chief Juan of the Pampopas was appointed governor of the mission pueblo; Chief Nicolás of the Suliajames, judge; Chief Alonso of the Pastías, sheriff, and two other Indians councilmen. Captain Valdez, through his interpreter, explained to them the duties of their several offices, and exhorted all the Indians to submit to the guidance and directions of their missionaries in all matters, temporal as well as spiritual.

The First Site

That the first site of Mission San José was on the east bank of the San Antonio River, a little to the north of its present location, is clearly stated in the *Crónica* which Fr. Espinosa completed in 1744 and had printed in 1746-1747.

In a short time the first temporary structures in the mission square, a chapel, a dwelling for the two missionaries, and huts for the Indians, were erected; and a large number of Indians, more than 200, were congregated in the new mission. Corn was planted on the mission farm, and the Indians willingly accepted the routine of mission life. From the beginning, the mission enjoyed considerable success.

Fr. Patrón, however, remained at San José for only one year. Following instructions received from Fr. Margil, he left Fr. Núñez de Haro in charge and accompanied Captain Domingo Ramón to Lavaca Bay in 1721 to prepare the way for the founding of another mission. However, Captain Nicolás Flores, who had been present at the founding of Mission San José and in 1722 succeeded Captain Valdez at the presidio, supplied two soldiers, who not only protected the mission but also aided its missionary as overseers and teachers of the Indians.

When the Marqués de Aguayo arrived at San Antonio in April, 1721, he paid a visit to Mission San José and found 227 Indians living there. To all of them he gave clothes and other articles which they prized highly.

By the spring of 1724, the mission had made remarkable progress. With the help of its two soldiers, Fr. Núñez and the Indians had completed the irrigation ditch and improved the farm to such an extent that the mission had a surplus of 160 bushels of corn. The latter was sent to the presidio and mission which had been founded on Garcitas Creek at Lavaca Bay in 1722 and was now in dire need of supplies. Fr. Núñez had also been able to bring back to the mission some of its Indians who, like truant school boys, had run away; and he had attracted new Indians to the mission.

The Second Site

Though the mission was faring so well at its first site, Fr. Núñez decided at some time between 1724 and 1727 to move it to the west bank of the San Antonio River. The reason may have been the efforts which were being made to establish another Querétaran mission, San Francisco Xavier de Nájera, on the east bank, between the missions of San Antonio and San José.

At any rate, when Inspector Pedro de Rivera visited San José in 1727, the mission square was situated on the west bank of the river, a little farther south; and the mission was doing so well that the economizing inspector thought it could do without the two soldiers. If they were removed as a result of Rivera's recommendations, they were restored soon afterwards. Rivera reported that more Indians were living in the two missions of San Antonio and San José than in the six missions of eastern Texas.

The second site of Mission San José was not the same as the present one. It was closer to the river bank, on land that was about 25 feet lower and a half mile distant from the present location of the mission. Some of the ruins of the adobe church which Fr. Núñez built at the second site could still be seen in 1859-1864, when Fr. Alto S. Hoermann resided at Mission San José. He tells us that one of the mission Indians who died in 1860 was 105 years old; and there were others still living who helped to construct the present (restored) church of San José. They were able to tell him much about the earlier history of the mission.

In 1731, therefore, when the town of San Fernando was established and the three Querétaran missions were transferred from eastern Texas to the San Antonio River, Mission San José was on the west bank; and its new neighbors followed the same pattern of choosing sites on alternate sides: Concepción on the east side, at the place originally selected for Mission San Francisco Xavier de Nájera; then San José on the west side; San Juan Capistrano on the east side; and San Francisco de Espada on the west side.

Successes and Reverses

At its second site San José, with about 300 resident Indians, continued to enjoy the same measure of success it had at the first, although it still had only temporary buildings. It had an adobe church, it is true, but that was not regarded as a permanent structure.

When Governor Franquis de Lugo came to San Antonio in 1736, Fr. Núñez had an assistant in the person of Fr. Joseph Cosmé Borruel; and when the governor demanded that one of the two soldiers at the mission return to the presidio, Fr. Borruel told him he could have both. However, the following year Franquis de Lugo was removed from office; and his successor sent three soldiers to San José as he did to each of the other San Antonio missions. Earlier the same year Fr. Borruel had gone on to Espíritu Santo Mission at Lavaca Bay, and another father whose name we do not know had taken his place at San José.

When the epidemic of 1739 swept through the San Antonio area, Mission San José was the hardest hit. Of the 300 Indians who had been at the mission only 49 remained in the early part of 1740; the rest had died or run away. The two fathers likewise took sick, but as soon as they could they went in quest of the runaways and of new converts; and by the end of 1740, no less than 249 Indians were once more living at Mission San José. By February of that year, the total number of Indians who had been baptized at San José was 431.

The Third Site

The fact that the mission square lay on low lying ground near the river was regarded as the reason why San José suffered such heavy losses during the epidemic; and it was after the epidemic that Fr. Núñez moved the mission for the second time, this time to the elevated spot it now occupies. Mission San José now entered upon its period of greatest development; and during the 1740's it's first permanent buildings were constructed.

When Fr. Espinosa wrote his *Crónica*, which was completed in 1744, he made only a brief remark about Mission San José; but what he does say is important. He tells us that this mission, which was founded by the zealous Fr. Margil and developed by the practical-minded and enterprising Fr.

Miguel Núñez at the cost of great effort, "has been maintained to the present day, with the sole difference that it has been moved from one side of the Rio de San Antonio to the other and farther down. There it has an adobe church (*iglesia de terrado*), with a house for the friars, and an irrigation system for the cultivated fields. It is one of the most successful missions in charge of the College of Zacatecas, and has numerous Christians. The Indians of the pueblo are fully instructed in Christian doctrine."

While the adobe church which he mentions may have been the one built at the second site, it could also have been the first constructed at the present site. The latter is mentioned in the first detailed description of Mission San José, which is contained in a report on the Zacatecan missions in Texas compiled by Fr. Ignacio Antonio Cyprián and sent by him on October 27, 1749, to the Franciscan commissary general of New Spain.

Fr. Ciprián was in Texas already in 1731; for, he administered the first baptism in the newly founded Villa de San Fernando. In 1749 he was in charge of Mission Nuestra Señora del Espíritu Santo at La Bahía (Goliad); and he seems to have held the office of Father President at this time.

Fr. Ciprián's Report, 1749

Mission San José, wrote Fr. Ciprián, has a very interesting church (*iglesia mui curiosa*) which can accommodate 2,000 persons. Though the statement that the church could hold 2,000 persons is repeated in two subsequent reports, it is probably due to an error that was made in the extant copy of Fr. Ciprián's report and perhaps also in the original. There was no need for such a vast edifice. The Indians who were living at the mission would not have filled one-tenth of the space. This church, like the one at the second site, seems to have been built of adobe.

However, the friary adjoining the church "with a serrated cloister and a porter's office," and the granary, both having flat roofs, were no doubt stone structures. The houses of the Indians, says Fr. Ciprián, are of stone and so strongly built that they make the mission a veritable fortress.

The reason why Mission San José, as well as the other missions on the San Antonio River were built like fortresses, were the raids which the Apaches and other Indians of the north made on them throughout their history. The missions were so well fortified that the hostile Indians did not dare to attack the compounds themselves but harassed them by stealing what they could from their farms and ranches which were outside the walls.

On San José's farm, writes Fr. Ciprián, 1,500 *fanegas* (2,400 bushels) of corn were raised annually; "and if they planted more they would have more." But he adds that all of the mission Indians "have everything they need in every respect; and they are very well instructed and are very good Christians." On the ranch were 2,000 head of cattle and 1,000 sheep.

The Indians living at the mission were over 200 in number. They were dressed in cotton and woolen cloth, which they wove themselves in their textile shop which had several looms.

This mission, declared Fr. Ciprián, has made greater spiritual and temporal progress than any of the other Zacatecan missions in Coahuila, Nuevo Reyno de León, Nuevo Santander, and Texas.

Fr. Ciprián's report was supplemented by two memorials which the Fr. Guardian of the College, Fr. Francisco Vallejo (who had been a missionary in eastern Texas) and his councillors sent to the king and to the Franciscan commissary general in Spain on January 15, 1750. The one addressed to the king states that 70 Indian families, or a little more than 220 persons, were living in the pueblo of San José in 1749.

It also declared that, to achieve greater spiritual and temporal progress, Mission San José had been placed in various locations (*puesta en varias situaciones*)—not merely two, but at least three. This statement confirms what has been said above, namely that the transfer of the mission from the east to the west bank was not the only one, and that before it was moved to its final site the mission occupied a place on lower ground, closer to the river, from about 1727 to 1740.

It was Fr. Miguel Núñez de Haro, San José's first missionary, who twice moved the mission; and he had the happiness of seeing it firmly established at its present site. After serving the mission for over three decades with untiring zeal, patience, and perseverance, he died on December 2, 1752, and was buried at San José. Later, however, his remains were taken to Zacatecas and laid to rest in the cemetery of the College.

Report of Governor Barrios, 1758

Five and a half years after the death of Fr. Núñez, when Governor Jacinto Barrios y Jáuregui paid a visit to San José on May 23, 1758, the missionary in charge was Fr. Ildefonso Joseph Marmolejo. Twenty years earlier he had been a missionary in eastern Texas, and from 1750 to 1753 he had held the office of guardian at the College of Zacatecas. The missionary showed the governor the records of the mission and every part of the compound; and so favorably impressed was Barrios that he wrote a detailed description of San José five days later and sent it to the viceroy.

The mission compound, writes the governor, is divided into eight squares. Four of these are formed by 84 Indian houses built of stone and having flat roofs, parapets, and loopholes. Each of the four groups of Indian dwellings consists of eighteen appartments ($4 \times 18 = 72$, and hence there must have been 12 others adjoining them or elsewhere.) All of these houses are arranged in the same way; and they have their interior patios in which are ovens, flowing water from the irrigation ditches, and bathing pools. The other four squares are formed by the church, friary, cemetery, soldier's quarters (for three Spanish soldiers), granary, and various workshops.

This description of the compound seems to indicate an arrangement that was quite different from the one which the mission had a decade later; but it is not likely that the stone Indian houses were torn down and then reconstructed along the walls. Furthermore, already in 1758, these houses had parapets and loopholes. When the governor speaks of eight squares within the compound, he is probably referring to a mental rather than a strictly physical division of one large square in order to indicate the location of its several parts.

Each of the Indian houses, says Governor Barrios, consists of one room and a kitchen, and is furnished with a *metate* (for grinding corn by hand), a *comal* (flat piece of iron for making *tortillas*), a pot, water jar, closet, pantry, bed, and dresser. All the Indians are well dressed, even better than one would expect of their station. The number of Indians living in the mission is 281, of whom 113 are men capable of bearing arms.

Regular Indian guards make the rounds at night. The Indians have their own civil and military officials who carry out their duties under the guidance of the missionary, who uses his influence to have the guilty ones punished and all drawn together by love. But there are no chains or stocks, no bloodshed, and at the present time no fugitives.

The church, the same as in 1749, has transepts and a well-proportioned tower with bells. The friary is a two-story building built of stone and lime, but has only one room on the second floor.

Opposite the church are the soldiers' quarters for three Spanish guards with another bathing pool; and between the church and these quarters is the cemetery, surrounded by a rubble fence with three entrances. The cemetery, which is 222¼ feet square, serves also as a *plaza de armas*, where the

Indians have their military drills, which are different from those of the Spaniards but are carried out with remarkable precision.

Within the compound are also a granary containing 2,500 *fanegas,* that is, 4,000 bushels of corn, a carpenter shop, a smithy, and other workshops; also a sugar mill for making cane syrup and brown sugar bars.

For work on the farm the mission has 30 yoke of oxen; and on the mission ranch are 1,500 branded head of cattle and 3,376 sheep. Since 1749, the Apaches have killed and stolen no less than 2,000 head of cattle. Every week seven beefs are slaughtered to provide the Indians with meat. Those who are sick receive chicken and the mutton of lambs.

Every Sunday the missionary doles out to each Indian one peck of corn, a slab of meat, and some tobacco. On Thursdays he distributes among them beans, brown sugar bars, and more corn to those who need it. If there is anything else that they need for their sustenance on the other days of the week, the missionary gives it to them.

On Saturdays the Indians pray and sing the Rosary; and "no one who has seen it can keep from weeping at the modesty, the composure, the religious fervor, the good voices, and the music of the Indians."

The mission records inspected by the governor, showed that during the 38 years since 1720, 964 Indians were baptized, 145 couples entered Christian marriages, and 466 received Christian burial. More than half (533) of the 964 Indians who were baptized received the sacrament in the last eighteen years, that is since 1740. "Everything at Mission San José," declares Governor Barrios, "is arranged with such perfect symmetry that it provokes the admiration of all who see it."

Another distinguished visitor who bestowed his meed of praise upon Mission San José was the Franciscan Bishop Francisco Martínez Tejada of Guadalajara, who made an official inspection of the Province of Texas in the fall of 1759.

From La Bahía he went to San Antonio, and arrived there on November 17. He visited San José, therefore, about a year and a half after the governor had seen and admired the mission. On this occasion, the bishop no doubt administered the sacrament of confirmation to the Christian Indians, as he did at the other places enroute.

The bishop's visit and praise is mentioned in a report of 1762, written by Fr. Simón de Hierro, the guardian of the College of Zacatecas. He declared that San José was "one of the most flourishing missions, in regard to both temporal and spiritual growth," among all those which the College had founded since its inception and it was so strongly fortified that the Apaches dared not make an assault upon the mission compound itself.

The Visit and Report of Fr. Solís, 1768

With a total of 350 resident Indians, Mission San José reached its peak in population in 1768. In that year Fr. Gaspar José Solís, who had been sent by the College of Zacatecas to inspect its seven missions in Texas, spent three weeks at San José in the spring and another two weeks in the summer. He wrote that "this mission is so pretty and in such a flourishing condition, both materially and spiritually, that I cannot finds words or figures with which to express its beauty."

Fr. Solís arrived at San José on March 18; and the next day, the feast of St. Joseph, the mission's patron saint, he blessed the foundations of the mission's new church, and the first two stones were laid by Governor Hugo Oconor and Fr. Solís. The church which had been built before 1749 had been torn down to make room for the new stone church, the present (restored) edifice; and a hallway of the stone friary was being used temporarily as a chapel. The missionary of San José at this time was Fr. President Pedro Ramírez de Arellano.

The mission compound, writes Fr. Solís, is built of stone and forms a perfect square, 220 *varas* (611 feet) on each side, with two towers on diagonal corners. On each of the four sides there was an entrance. The Indian houses of stone, which formed a part of the wall, extended 11 feet into the square and were from 14 to 16½ feet in length.

Each Indian apartment consisted of one room and a kitchen with a fireplace. All of them had beds, raised above the ground, covered with buffalo hides, and provided with sheets of gunny sack and large blankets of wool and of cotton which were woven in the mission shops. From these shops came also the clothes worn by the Indians, of which each one had two sets, one for week days and one for fiesta days.

Besides the textile and tailor shops, the mission had a carpenter and a blacksmith shop, a stone granary with a vaulted roof, and lime and brick kilns. Inside the square was a well "from which there comes as large a flow of water as from a small river." This water flowed through the square and joined the irrigation ditch outside the walls, in which there was an abundance of fish.

The irrigated farm outside the walls was more than two and a half miles long and produced abundant crops of corn, beans, lentils, potatoes, sugar cane, cotton, melons, vegetables, and fruits, especially peaches. The latter weighed as much as a pound each. The surplus products of the farm were sent to the four presidios in Texas.

The ranch of the mission, called El Atascoso, was at a considerable distance from the square and farm, 25 to 30 miles farther south on the Atascoso River, near present Pleasanton or Poteet. Here all the stock was kept, including 1,500 head of cattle, 5,000 sheep and goats, about ten droves of mares and four droves of asses. "White overseers or administrators are not needed," says Fr. Solís, "for the Indians take complete charge of the ranch."

Arch and well of the old convento or friary of Mission San José. (H. L. Summerville photo; courtesy of San José Mission Friary.)

The three Spanish soldiers, who were still at San José in 1763, apparently were no longer stationed at the mission in 1768. Fr. Solís does not mention them, but declares that "there is no need to employ anyone who does not belong to the mission," and of the 350 Indians at the mission 110 are warriors, 45 armed with guns and the rest with bows and arrows, spears, and other weapons. Mounted Indian sentinels keep guard outside the walls to prevent a surprise attack by hostile Apaches and other Indians of the north.

The priests of San José, namely Fr. Ramírez and his assistant, continued their efforts to bring new converts from the seacoast into the mission. Except for the new arrivals, the mission Indians spoke Spanish quite well; they were well instructed in Christian doctrine, well trained in various crafts, played various musical instruments, had a choir of four voices, and could dance "just as the Spaniards, perhaps even more beautifully and gracefully. These Indians are so polite, so well-mannered, and so refined that one might imagine that they had been civilized and living at the mission for a long time."

Fr. Morfi's Eyewitness Account, 1777

The new stone church, begun in 1768, was nearing completion at the end of 1777, when Fr. Juan Agustín Morfi, chaplain and diarist of the Commandant General Teodoro de Croix, visited Mission San José.

In his *History of Texas, 1673-1779,* which he wrote about five years later, Fr. Morfi described the new church and mission as he had seen it. Mission San José, he declares, "is, in truth, the first mission in America, not in point of time, but in point of beauty, plan, and strength, so that there is not a presidio along the entire frontier line that can compare with it."

Since he had visited all the frontier establishments with De Croix, he was well able to make the comparison. It is on this statement that San José's title of "Queen of the Missions" is based.

It is true that the same title has been given to Mission Santa Barbara in California; but it was founded at a later date (December 4, 1786) and its present (restored) church was constructed in 1815-1820. Besides, Santa Barbara was named the Queen among the twenty-one missions which were established on the coast of California between 1769 and 1823.

Fr. Morfi tells us that the sacristy of the new church had been completed and was being used as a church at the end of 1777. Fr. President Pedro de Ramírez was still in charge of the mission; and though he was absent on important business in eastern Texas in 1771-1772, he deserves the title of the builder of the present (restored) church of San José. Fr. Morfi wrote of him that his "dedication, zeal, and religious spirit deserve all praise."

When Fr. Ramírez died on September 30, 1781, he was buried in the sacristy, just outside the railing, about a foot from the south wall. He was a contemporary of Fr. Junípero Serra, the president of the California missions; and like Fr. Serra, he received the faculty to administer the sacrament of confirmation in 1778. On May 10 of that year he exercised this faculty for the first time at Mission San José.

Of the new church, Fr. Morfi writes: "The whole structure is admirably proportioned and strongly built of stone and mortar, chiefly of a sandy limestone that is light and porous when freshly quarried but in a few days hardens and becomes one with the mortar. . . . This stone is obtained from a quarry near the Mission of Nuestra Señora de la Concepción."

It has a beautiful, ornamented cupola, says Fr. Morfi, and its façade is very costly because of the statues and ornaments with which it is decorated. Over the main entrance there is a large balcony which bestows much majesty on the building. "In a word, no one could have imagined that there were such good artists in so desolate a place."

The ornamentation of the cupola and of the flat surfaces of the façade consisted of geometrical color designs of yellow, red, blue, and black. These could still be seen by visitors in the nineteenth century; and Ernst Schuchard has recreated some of them in the same manner in which the original designs were drawn.

The statues on the façade, as shown by old photographs, were the same as those which have been restored. At the top of the oval window are angel heads supporting the figure of St. Joseph, the husband of Mary and patron of the mission. On his right is a statue of St. Dominic, the friend of St. Francis, and on his left one of St. Francis of Assisi, founder of the Franciscan Order. Above St. Joseph is a representation of the Sacred Heart of Jesus, encircled by a crown of thorns. At the top was a richly carved stone cross, of which only a part remains.

In the center of the façade were two large carved doors, which have been reproduced. A smaller door is in the lower part of each of the larger ones. Above the doors is a relief reproduction of the miraculous painting of Our Lady of Guadalupe, which is venerated in the pilgrimage shrine on the northern outskirts of Mexico City. On its right is a statue of St. Joachim and on the left one of St. Anne, the parents of the Blessed Virgin Mary. The hearts above these two statues represent the hearts of Joseph and Mary. The shell above the image of Our Lady of Guadalupe is symbolic of the sacrament of baptism.

Fr. Morfi does not mention the famous so-called Rose Window, which is the exterior ornamental frame of the sacristy's south window. It was probably sculptured after the church had been completed in 1782.

The further description of Mission San José by Fr. Morfi agrees with that of Fr. Solís, except for the additions which had been made during the intervening decade. There were now four towers, one at each of the corners of the square; and in the west wall was a fifth gate with an iron grating, the only one that was kept open every day. The granary had three vaulted sections.

More rooms had been added on the second floor of the friary; and both floors had spacious galleries, of which the upper one opened out on the flat roofs of the Indian houses. According to Fr. Morfi's description and measurements these houses were principally on the east and south side. The upper floor of the friary was connected with the ground floor by an ornate stairway of stone. The farm outside the walls was not merely 2½ miles long but 2½ miles square. It was fenced, and irrigated by a beautiful ditch which led the water from the San Antonio River to every part of the fields.

As traced by workers of the Texas Civil Works Administration and the Texas Relief Commission during the Depression days, the irrigation ditch of San José began above a dam built across the San Antonio River about a half mile below Arroyo Concepción, and flowed south for about 3½ miles before it rejoined the river. Outside the north wall of the mission square it ran from west to east, and then south along the east wall.

Everything at the mission, writes Fr. Morfi, "is in such good order and so well planned, that even if the enemy would be able to lay siege to the mission, the besieged, having their granary well filled with food and plenty of good water in their wells, could afford to laugh at their opponents."

However, the decline of Mission San José set in soon after it reached its most flourishing condition. The 350 Indians who resided at San José in 1768 were reduced in 1777 to about 275, not counting about 25 who lived at the mission ranch.

In 1783, after an epidemic it seems, the mission Indians of San José numbered only 128. They were increased to 189 in 1786; but two years later their number was decreased to 114, probably by another epidemic. In May, 1789, San José had 138 Indians, while the combined total in the other four San Antonio missions was only 238.

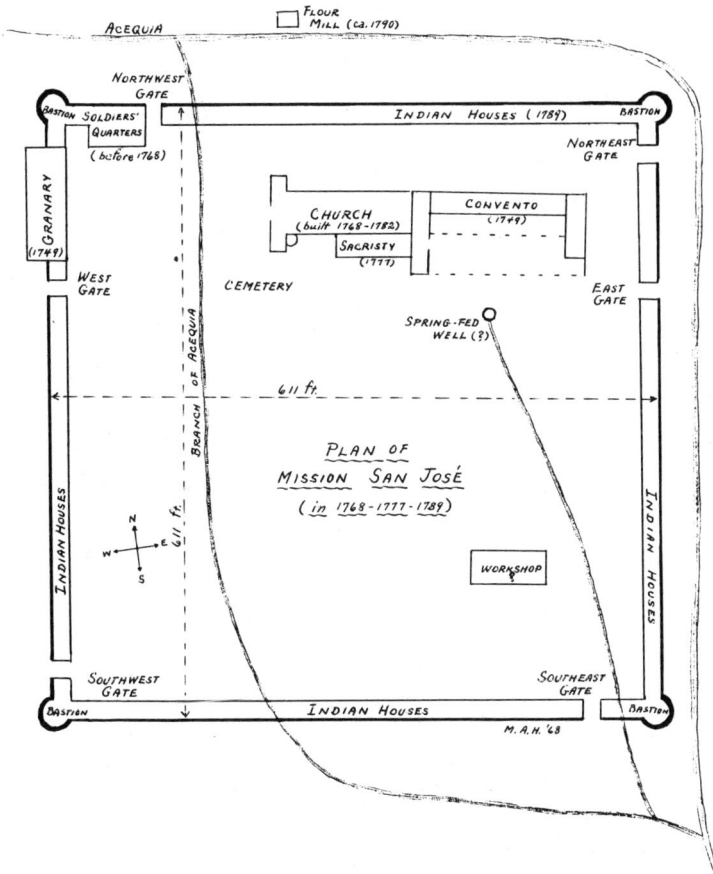

Author's diagram of the mission square of San José y San Miguel de Aguayo. According to the report of Fr. López (1789), the four corner gates directly faced the points of the compass.

Report of Fr. López, 1789

It was on May 5, 1789, that Fr. José Francisco López, who resided at Mission San Antonio, signed a long report on the seven remaining missions in Texas, of which he was the president.

Not only does he describe the condition of the missions, but he also points out the causes of their decline. Sickness and plagues of smallpox and buboes was one of these, especially at San José. Others were the recurrent flight of mission Indians and the wholesale slaughtering of mission cattle, not only by the Apaches, but also by the soldiers and the settlers.

But the principal cause was the decree of Commandant General Teodoro de Croix, issued after his visit of the San Antonio area in 1777-1778. It declared all unbranded cattle to be government property and imposed a tax of four *reales* (one half a peso) for every head of unbranded cattle taken or killed by anyone, including the missions. The result was that the once opulent missions were impoverished.

Mission San José, however, "standing on a broad plain, rather sparsely wooded, its grounds and buildings surrounded by a rampart of stone-and-mud houses," still offered "an attractive sight." Of its church and sacristy, Fr. López writes that "because of their architecture, they are the most beautiful structures to be seen anywhere this side of Saltillo."

From the private rooms on the second floor of the friary, the missionary could enter a pulpit attached to the east wall of the sanctuary of the church. Between the church and friary on one side and the Indian houses along the north wall of the square there was a street. A sixth gate had been added, probably on the east side. The Indians of San José were less indolent and could speak Spanish better than those of the other missions. Though most affected by the plague of buboes, this mission had always been the richest and the most populous.

The missionary in charge of San José at the time Fr. López made his report was Fr. José María Salas. About a year later, June 17, 1790, he died and was buried in the sanctuary of the church on the north side.

That Fr. Salas had made a special effort to gain new converts for San José after Fr. López wrote his report is shown by the fact that in December of 1789 the number of mission Indians had been increased to 198. Subsequently San José did not again reach that total, but declined steadily. In 1790 it had 144 Indians, and in 1791 there were 106.

The Flour Mill

The successor of Fr. Salas at San José from 1789 to 1794 was Fr. José Manuel Pedrajo, a young priest not yet thirty years old. Despite the handicaps he had to face, he succeeded in training the mission Indians to weave cloth and blankets that were as good as those of Querétaro. He also improved the products of the mission farm, which now included wheat; and he built an ingenious flour mill along the irrigation ditch outside the north wall of the square.

This mill was a so-called Norse Mill and a forerunner of Pelton's turbine; it was powered not merely by the flow of water but by the impulse energy derived from water falling from a height. The old mill's lower part was discovered in 1933, and the mill has been restored by Ernst Schuchard.

Partial Secularization, 1794

After Mission San Antonio had been suppressed in 1793, the other four missions in the area were partially secularized in 1794. Governor Múñoz carried out the secularization of Mission San José on July 16-22. After Pedro Huizar had surveyed the mission farm, parts of it as well as the available domestic animals and various tools were distributed to the heads of families and unmarried adults among the 93 Indians then residing at San José.

José Herrera was appointed "justice," with the task of looking after the temporal interests of the Indians. The missionary remained as the pastor of the Christians and had complete charge, as before, of the six families who were still under instruction, and such new converts as would be brought to the mission.

Fr. José Mariano Cárdenas, who had succeeded Fr. López as *presidente,* resided at San José at this time; and shortly afterwards he began to take care also of Mission Concepción as a sub mission. Fr. Pedrajo went to Mission Rosario and then to Refugio, a new mission founded in 1793. The following year, when Fr. Pedrajo came back to San Antonio to hire workers for the building of Refugio, he settled the accounts of San José. The report which he gave Governor Múñoz showed that Mission San José had a balance of 3,888.55 pesos in loans which the mission had made to Spanish settlers.

After the partial secularization, life at Mission San José continued very much the same as before, except that it was carried out on a smaller scale. In 1797, eight Indians (three men and five women), who were under instruction, were under the care and the supervision of Fr. Cárdenas in temporal as well as spiritual matters just as in former days. A small number of new Indians came into the mission almost until the very end.

Spaniards too began to settle at and near the mission, and the missionary of San José included them in his pastoral ministrations. During the five years that Fr. Cárdenas served San José and Concepción, he baptized 44 persons.

The first "justice" of the partially secularized Mission San José, José Herrera, seems to have been succeeded in 1796 by Pedro Huizar, who held the same office for Concepción; and he may have continued to look after Concepción also after 1796. In 1809, the justice of San José Indian pueblo was Santiago Mandujano. He was succeeded the same or the following year by Pedro Huizar's son, José Antonio, who was

called Spanish *alcalde* of the Indians instead of "justice," and
served in that capacity until December 13, 1819. His successor,
Tomás de León, was still Spanish *alcalde* of San José in
1822.

Fr. Bernardino Vallejo, 1800-1816

The successor of Fr. Cárdenas, both as Fr. President and as
missionary of San José and Concepción, was Fr. Bernardino
Vallejo. For sixteen years, from 1800 to 1816, when he
returned to Zacatecas and was elected guardian of the
College, Fr. Vallejo resided at Mission San José, fulfilling his
duties in such an exemplary manner that he won the esteem
and love of all. Twice he was recalled to the College, but at
the governor's request he was allowed to remain at his post.

In his report of December 31, 1804, about the missions in
Texas, Fr. Vallejo states that Mission San José had a population of 73 persons, of whom 57 were Indians and 36 were
Spaniards. The number of Indians was the same as two years
earlier.

The friendly priest mentioned by Lieutenant Zebulon M.
Pike when he speaks in his diary of his visit to Mission San
José in June, 1807, was none other than Fr. Bernardino
Vallejo. Pike says that he was respected and loved by all who
knew him and he treated him with the kindest hospitality. The
buildings of San José and two other missions that he saw
elicited the admiration of Lieutenant Pike; for he declares
that, in regard to solidity, accommodation, and even majesty,
these formerly prosperous missions were surpassed by few he
had seen in Mexico.

Governor Manuel Salcedo, in a report of June, 1809,
described the mission churches of San José and its three
neighboring missions as being in fair condition, and he says
they were being administered by two Franciscan missionaries.
Mission San José owned and operated a good flour mill, the
same which had been built by Fr. Pedrajo between 1790 and

Aerial view of Mission San José before restoration, after the new friary had been built in 1931. (From the Archives of San José Mission Friary.)

1794. San José had a population of 70, of whom 55 were Indians and 15 were Spaniards.

During the Casas rebellion of 1811 and the Gutiérrez invasion of 1813, the padres and residents of San José and the other three missions remained loyal to the Spanish crown. It was during the revolution of 1813 that most of the records of these missions, which were kept at San José, were destroyed. However, those which had been commenced by Fr. Ramírez at San José and the marriage register of Concepción from the year 1733 survived; and these are now in the archives of the Cathedral of San Fernando.

The last report on the missions of Texas was submitted by Fr. Vallejo in February, 1815. San José Mission had a population of 109 persons, 49 of them Indians and 60 Spaniards. Only some of the fields which had been given to the Indians were irrigated, and the Indians were practically destitute. The church of San José was still in good condition.

Fr. Vallejo and his companion missionary at Espada still received the customary annual allowance from the government; but the very next year, this aid was discontinued. The missionaries collected no fees, neither from the Indians nor from the Spaniards. Every Sunday they gave instructions in Christian doctrine to all the people at the four missions, Indians and Sparniards.

The Last Missionaries

Fr. Manuel María Fellechea, who came to Mission San José when Fr. Bernardino Vallejo left in 1816, had to take care of all four missions. He did not remain long; he was followed the next year by Fr. President Francisco Frexes. Not only did Fr. Frexes have to get along without the annual allowance from the government, but the Indians refused to render any service to him and lodged false charges against him with Governor Antonio Martínez. Unfortunately the governor accepted them at face value; and Fr. Frexes left in the summer of 1819, after Fr. Miguel Muro had arrived to take his place.

Fr. Muro adapted himself to the situation, and won the friendship of the governor. There was a disastrous inundation of the San Antonio River on July 5, 1819; and Fr. Muro distributed 150 pesos, collected in Coahuila for the flood-sufferers, among both Indians and Spaniards at San José Capistrano, and Espada.

In the summer of 1820, Fr. José Antonio Díaz de León, the missionary at Mission Nuestra Señora del Refugio, received the news of his appointment as Fr. President; and some time later he exchanged places with Fr. Muro. He was the last missionary of Mission San José and its neighboring missions.

Early in 1822 Fr. Díaz had to substitute also for the pastor of San Fernando, the Rev. Refugio de la Garza, who went to the National Congress of the independent Republic of Mexico as a delegate; and until November of that year when the military chaplain Francisco Maynes came to San Antonio, he was the only priest in the area. Fr. Díaz continued to assist Fr. Maynes until Fr. Garza returned in 1824.

Complete Secularization, 1824

Due to the efforts of Delegate Garza, the Mexican government ordered the complete secularization of Mission San José and its three neighboring missions on September 13, 1823. These orders were transmitted two days later to the newly appointed Political Chief José Antonio de Saucedo, who administered Texas now that it had been joined to Coahuila in one state.

Fr. Díaz, who still hoped to rehabilitate the remaining missions, tried in vain to save San José and its neighbors. He pointed out that the missions had by no means been abandoned and closed for a period of one year, as Delegate Garza had claimed, and that their complete secularization could not be carried out because there were no secular priests on hand to take them over. But after the College of Zacatecas gave its consent to their full secularization on December 31, 1823, Fr.

Díaz complied with the orders that he prepare an inventory of the four mission churches and their furnishings.

On February 29, 1824, he signed the inventories and surrendered to Chaplain Maynes, the representative of the bishop of Monterrey, the mission churches of San José, Concepción, Capistrano, and Espada. On that day they ceased to be in the care of Fr. Díaz, the missionary of the College of Zacatecas. San José was no longer a mission. It had been in existence for over a century, from 1720 to 1824.

Number of Indians Baptized

How many Indians were baptized at Mission San José? During the first twenty years, 1720 to 1740, there were 431 baptisms, an average of 23 per year. During the next 18 years, there were 533 more, a yearly average of about 30, making a total of 964 in 1758.

According to Fr. Solís, the total in 1768 was 1,054, a figure that is repeated by Fr. Morfi; but Fr. Solís qualifies his statement by saying "if I am not mistaken," showing that he was not quite sure for some reason. The fact is that his total cannot be correct, unless he means the baptisms of adults only. It would imply that during one of San José's most flourishing decades there were only 90 baptisms, an average of nine a year.

Anyhow, a new baptismal register beginning with the number "one" seems to have been started after 1758. When Fr. Ramírez commenced a third book of baptisms, the only one which is still extant, he gave the first entry the number 832, indicating that there were at least 831 baptisms, or about 42 a year, between 1758 and 1777, the period of the mission's greatest success.

The last recorded baptism in the third book is numbered 1,211, showing that there were 380 baptisms, or an average of eight per year, during the last 47 years from 1777 to 1824, the period of the mission's decline.

Now, if we add the total of 964 in 1758 to the total of 1,211 in 1824, we arrive at a grand total of 2,175. A few of the entries during the last years were those of baptisms administered at the neighboring missions; but we can safely say that during the 104 years of the mission's existence, more than 2,000 Indians, young and old, were baptized at San José.

After the Secularization

During the sixteen years which followed the complete secularization of San José in 1824, this mission and the other three were completely neglected although there were two priests in San Antonio, the Rev. Refugio de la Garza and the Rev. José Antonio Valdez. They were removed from office in the summer of 1840, when Father John M. Odin, vice-prefect of Texas, came to San Antonio and appointed Father Michael Calvo pastor of San Fernando and the old missions. From that time on, Father Calvo occasionally visited San José and conducted divine services in its church, which was still in good condition. The title of the Catholic Church to San José and the other former mission churches was confirmed by the Congress of the Republic of Texas in 1841.

Originally a part of the diocese of Guadalajara, the Province of Texas was placed under the jurisdiction of the new see of Linares, Nuevo León, in 1777; and in 1791 the seat of this diocese was transferred to Monterrey. When Texas gained its independence in 1836, it was put under the bishop of New Orleans; and after it became a State of the Union in 1845, the diocese of Galveston, comprising the whole State, was created in 1847. The diocese of San Antonio was erected in 1874.

At the request of Bishop Odin of Galveston, the Benedictines of Latrobe, Pennsylvania, came to San José in 1859 and established a priory in the former *convento* or friary. They did some building here and remained until 1868. The first prior was Fr. Alto S. Hoermann, author of a novel about San José,

The Daughter of Tehuan. He was succeeded by Father Armand Kramer in 1864, and some time later by Father Aemilian Wendel.

After the departure of the Benedictines, diocesan priests visited San José at times until the Holy Cross Fathers took charge in 1872. They continued to conduct religious services regularly at San José until 1888. Diocesan priests then once more served San José, especially after 1918, when Father William Wheeler Hume, with the aid of Mrs. H. P. Drought, renovated the sacristy, which was used as a church.

From 1923 to 1931, the Redemptorist Fathers attended San José regularly. Since 1931, when they built a new friary near the old church, the Franciscans of the St. Louis-Chicago Province have been in charge of San José, and of its parish which was formally erected in 1932.

San José Mission in Ruins

While divine services were held at San José more or less continuously since 1840, the several buildings of the mission except the sacristy gradually fell into ruins during the latter part of the nineteenth and early part of the twentieth century.

The walls of the mission square, with the Indian houses, disappeared. The vaulted roof of the granary collapsed. The old friary, too, became roofless. A part of the north wall of the church fell down on December, 10, 1868; and the dome with the greater part of the roof crashed on December 25, 1874, while midnight services were going on in the sacristy.

The façade was wantonly mutilated between 1841 and 1850 by soldiers who were quartered at the old mission, and more so by others after 1880. The doors of the main entrance of the church were stolen between 1880 and 1890. The steps of the spiral staircase beside the tower lay scattered about since 1903, but were put back about 1920. The tower itself fell down in 1928, but was restored immediately with a squat

Aerial view of Mission San José after its restoration had been completed in 1937. (From the Archives of San José Mission Friary.)

conical top. The original pyramidal apex of the tower was restored only after it had been struck by lightning in 1940.

Restoration of the Mission

The complete restoration of Mission San José has been the work of many minds and hearts, of individuals as well as organizations and societies. The book about San Antonio which William Corner wrote and published in 1890 aroused some interest in the preservation of what was left of San José. But it was not until 1917 that the Texas Historic Landmarks Association and the De Zavala Chapter of the Daughters of the Republic of Texas took some definite steps towards this end. A donation from the latter was used to have some work done on the church.

About the same time, Father William W. Hume undertook to make the people of San Antonio and Texas conscious of the treasures they possessed in the old missions; and with the aid received from Mrs. H. P. Drought, he had considerable restoration work done on the church and friary.

When the Franciscans returned in 1931, Archbishop Arthur J. Drossaerts decided to have the roofless church completely restored and placed the project under the direction of Father Mariano S. Garriga, who was in charge until 1935 when funds gave out. The work was resumed the following year under the supervision of Father Alois J. Morkovsky, and in 1937 the church was rededicated. Archbishop Robert E. Lucey had further work on the church and its façade done especially during the years 1941-1952.

The San Antonio Conservation Society, founded in 1924, concentrated its attention on the acquisition and restoration of the granary and adjoining parts of the mission square on the north side. The granary was restored and roofed in 1933; and in 1936, with aid received from the National Society of Colonial Dames in Texas and the Pioneer Flour Mills of San Antonio, Fr. Pedrajo's flour mill was reconstructed. A gravel pit on the north side was converted into an outdoor theater in the 1930's; and after it was completely rebuilt in 1958, the theater was given by the Conservation Society to the State of Texas and made the official Texas State Historical Theater.

The County of Béxar restored the walls and Indian quarters on the west, south, and east sides of the square in 1932; and after the Conservation Society had given the title to the granary and north side to the County, the latter surrendered the entire square, except the church and friary, to the State.

With the cooperation of the Archdiocese of San Antonio, which entered an agreement with the State concerning the church and friary and adjoining property, the entire mission compound was made a Texas State Park as an Historic Site, in 1941. The same year San José Mission was designated a National Historic Site, not federally owned.

State and National Historic Site

While the restored church is used as a regular parish church, San José Mission, State and National Historic Site, is administered by the Texas Parks and Wildlife Department in cooperation with the Archdiocese of San Antonio and the National Park Service, and with the assistance of an advisory board consisting of one representative of each of these three organizations together with one of the County of Béxar and another of the San Antonio Conservation Society. San José is the only Historic Site in the United States that has this unique arrangement for its continuance; it is also the only one of the old missions in our Spanish Borderlands which has been declared a National Historic Site.

Many people, in groups and as individuals, from the United States and foreign countries, visit the restored old mission of San José in the city of San Antonio. The total number of visitors during the year 1967 was about 125,000. The mission is open to visitors daily from 9:00 a.m. to 8:00

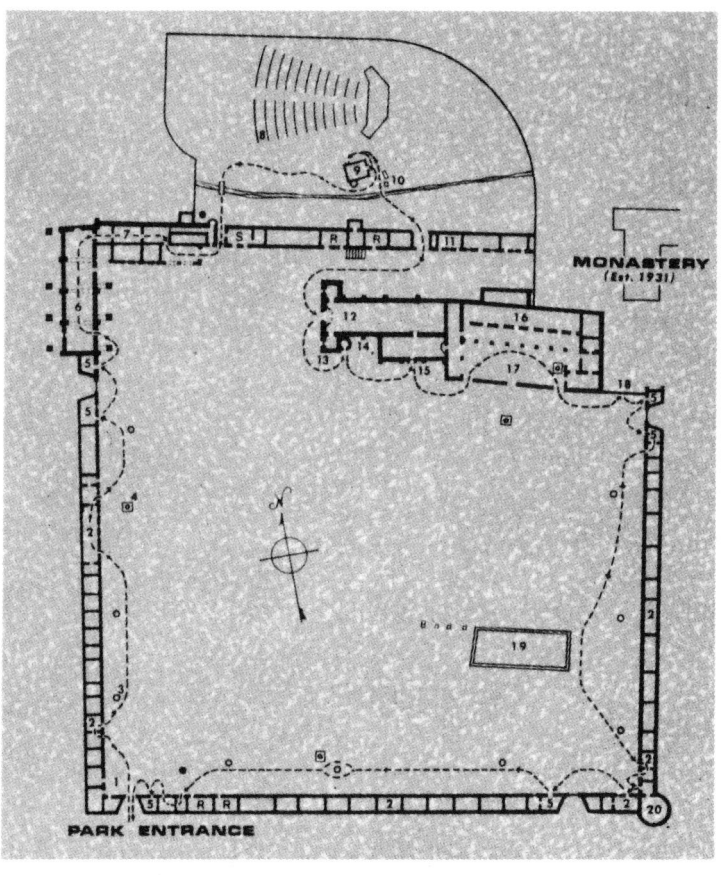

Plan of San José Mission State and National Historic Site. (Courtesy of Pierson DeVries, Superintendent.)

p.m., April 1 to September 30, and from 9:00 a.m. to 6:00 a.m., October 1 to March 31. It is situated on Roosevelt Avenue, a part of Highway 281, about 4½ miles from downtown San Antonio. There are ample parking facilities outside the walls near the entrance at the southwestern corner of the mission square.

"When one leaves San José," to quote Charles Mattoon Brooks, Jr., "he has seen the finest of the southwestern monuments. . . . At no other mission is there sculpture to compare with the rich carving here enshrining San José and the Virgin of Guadalupe. At no other establishment in the whole territory was there a more comfortable or impressive convent. . . . Few developments achieved the ingenious fortifications that surrounded this patio. And finally, seldom were the efforts of the padres crowned with more success in the matter of Christianizing the heathen."

(A more complete, book-length, authentic history of Mission San José from the time of its founding to the present day is available in the writer's *San Antonio's Mission San José, State and National Historic Site, 1720-1968*, published by the Naylor Company of San Antonio and Franciscan Herald Press of Chicago in the spring of 1968.)

Important Dates

1720, Feb. 23: Mission San José was founded on the east bank of the San Antonio River, about 3½ miles south of Mission San Antonio, as a Zacatecan mission.

1727: Some time before this year, the mission was moved to the west bank, about one-half mile from the present site, nearer to the river.

1740: The mission was moved to its third site, the present one; and the construction of permanent buildings was begun.

1749, Oct. 27: Fr. Ciprián reported completion of a granary, friary, and Indian houses of stone, and a large adobe church.

1752, Dec. 2: Fr. Miguel Núñez de Haro, missionary of San José during its first 32 years, died.

1768, March 19: Governor Oconor and Fr. Solís laid the first stones of San José's new church, the present restored building. Mission Indians numbered 350. No soldiers at the mission.

1764, Nov. 7: Fr. Juan de Dios Camberos died at San José.

1781, Sept. 30: Fr. Pedro Ramírez, the builder of the stone church, died at the mission, and was buried in the sacristy.

1782: The stone church of San José was completed.

1789, May 5: Fr. López reported four bastions, one at each corner, and six gates. Indians of mission reduced to 138.

1790, June 17: Fr. José María de Salas died, and was buried in the sanctuary of the new church.

1790-1794: Fr. Pedrajo built a flour mill outside the north wall.

1794, July 23: San José Mission was partially secularized.

1824, Feb. 29: The mission was completely secularized.

1859-1868: The Benedictine Fathers had a priory at the former mission.

1868, Dec. 10: Part of the north wall of the church collapsed.

1874, Dec. 25: The dome and roof of the church crashed to the floor.

1931, Oct. 25: Cornerstone of the new Franciscan friary at the mission was laid.

1937, April 18: The restored church of San José was rededicated.

1941, May 8: San José was dedicated as a National Historic Site. Previously, the same year, it was declared a State Historic Site.

Mission Nuestra Señora de la Purísima Concepción de Acuña. (H. L. Summerville photo; courtesy of San José Mission Friary.)

V

Mission Nuestra Señora de la Purísima Concepción
1716-1824

Two years before the founding of Mission San Antonio de
Valero, the permanent occupation of the Spanish Province of
Texas was begun by the expedition of Captain Domingo
Ramón. This expedition accompanied a group of missionaries
from the two colleges of Querétaro and Zacatecas to the
country of the Tejas Indians in eastern Texas, for the purpose
of establishing a chain of six missions. Three were staffed by
Querétaran friars, with Fr. Isidro Félix de Espinosa as their
president, and the other three by Zacatecan missionaries, with
Fr. Antonio Margil as their superior. Four missions and a
presidio were established in the summer of 1716, and the other
two missions early in 1717.

Concepción Mission in East Texas

One of the Querétaran missions was that of Nuestra Señora
de la Purísima Concepción. It was founded in the principal
village of the Ainay Indians, one of the many Tejas tribes, on
July 7, 1716. The site of this mission was near two springs, a
mile or two east of the place where the highway crosses the
Angelina River, not far from the present Linwood Crossing,
west of Douglass, in Nacogdoches County.

The presidio, which received the name of Nuestra Señora de los Dolores de los Tejas, after occupying a temporary site on the margin of a large lake, was established by the fall of 1716 near the Mission of San Francisco, and then moved to a place about 2½ miles northeast of Mission Concepción, on Thomas Creek, about four miles from the Angelina River, just west of Douglass.

Fr. Espinosa chose Mission Concepción as his headquarters, and had Fr. Gabriel Vergara as his companion. The Indians built a church and a house for the missionaries of timber, which abounded in this territory; but the missionaries found it difficult to gather the Tejas, who lived in widely scattered small villages, into a mission compound, as they did in the San Antonio area. Being more than four hundred miles from San Juan Bautista on the Rio Grande, they suffered much from lack of food and other supplies. In his *Crónica,* Fr. Espinosa relates the hardships which they had to bear and the difficulties they encountered.

"For two years," writes Father Espinosa, "the want and hardships which the fathers endured in the missions of (eastern) Texas were keenly felt; but it seems they were unavoidable. From the time that the missionaries entered that country, in 1716, no aid whatever reached them; and since the supplies which they had brought along were very meagre, they soon gave out and we were reduced to great straits.

"During the year 1717 and 1718, because of the severity of the drought, the harvest of corn and beans among the Indians was very poor. Since we usually received some provisions from the natives, it was inevitable that, when they themselves suffered want, we too should feel the pangs of hunger. . . .

"Many a day dawned when we had absolutely nothing to eat on hand. Necessity, however, is the mother of invention. It occurred to one of the fathers that possibly the flesh of the crow might after all furnish us a meal. These birds were somewhat smaller than our crows; but they abounded in the trees, especially during the morning hours. With the use of a gun, surely, we should be able to feast on meat every day. True, the color, flavor, and toughness of this meat were quite repugnant; but hunger made it so appetizing, that for the greater part of the year crow's meat was one of our most delicious dishes. When the fathers in the other missions heard of our discovery, they also provided their tables with crow's meat for the ordinary meals.

"On days of abstinence, however, our difficulties increased. Since we had neither bread nor vegetables, we sought to appease our hunger by means of herbs, adding nuts as a seasoning. On some days, the leaves of the mustard plant served as a most tasteful morsel, particularly when salty soil was found which rendered them more palatable."

To hunger was added sickness. Fr. Manuel Castellanos, who served also as chaplain of the presidio, and Fr. Hidalgo were afflicted with what seems to have been malaria. During the winter of 1717 and the spring of 1718, a serious epidemic took its toll among the Indians; and the missionaries baptized more than a hundred dying persons.

New supplies finally reached the missions in the summer of 1718; but Alarcón's expedition to eastern Texas in the fall of the same year, following the founding of the mission and presidio of San Antonio, turned out to be of little help to the missionaries and presidio soldiers in eastern Texas.

When Alarcón visited Mission Concepción on October 18, 1718, he was godfather for three children who were baptized. In the fifteen months which had elapsed since the founding of this mission, despite many obstacles, no less than 62 baptisms had been administered. In the mission pueblo, which was now reorganized and named Concepción de Agreda, there were five Indian houses; and an influential chief by the name of Angelina was induced to take up his residence in one of them.

Temporary Abandonment

In June of 1719, the French who had a post at Natchitoches, learning that France and Spain were at war in Europe, seized the Zacatecan Mission San Miguel de los Adaes, which was the farthest east, in present Louisiana. Although Frs. Espinosa and Margil wanted to remain at their posts, the others all believed it was best to abandon the missions and presidio temporarily and to retreat to the Trinity. When they decided to retire still farther west, all the way to the new mission and presidio of San Antonio, the two presidents had to follow. The refugees from eastern Texas arrived at San Antonio by November 1719, and there waited for the expedition of the Marqués de Aguayo.

With Aguayo's army, the missionaries, soldiers, and settlers of eastern Texas returned. They left San Antonio May 13, 1721; and by the beginning of August they had reached the country of the Tejas Indians. Not only were the six missions and the presidio near Mission Concepción re-established, but a new presidio was founded near Mission San Miguel de los Adaes, not far from Robeline, Louisiana; and this presidio served as the capital of Spanish Texas for the next half century.

Re-establishment of the Mission

On August 2, Fr. Gabriel de Vergara and Fr. Benito Sánchez were sent ahead to Mission Concepción to make preparations for its restoration. Unlike the other missions, Concepción had not been completely destroyed; and with the help of a group of men sent by Aguayo on the 6th, the missionaries had the mission ready for a colorful ceremony which was enacted on the 8th.

With his entire army, Aguayo went to Mission Concepción. The soldiers were lined up in three files before the church. Between the troops and the church six pieces of field artillery were placed. Fr. Margil sang a high Mass, and Fr. Espinosa preached an eloquent sermon. During the Mass several salutes were fired by the cannons and the soldiers' muskets. Several Indian chiefs then paid their respects to Governor Aguayo; and the latter had a good dinner served to them and the padres. Afterwards the Indians inducted Aguayo into their own ranks in a fashion of their own.

There was nothing niggardly about the gifts which Aguayo gave the Indians. In fact, as the missionaries learned by bitter experience afterwards, he was too lavish with them. He distributed clothing to about four hundred Indians. To the principal chief of the Tejas he gave his best suit which was trimmed with gold braid and a jacket that was adorned with gold and silver cloth. To Chief Cheocas, who was appointed governor of the mission pueblo of Concepción he gave a new suit of blue cloth with gold and silver braid and, as a symbol of his authority, a silver-headed cane or baton.

Aguayo accomplished more than any of his predecessors, but the missions in eastern Texas were not to benefit by the improved conditions for long. In the spring of 1727, Brigadier General Pedro de Rivera arrived in Texas for the purpose of inspecting the province and cutting expenses wherever he could. He decided that the number of soldiers at the presidio of Los Adaes, near Mission San Miguel, should be reduced, and the Presidio de Nuestra Señora de los Dolores de los Tejas, near Mission Concepción, should be abolished altogether.

Transfer of the Mission

The recommendations of Rivera were accepted and on April 26, 1729, the viceroy decreed the suppression of the Presidio de los Tejas. Three months later the missionaries of the three Querétaran missions, which were in the vicinity of the suppressed presidio, gathered at Mission Concepción and drew up a memorial in which they asked the viceroy to restore the presidio, and if this could not be done to permit them to move their missions to a more suitable site.

This petition was signed on July 20, 1729, by the following six missionaries: Fr. Gabriel Vergara, Fr. Joseph Andrés Rodríguez de Jesús María, Fr. Juan Bautista Garzía de Suarez, Fr. Alonso Giraldo de Terreros, Fr. Manuel de Ortuño, and Fr. Joseph de San Antonio y Estrada. Fr. Vergara was the president of the Querétaran missions at this time. He had been the companion of Fr. Espinosa, when the eastern missions were re-established in 1721; and when Fr. Espinosa was elected guardian of the College of Querétaro soon afterwards, Fr. Vergara succeeded him as Father President.

Rivera, who was now the viceroy's councillor, suggested the the missions be transferred to the Colorado River. This was done by July 27, 1730; but the new location did not prove to be satisfactory. Fr. Miguel Sevillano de Paredes, who was the guardian of the College at this time, sent a new petition to the viceroy, requesting permission to move the missions to the San Antonio River. Rivera had no objections, and so the three missions were moved to their present site on the San Antonio River.

On the San Antonio River

The re-establishment of the three missions on the San Antonio River took place on March 5, 1731, as is stated in the marriage record of Mission Concepción. But it took time to erect temporary buildings and to bring new Indians into the missions; and it was only by May 4 that this was accomplished.

The moving of the missions really meant the founding of new missions with the moveable property and supplies of the old ones. For, the Tejas Indians who had become Christians remained in eastern Texas; and they were henceforth to be taken care of by the three Zacatecan missions which remained where they were, especially by the Mission of Nuestra Señora de Guadalupe at Nacogdoches.

The moving of Mission Concepción and the other two, all the way from the Neches and Angelina rivers to the San Antonio, was a remarkable feat. The furnishings of the churches and the herds of cattle, horses, mules, and burros had to be taken across large rivers for a distance of 375 miles; and this was done without any serious mishap, and without any additional expense to the government.

However, the missions had to incur a debt in order to obtain the corn and cattle they needed during their first year at the new site. From San Juan Bautista on the Rio Grande they purchased 1,280 bushels of corn and 250 head of cattle. This was needed to feed the new mission Indians.

During March and April the missionaries, accompanied by soldiers, made two extended trips to bring Indians of various Coahuiltecan tribes to the three missions; and according to Fr. Espinosa they succeeded in gathering close to a thousand Indians who were willing to settle down and to work under the supervision of the missionaries. That meant over 300 Indians in each of the missions.

In a short time they constructed rough temporary shelters with thatched roofs—chapels, quarters for the padres, store-houses, and huts for themselves. Irrigation ditches were dug, fields were plowed, and corn was sown so that they would have a harvest in the summer. All this was done by May 4. Mission Concepción and the other two had a good beginning.

At its new location Concepción Mission received the name of Nuestra Señora de la Purísima Concepción de Acuña. The addition of "de Acuña" was made in honor of Juan de Acuña, Marqués de Casafuerte, who was the viceroy of New Spain at this time.

Difficulties and Obstacles

Not all the Indians, however, who had come persevered. Some deserted and went back to their haphazard and nomadic way of life, even though it meant periods of starvation; they succumbed to their disinclination for work and the lure of the wild. That always remained a problem with which the missions had to contend. The padres went in quest of them, and some of them as least welcomed them and gladly returned with them to the missions.

The missionaries were aided by a few Spanish soldiers who served not only as protectors of the padres and their charges but also as instructors of the mission Indians in agricultural pursuits and various trades. After Rivera visited Texas, the guards were removed from all the missions; but, at the request of the missionaries, they were restored. And when the three Querétaran missions were moved to the San Antonio River, three soldiers were assigned to each of them.

However, when the cantankerous Governor Franquis de Lugo came to San Antonio in the latter part of 1736, he reduced the number of these mission guards to one in each; and although he was ordered to give each mission three guards, he refused to do so. The soldiers were sent back only after Franquis de Lugo had been supplanted by his successor. Though he served as governor for less than two years and was then removed from office, Franquis de Lugo managed to do more harm to the missions by the highhanded manner in which he treated the missionaries than the Apaches. The latter made frequent raids on the missions, especially their herds of cattle; and that is the reason why the mission compounds were built in the form of walled fortresses.

Mission Concepción and the other San Antonio missions suffered another serious setback in 1739 when an epidemic swept through them. Of the 250 Indians who had lived at Concepción before the epidemic, only 120, about one half, remained after it had run its course. But in the spring of 1740, Fr. Benito de Santa Ana Fernández was able to report that the missions had recovered from this calamity.

Fr. Fernández had succeeded Fr. Vergara as the missionary in charge of Mission Concepción and as Fr. President of the Querétaran missions in Texas, in 1733; and he continued to reside at Concepción in this capacity for seventeen years. In 1749 he went to Mexico City to plead the cause of the new San Xavier missions which the College of Querétaro founded at this time on the San Gabriel River, north of San Antonio.

Although the missions had recovered from the epidemic, Fr. Fernández found it necessary in May, 1740, to complain to Captain Joseph de Urrutia of the presidio in San Antonio that the mission guards supplied by Captain Costales of La Bahía were practically useless. Thus, of the guards at Concepción, Juan Muro was not far from being an invalid and had been sick for the past six months, and Santiago Moya had neither a horse nor a gun.

Four soldiers from La Bahía happened to be in San Antonio at the time; and Fr. Fernández requested that two of them take the places of Muro and Moya. Captain Urrutia, a friend of the missions, took the matter into his own hands and ordered Joseph Bueno de Rojas and Marcelino Martínez, both fully equipped and armed, to Mission Concepción. The names of at least four soldiers who were stationed at Concepción have thus been recorded.

At the end of 1740, Captain Urrutia informed the viceroy that due to the self-sacrificing labors of the missionaries all the missions in the San Antonio area were faring well, even though the mission buildings were still of a temporary nature. Mission Concepción at this time had a population of 210 mission Indians.

The captains at La Bahía, however, continued their attempts to evade their obligation of sending suitable guards to Mission Concepción and the other two missions established on the San Antonio River in 1731. Fr. Fernández finally wrote to the viceroy in 1743, and strict orders were issued that the soldiers be furnished and that the soldiers should assist the missionaries as instructors of the Indians.

The missionaries compensated these men with clothing and provisions; and hence they did not have to buy these items from their captain's store. That, says Fr. Fernández, was the reason why the captain of La Bahía was so unwilling to supply competent men for the missions.

Report of Fr. Ortiz, 1745

In the middle of 1745, Fr. Francisco Xavier Ortiz, who was sent by the College of Querétaro to make an inspection of its Texas missions, spent a whole month in San Antonio. In his report we find the first detailed description of Mission Concepción.

Considerable progress had been made at this mission during the fourteen years that it had been on the eastern bank of the San Antonio River. The number of Indians who had been baptized during this period was 393; and 265 had received Christian burial after receiving the sacraments. There were now 207 Indians living in the mission, of whom 176 were baptized and 31 were receiving instructions.

A wall, built of stone and mortar, surrounded the mission enclosure. Inside this enclosure were, besides the church and friary, a large stone granary, three stone houses for the soldiers, and the huts of the Indians which were still *jacales* of wooden poles, brush, and mud, with thatched roofs. An irrigation ditch flowed through the middle of the compound.

The friary or residence of the two missionaries, Fr. Fernández and his assistant Fr. Joseph Francisco de Ganzabal, was a two-story stone house, two private rooms upstairs and two office rooms downstairs.

A new church of cut stone and mortar was being built, and it was about half finished. In the meantime a large adobe hall with a terrace (flat, earthen) roof served as a church; and a separate room was used as a sacristy.

On the altar in the church there was a carved statue of Mary Immaculate; and in the sacristy, on a smaller altar, a life-size statue of Our Lady of Sorrows, and also a large crucifix. In the church was one confessional and one bench — no pews. Two large carved cedar chests in the sacristy contained the vestments and sacred vessels. Everything needful for divine service was on hand.

On the mission farm outside the enclosure, eight bushels of corn seed were planted every year and produced eight hundred bushels. One and three-fifths bushels of beans yielded twenty-four. There was also a good patch of melons and watermelons, and a very productive field of sweet potatoes and pumpkins. The farm was irrigated with water from the San Antonio River.

Later at least, if not already at this time, the irrigation canal of Mission Concepción began at a stone dam built across the river in the south section of its loop, in present downtown San Antonio. It flowed south, down what is now South St. Mary's Street, past and through the mission compound; and after continuing in a southeasterly direction for about 1,250 yards, turned west and slightly northwest, and rejoined the river below the dam of Mission San José.

Thirty yokes of oxen were on hand for work in the fields; and there were blacksmith, carpenter, and masonry shops, these no doubt inside the enclosure.

The stock of the mission was on a ranch at some distance from the mission compound and farm. For this reason it could not be counted on the occasion of Fr. Ortiz' visit. But a previous inventory showed there were 900 head of cattle, 300 sheep, and 100 horses. The mission had its own brand.

Mission Nuestra Señora de la Purísima Concepción de Acuña. (Painting by Theodore Gentilz in the Daughters of the Republic of Texas Library at the Alamo.)

Second Report of Fr. Ortiz, 1756

Eleven years later, in 1756, Fr. Ortiz paid another official visit to Mission Concepción, and found that the stone church had been completed. In fact, it had been dedicated on December 8 of the previous year, and was now in use. This church is still standing at the present day; and it is the best preserved of all the old mission churches in Texas. It is the oldest church of the Immaculate Conception of the Blessed Virgin Mary in the United States.

Fr. Ortiz describes the exterior and interior of the new church in detail. It was a cruciform building of stone and mortar, having a vaulted roof with a cupola, and two similar towers topped by crosses of iron. He says it was 30 *varas* (83⅓ feet) long, 7¼ *varas* (17½ feet) wide in the nave, and 17 *varas* (46½ feet) wide at the transepts. These seem to have been the measurements on the inside. Later the church was described as being 89 feet long, and 22¼ feet wide. The walls are 45 inches thick. We may add that they consist of adobe and small stones, and only their facing inside and out is of solid stone.

Between the towers, writes Fr. Ortiz, is a portal of hewn stone, and above it a niche with a statue of Mary Immaculate. In a smaller niche are figures of two angels holding a chalice with a host. On one side is painted a sun and on the other a moon. The entire façade is decorated with painted "flower work," that is, with colored geometric designs, similar to those which were painted on the exterior walls of the later church of Mission San José. In the drum of the cupola are four closed windows.

At the base of each tower, on the inside, is a vaulted chapel, with a latticed window. In one of these is an altar, dedicated to St. Michael; it has a framed picture of the Holy Archangel about 33⅓ inches square. In the other, which serves as a baptistery, is a beautiful font of sculptured stone having a lining of copper.

The choir loft has a vaulted ceiling and two latticed windows facing west. At the entrance of the church is a large holy water font of white stone, with a copper lining. In the body of the church stands a pulpit with a sounding board and a statue of Christ with a baldachin. On the walls are the fourteen stations of the Way of the Cross with good pictures. There are also two enclosed confessionals, newly made, with doors and grilles, and some benches.

The sanctuary is ample and raised two steps; it has a Communion railing of carved wood. The table of the altar is of stone. Standing upon it at the back are three steps of painted wood. On these stands a carved image of Mary Immaculate, more than $33\frac{1}{3}$ inches high. A painted pavilion forms a background, and there are several other statues.

In each of the transepts is another altar at which holy Mass can be cebrated. One has a painting of Christ and various saints; and on the altar is an image of the thorn-crowned, suffering face of our Lord. The other side has a painting of Nuestra Señora del Pilar; and on the altar is a carved image of our Lady under the same title.

Adjoining the sanctuary is the sacristy, where there is a framed painting of Christ Crucified, about 1¼ *varas* (41½ inches) square. In three large walnut chests with drawers are the various articles needed for divine service, including ten chasubles of different colors of which five are new.

The former friary is almost in ruins; but a new one-story friary with three good private rooms and several offices, with arched ceilings, is now being constructed. Most of the Indian houses in the mission square are of adobe, and the rest are *jacales*, huts of wood and tule.

The number of Indians now living at the misssion is 247, of whom 40 are not as yet baptized. But in August, two or three months from now, some Indians of the Mano de Perro tribe, who have a ranchería of about 200 persons on the coast, are expected to come to the mission. One of the two missionaries of Concepción will go to them at that time and conduct them to the mission. They have promised to join the mission Indians of Concepción.

Inside the square is also a building of stone and lime which serves as a granary, and another in which are three looms; also a carpenter shop, and a smithy.

Through the square flows an irrigation ditch which waters the farm and orchard outside the walls. The farm is sufficiently large to provide the needed corn, beans, and cotton; and the orchard in which there are various kinds of fruit trees has a stone fence. For work on the farm there are 40 yokes of oxen.

On the mission ranch are 700 head of cattle that have been counted, and there are others in the hills. Here are also 1,800 sheep, a dozen pigs, a drove of horses and another of mares.

Since 1731, 653 Indians have been baptized at the mission, 578 received Christian burial, and 125 entered Christian marriages.

To the description of the church, in the report of Fr. Ortiz, it will be well to add that on the arch over the main entrance one can still read the following inscription:

A SU PATRONA, Y PRINCESSA
CON ESTAS ARMAS, ATIENDE
ESTA MISSION, Y DEFIENDE
EL PUNTO DE SU PUREZA

These words may be translated as follows: "To its Patroness and Princess, with these arms, this mission gives honor, and defends the doctrine of her purity," that is, of her Immaculate Conception. The encircling cord with twelve knots represents the Franciscan Rule of twelve chapters. The shield at the top with an M and AVE stands for "Ave Maria" (Hail Mary). The medallion at the upper left is the coat of arms of the Franciscan Order; and the one at the upper right is a representation of the Five Wounds of Christ.

The missionary under whom the greater part of the church was built was the Fr. President Benito de Santa Ana Fernández, who resided at the mission till 1749; and it was completed by his successor, Fr. Francisco Cayetano del Aponte y Lis. The latter was followed by Fr. Pedro Parras, 1758-1765.

The Report of 1762

In 1762, Fr. Parras and Fr. Joseph Guadalupe Ramírez de Prado supplied the information about Mission Concepción for a report which was compiled by Fr. President Mariano de los Dolores y Viana and sent to the Fr. Guardian of the College of Querétaro, who was none other than Fr. Ortiz, the visitor in 1745 and 1756.

The measurements of the church given above, 89 x 22¼ feet, are contained in this report. It also states that beneath each tower there was a chapel, one with an altar and a statue of St. Michael the Archangel, and the other with a baptismal font and cover of copper with a silver shell.

Above the main altar in the church were a fresco painting on the wall and two oval-shaped niches with statues of Our Lady of Sorrows and Our Lady of the Pillar. There were also a pulpit, two confessionals, and several benches.

Adjoining the church was a large and fully equipped sacristy with an arched ceiling, measuring about 61 feet on each of the four sides. The friary was a long one-story structure, fronted by an archway, with rooms for the missionaries, offices, and space for storage.

Like the church, the friary faced west and stood beside the front part, the towers, of the church. Next to the friary, and extending out farther west, was a large hall with two store rooms. Here were the looms operated by the Indians to manufacture cloth of various kinds.

There was also a granary, in which 1,280 bushels of corn and 80 bushels of beans were stored. Also a blacksmith shop, and a carpenter shop for cabinet-making.

The Indian houses were arranged in two rows, on two sides of the church and friary. Each of these houses was furnished and had the ordinary household utensils. The enclosure formed a rectangle and was surrounded by a wall for protection against hostile Indians.

Just outside the walls was the fenced and irrigated farm, on which 45 yokes of oxen were used. The ranch, however, was farther away; and for this reason it had several houses for the Indian cowboys and shepherds. On the ranch were 120 horses, 200 mares, 610 head of cattle, and 2,200 sheep and goats.

Since the establishment of the mission on the San Antonio River in 1731, a total of 792 Indians had been baptized and 558 had received Christian burial. In 1762, 58 Indian families were living at the mission; and these with the unmarried gave the mission a total population of 207 persons. They were chiefly Pajalat, Tacame, and Sanipao Indians.

Declining Indian Population

With 207 Indians residing in the mission, Concepción still had a sizeable population in 1762; but it was considerably less than in the earlier days, and the number continued to diminish. The same situation prevailed in the other San Antonio missions; and the reason for it lay in the fact that the missionaries were unable to make extended trips for the purpose of bringing back runaways and adding new converts, because a military escort was not provided for them.

Any traveling outside the missions had to be done in the company of a guard of soldiers because of the ever-present danger of encountering bands of hostile and thieving Apaches and other northern tribes.

In 1771, however the missionary of Mission San Juan Capistrano was able to organize an unusual expedition in behalf of all the San Antonio missions. Accompanied by Captain Luís Antonio de Menchaca and thirty soldiers, he set out for the coast and the coastal islands on July 9, and on August 7 he returned with 107 Indians who were willing to join those in the missions. These were distributed over the several missions, and Concepción received 16. Fr. Juan Joseph Sáenz de Gumiel, then in charge of the mission, signed a statement to that effect. Ten of them had deserted the Rosario Mission at La Bahía, and that mission was notified that they were now at Concepción.

A year and a half later, the missionaries of the College of Querétaro turned over Mission Concepción and its other missions on the San Antonio River to those of the College of Zacatecas, which already had the care of Mission San José. A note in the marriage record of Concepción, at the beginning of 1773, states that the signatures in the record from that time on are those of Zacatecan friars.

Fr. Morfi's Description, 1777

The first of the latter was Fr. Joseph Francisco Lopéz, who remained at Concepción for a full decade. While he was stationed at Concepción, Commandant General Teodoro de Croix and his chaplain Fr. Juan Agustín Morfi visited the mission at the close of 1777; and after his return to Mexico, Fr. Morfi included a short description of Concepción in his *History of Texas.*

"The church," writes Father Morfi, "is beautiful. It is 32 *varas* long and 8 wide [89 x 22¼ feet, the same measurement as that given in 1762], built of stone and mortar, with a vaulted roof, transept, cupola, and two towers. The sacristy is likewise a handsome room with a vaulted roof, as is also the living room of the friars, which is large and comfortable but not very high. The latter opens on an arcade. The Indian quarters are arranged in two parallel rows on two sides of the friary, the square being completed by the granary on the other [the east side], thus forming a closed rectangle with only two gates that are well defended. . . . This mission has also suffered a great reduction in the number of its Indians."

Thus Fr. Morfi indicates the arrangement of the mission's rectangular walled enclosure. The church and friary, facing west, were on the east side; the granary was behind the church, also on the east side; the Indian houses were along the north and south walls, which were longer than the east and west walls. A third gate in the walls was added later. The decline of the mission had continued, and it probably had about 170 resident Indians at this time, perhaps less.

Report of Fr. López, 1789

The reasons for the further decline, and the addition of the third gate, are mentioned in the last detailed report about the Texas missions, which was written by Fr. Joseph Francisco López in 1789. Fr. López, former missionary of Concepción, was then Fr. President and resided at Mission San Antonio. Concepción had only 71 mission Indians in that year; and the principal cause of this great diminution, he says, was the decree of Teodoro de Croix which made all unbranded mission cattle the property of the government.

Mission Concepción, writes Fr. López in 1789, "stands on a clearing, protected by the woods along the river. The mission is square [rectangular] in shape and enclosed by a stone and mud wall, low in parts, and provided with three ample openings, one on the east, another on the west, and a third on the south. These have gates of carved wood with good locks. This rampart serves as a wall for houses of the same material. These furnish ample shelter for the Indians. In fact, there are

23 rooms [Indian houses], with flat roofs; and although some of them are in a ruinous state, they are not difficult to restore or repair. In the present year all or nearly all will be rebuilt.

"On the east side stands the roomy house of the missionaries and the offices of the community, all made of stone and lime, nearly all provided with arched roofs. This is a one-story building, except for one room built above. The sacristy and the church adjoin the main stone and lime structure [the friary]. They are both very notable for this country, because of the two towers and the beautiful cupola. The church and sacristy together are valued at 30,000 pesos, and their furnishings and ornaments at 3,000 or 4,000.

"East of the church is a spacious granary, about 15 or 20 *varas* [about 50 feet] in length and 8 or 9 *varas* in width [about 24 feet], with walls of stone and lime, and a flat wooden roof. This building may be valued at not less than 1,000 pesos.

"The mission consists of:

17 married couples, from 25 to 60 years of age 34
Widowers and one widow, from
   30 to 80 years of age 13
Bachelors, about 20 years of age 2
Children 22
Total number of persons 71

"Although these people are descendants of the various tribes for whom this mission was founded, such as the Paxalotes, or Paxalaches (the corrupt form), Sciquipiles, Sanipaos, Pacaos, Tacames, Borrados, and Manos de Perro, they are now reduced to Paxalaches and generally so called. The language of the latter is the one most commonly used; and although nearly all speak Spanish, it is with notable imperfection. It should be noted that most of the Indians were baptized after they were fullgrown, and that those over forty years of age are children of uncivilized Indians."

The Mission Square

Comparing the account of Father López with earlier reports, we can now form an exact picture of the Concepción Mission compound, which was about one-fourth of a mile east of the San Antonio River. Since the church and friary faced west, they must have stood in the eastern section of the rectangular walled area, with an open space (not a wall) lying before them. The granary formed a part of the wall behind the church at the east end. The Indian houses were built up against the longer north and south walls.

Behind the church and friary, there was a gate in the wall. Another was at the western end of the rectangle. The third gate was next to Indian houses on the south side. Each of the three gates, according to Portillo, was defended by two bronze, eight-ounce calibre cannons, each weighing 83 pounds.

A branch of the irrigation ditch entered the rectangle on the north side and left it on the south side, either straight across the open area or at an angle.

The large hall which served as a textile shop, standing next to and south of the friary, extended westward. The friary, previously a one-story building, now had a second floor consisting of one room.

What Father López says of the Paxalaches Indians is of special interest, because the irrigation canal of Mission Concepción was also known as "the Pajalache Ditch."

Available statistics show that the decline of Concepción's population was not a steady one; at times it increased a little, and then again grew less. In 1783, the number of its mission Indians was 87; in 1786 it had increased to 104; in 1788 it dropped to 51; in 1789 it rose to 71; in 1790 it went down to 47; and in 1794, there were only 38 Indians in the mission.

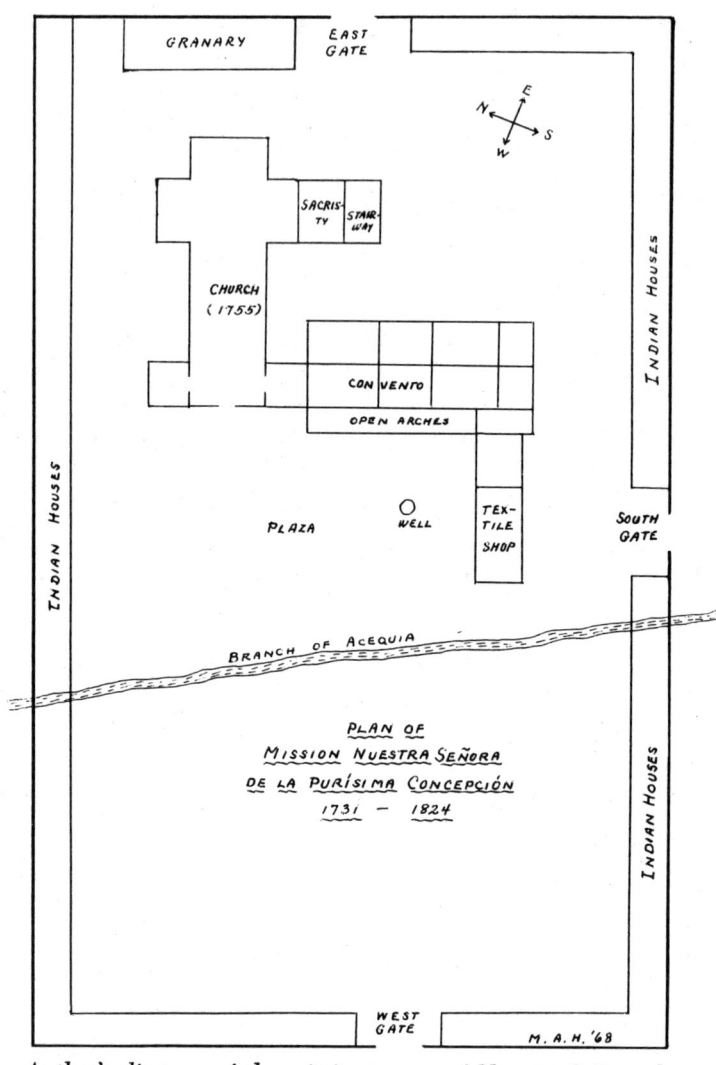

Author's diagram of the mission square of Nuestra Señora de la Purísima Concepción. The exact spot in the rectangle where the church and friary were located is not indicated.

Partial Secularization

It was in 1794 that the first secularization of Mission Concepción took place. The previous year Mission San Antonio had been suppressed entirely; but the other four missions on the San Antonio River were only partially secularized in 1794.

Some of the mission property was divided among the Christian Indians of the mission, and they became private landowners. The missionary was relieved of the task of administering their temporal affairs, and a so-called "justice" was appointed to assist them in these matters.

However, the missionary remained at his post, served the Christian Indians as their pastor, and continued to have complete supervision over those Indians who were still under instruction and such others as would take up their abode in the mission to be instructed. Thus the missions continued to be such in a modified form, and were considered and classified as missions until their final and complete secularization three decades later.

The formal secularization of Mission Concepción was carried out on July 31 and August 1, 1794. Governor Manuel Múñoz went to the mission on July 31; and after Fr. José María Camarena, the missionary in charge, had called together the resident Indians, the governor informed them that they would now receive farms of their own which they would have to cultivate to provide for their needs, without the missionary's supervision. However, the surveyor and carpenter, Pedro Huizar, would be on hand as their "justice" to give them advice, guidance, and protection. To a certain extent he would take over the temporal administration of the mission which till now had been in the hands of the missionary. It was found that the resident Indians included 16 men, 15 women, one boy, and 6 girls—a total of 38 persons.

The next day, Pedro Huizar surveyed the mission farm and divided it into 26 plats. Of these 8 were each 1,111 feet long and 555½ feet wide, and they constituted the common lands of the pueblo. The other 18 plats were each 833⅓ feet long and 555½ feet wide. Each of the 16 heads of families received one of these. One plat went to a Spaniard by the name of Javier Longoria, who had assisted the missionary as an overseer and agreed to remain and supervise the Indian's work on their farms. Another plat was given to Pedro Huizar for his services as surveyor of the lands of all the San Antonio missions.

The fields which were thus divided were not fallow; for, the mission farm had been planted with 6⅞ bushels of corn and 10 pecks of beans, and there were also two fields on which cotton was growing.

The stock that was distributed among the Indians consisted of 18 yokes of oxen, 24 horses of which 11 were saddle horses, 11 mares with a stallion and a jack, and 5 mules with pack equipment. There were also 128 cows with calves; but these were placed in the care of a single cowboy, who was to be paid for his services out of the common funds of the Indian pueblo. Governor Múñoz reminded the Indians that, if they caught or slaughtered any unbranded cattle, they would have to report this and pay a fee of four *reales* per head.

A Sub Mission of San José

Fr. Camarena was the last resident missionary of Concepción. Soon after the partial secularization of the mission, he left; and Concepción was henceforth taken care of by the missionary who resided at San José. Thus Concepción became a sub mission. Now that the missionary at San José was no longer burdened with the temporal administration of the mission, he could easily serve his mission as well as Concepción, especially since the number of Indians had been so greatly reduced. San José's missionary also ministered to the Spaniards who began to settle at both missions.

On January 1, 1796, Fr. President José Mariano de Cardenas, the missionary at San José, submitted to the governor for confirmation the names of the Indians who were elected governor and *alcalde* of the Concepción pueblo for that year. They had the Spanish names of Felix del Castillo and Lorenzo Villegas.

The following year, Captain Juan Cortes of the presidio at La Bahía informed Commandant General Nava that they had only two small cracked bells and suggested that two bells at the "abandoned" Mission of Concepción be given to them. Nava wrote to Governor Múñoz to tell him he should try to get the two bells from Fr. President Cárdenas. It is interesting to note that even such small matters were referred to the commandant general in Mexico. Cortes probably got the bells, but he was not correct when he called Concepción an "abandoned" mission.

As late as June, 1809, Governor Salcedo listed Mission Concepción in a general census, and reported that 21 Indians (9 men and 12 women) were living within the walls of the mission and that 32 Spaniards (18 men and 14 women) had likewise settled at this mission. Thus Concepción had a total population of 53.

Governor Salcedo also stated that the land belonging to Concepción included an area of about 38 square miles. From the mission the boundary line extended 2½ miles south to El Paso de Nogal, then 2½ miles east to Salado Creek, then 2½ miles north to the La Bahía Road, then 20 miles farther to Cibolo Creek (northeast and east of San Antonio), and back to the mission. Most of this land was not being used, since Concepción no longer had a large herd of cattle.

After the Casas Revolution had been suppressed in 1811, the Villa of San Fernando was rewarded for its loyalty and raised to the rank of a "ciudad," a city. But, unlike other cities and even villas or pueblos, it had no common lands, of which the proceeds would help to defray its expenses as a community. Governor Herrera, on January 4, 1812, suggested that some of the lands of Mission Concepción be set aside for this purpose. He said, the mission was practically deserted and the single family living on the land was willing to move to Mission San José. His proposal was probably carried out, but he could not have meant that there was only one family living at Mission Concepción. Four years later there were still 16 mission Indians in this pueblo as well as 20 Spanish settlers.

When Bernardo Gutiérrez, in 1813, led his revolutionary army of some 500 men (including those enlisted by Magee) from La Bahía to lay siege to the City of San Fernando and its presidio of San Antonio de Béxar, he established his headquarters at Mission Concepción. But a siege was not necessary. On April 1, when the army boldly marched up to the walls of the city, Governor Salcedo immediately sent out envoys to propose terms of capitulation. The next day the city surrendered to the invaders, and the flag of the short-lived First Republic of Texas was hoisted in the military plaza.

The troops of Gutiérrez must have taken over also Mission San José for a short time; for, at this time, according to the testimony of Fr. Bernardino Vallejo, most of the records of the San Antonio missions which were kept at San José were destroyed. Of the records of Mission Concepción, fortunately the marriage record, at least, survived.

In the spring of 1814, after Spanish rule had been re-established, an incident occurred at Mission Concepción which seems to indicate that a sentinel was always on duty in one of the towers of its church. The sentry in the tower noticed that the bells of San José were being rung to call its residents to arms, and those of Concepción also rang the alarm. Afterwards it was learned that there had been merely a test drill at San José, in compliance with orders received from the comandant general.

The incident was reported to the governor on March 13 by José M. Hernández, the "justice" or Spanish *alcalde* of Concepción. He seems to have been the last to hold this office.

Merged with Mission San José

A census of Concepción as well as Espada was prepared on February 27, 1815, by José Antonio Bustillos, Spanish *alcalde* of Espada. The next year, on March 31, Governor Mariano Varela sent a message, about an attack of Lipan Apaches on the Refugio Mission, to the Spanish *alcaldes* of San José, Capistrano, and Espada, but none to Concepción.

Similarly, on January 28, 1820, Governor Martínez apprised the *alcaldes* of the same three missions of the appointment of the Rev. Refugio de la Garza, pastor of San Fernando, to the office of ecclesiastical judge; but no mention is made of an *alcalde* at Concepción.

Likewise, in the burial register of San José, Fr. Vallejo noted that he officiated at the funerals of two persons from Concepción in 1815, and Fr. Miguel Muro had one such funeral in 1819; but the burial in each case took place at San José (nos. 1,222, 1,229, and 1,276).

All this seems to indicate that, from the year 1815 on, the Concepción mission, having only a few residents, was more or less merged with San José, and its residents attended divine services at nearby San José Mission. However, it cannot be said that Mission Concepción was entirely abandoned at this time. That was done only after February 29, 1824, when its final and complete secularization took place.

That the church of Mission Concepción was no longer used for divine services after 1819, appears to be evident from a series of letters exchanged during the first part of 1820 between Governor Martínez on the one hand and the Rev. Refugio de la Garza of San Fernando and Father Miguel Muro of Mission San José on the other. In February the Rev.

de la Garza asked the governor's permission to select what he needed for the parish church from the vestments and sacred vessels of "abandoned" Mission Concepción which were now kept at San José.

The governor requested Fr. Muro to give him an itemized account of the belongings of Concepción now at San José. Fr. Muro replied that he needed time to prepare the statement and that he could not give these articles to anyone without his superior's consent.

Father Garza evidently got what he wanted; for, in June Fr. Muro informed both the governor and Father Garza that the superiors of the College in Zacatecas had disapproved of the giving of the religious goods of Concepción to the pastor of San Fernando.

Father Garza returned about one-half of what he had received, and then refused to give back the other half until he could find out whether the bishop of Monterrey had jurisdiction over them and could dispose of them. Whether Father Garza eventually surrendered the items he had, we do not know; but it is plain that the vestments and sacred vessels were no longer being used in the church of Mission Concepción at this time.

Final Secularization

Four years later, on February 29, 1824, Fr. José Antonio Díaz de León, the last missionary of the College of Zacatecas at San José and in Texas, signed the inventories he had made of missions San José, Concepción, Capistrano and Espada, and surrendered their churches, with furnishings and other property, to the care of the military chaplain in San Antonio, the Rev. Francisco Maynes, who was the acting pastor of San Fernando and as such the representative of the bishop of Monterrey.

Thus Mission Concepción, which had merely lingered for

an entire decade, finally died. Its existence as an Indian mission came to an end. Including the 11 years during which it was located in eastern Texas, the mission's span of life had been 104 years.

It has been said that the last words which Fr. Díaz de León wrote into one of the record books of Mission Concepción were: "Como la muerte" (like unto death); but we have not found them in the register of marriages, the only surviving record.

Spanish Settlers at Concepción

The City of San Fernando, which had already received some of the lands of Mission Concepción in 1812, three years later asked if additional lands of this mission could be sold to raise funds for school supplies; and this probably was done.

But some real estate still remained in 1824; and two years later an order was issued for its sale, except the buildings, and in 1827 another order directed that the walls and buildings be sold at auction and the proceeds sent to the treasurer of the State of Coahuila-Texas. But these orders were rescinded until 1831, when the sale of all the buildings, except the churches, of the four former missions was ordered and the monies received were to be placed in the care of the city treasurer of San Antonio until further notice.

At Concepción, where the irrigation canal was still in use, the number of Spanish settlers increased after the secularization of the mission. They had to pay a tax for the water they used to irrigate their fields, and they regarded this tax as being too high. In 1825 it was cut in half.

The Apaches continued their raids as they had done in mission days; and in 1826, when there were about 50 families of settlers in and around Concepción, troops were sent to their aid. Before they arrived, the Apaches made an attack on the workers in the fields at Concepción. After the soldiers came the Apaches ceased molesting the farmers, at least for some time.

Visitors of Concepción

During the fight for independence, the Battle of Concepción on October 27, 1835, took place about a quarter of a mile from the mission. A reference to this battle is found in George Kendall's account of his visit to San Antonio in 1841. He wrote that all the missions were most substantially built and had walls of great thickness. Of Concepción in particular he says: "The Mission of Concepción is a very large building with a fine cupola; and, though plain, magnificent in its dimensions and in the durability of its construction. It is here that Bowie fought one of his first battles with the Mexican forces; and it has not since been inhabited."

In the same year, on January 13, 1841, the Congress of the Republic of Texas confirmed the title of ownership of Concepción and other mission churches, with surrounding land not exceeding 15 acres, to the Catholic Church; but for a decade or more, the Concepción church continued to be used by the settlers as a cattle enclosure and barn. In the late 1840's, after Texas had joined the Union in 1845, the United States Army temporarily used the church as a supply depot.

John R. Bartlett, who visited San Antonio in 1850, wrote the following about Concepción: "The two towers and dome of the church make quite an imposing appearance when seen from a distance; but, on approaching it, we found it not only desolated but desecrated, the church portion being used as an inclosure for cattle, the filth from which covered the floor to a depth of a foot or more. Myriads of bats flitted about, which chattered and screamed at our invasion of their territory; and we found nothing of interest within the church to repay us for encountering their disagreeable presence."

Five years later, however, Herman Lungkwitz made a beautiful painting of the old mission, showing the church with its towers and dome still intact, and beside it a few arches of the friary.

The Brothers of Mary at Concepción

The same year, before the end of February, 1855, Bishop Odin gave the use of the mission land of Concepción to the Brothers of Mary, who had founded St. Mary's School in San Antonio (the present University) three years earlier; and on September 8, 1859, he transferred the title to these lands and the mission buildings to them. The Brothers improved the land and purchased additional acreage, using it as a farm to supply the school in the city. The farm included about 100 acres. They also restored the church; and on May 28, 1861, it was blessed and opened once more as a place of worship. Here they also established a postulate and novitiate for the training of candidates of the Society of Mary, which was continued until 1866 when the candidates were sent to Dayton, Ohio.

Brother Edel, the farm manager, and a few assistants resided at the mission until 1869, when the farm was leased, but not the buildings of the old mission. For several years before the farm was closed, the faculty of St. Mary's and some of the boarders from distant places spent the hottest part of the summer at Mission Concepción, enjoying a vacation of swimming, fishing, and hunting on the San Antonio River.

Even after 1869, the Brothers spent some of their more pleasant hours at the mission. In 1911 the Society of Mary gave the title of the mission buildings and the surrounding property back to the bishop of San Antonio.

In the meantime Bishop John C. Neraz had done further restoration work on the church; and on May 2, 1887, he rededicated the church in honor of Our Lady of Lourdes (the Immaculate Conception).

William Corner's Description, 1890

William Corner, who wrote an interesting book about San Antonio and published it in 1890, had the following to say about Mission Concepción: "The barracks [Indian houses and walls] that surrounded the square have long since disappeared; and what was for a period the home of hospitality and the stronghold and refuge of many wayfarers and travellers, and alive with the daily toil of its little community and the quick purpose of its founders, is now quiet and deserted, a relic; and but for the occasional service in the chapel [church] is an institution that has served its day. . . .

"Mission Concepción is the best preserved Mission of Texas. Its 'twin towers' and Moorish dome, rising out of the brush and small timber in its vicinity, arouse within one a mixture of curiosity, a sense of the incongruous, and a delight of the picturesque. . . .

"The only stained glass in all the Missions is the panes of two little windows each side of the upper part of the façade. The front of the Mission Concepción must have been very gorgeous with color, for it was frescoed all over with red and blue quatrefoil crosses and with large yellow and orange squares to simulate great dressed stones. This frescoing is rapidly disappearing, and from but a little distance the front looks to be merely gray and undecorated stone.

"The topmost roofs of the towers are pyramidical and of stone, with smaller corner pyramidal cap-stones. The upper stories of the towers have each four lookout windows of plain Roman arches. The tops of the side walls of the Church and the circle wall of the central dome have wide stone serrations in the Moorish character, the points of which around the finely proportioned dome stand out like canine teeth. . . .

"The baptistry walls are frescoed with weird looking designs, dim and faded, of the Crucifixion and 'los dolores.' It is quite dark in this room, there being no window, and a light must be procured to examine it. A semi-circular font projects from the south wall, its half bowl carved with what appears to be a symbolical figure with outstretched arms supporting the rim. It is a rude piece of carving, but is artistic.

"Inside, the stone roof of the Chapel [church] with its series of arches and central dome, is massive but plain. In each wing of the cross [the transepts] are altars or altar places. In the west end is a choir loft. In the east, an altar gorgeously decked and painted in the Catholic manner, for Mass. The walls, roof, and ceiling are newly white-washed, the floor is 'Mother Earth,' but some brand new seats have been provided. The Chapel [church] up till recently, was in a very neglected state. . . .

"In the holes in the walls outside are to be found the nesting places of owls, pigeons, doves, and other birds. To the south of the chapel [church], westerly, are a series of arches which were formerly cells, chambers, and cloisters for the Mission inmates, but now used as storage rooms and stables.

"To the south, forming a wing easterly, are other buildings probably the sacristy, superior's vestries and quarters; these have two stories, the upper being approached by a stone staircase.

"The square of the Mission at this date can very hardly be defined, but that the Mission was situated in the southeastern corner of a ramparted square is without doubt. The Mission square enclosed about four acres. . . ."

The room adjoining the sanctuary of the church was definitely the sacristy; and the one above it may have been an infirmary. It is not uncommon to find such rooms in the older friaries, with windows looking down on the sanctuary of the church and enabling the sick friars to attend holy Mass; however, the upper story of the sacristy may also have been used as the private room of the missionary in charge.

The extant reports about Mission Concepción do not mention the second story of the sacristy; and it may have been added after 1789. In the latter year, however, there was a

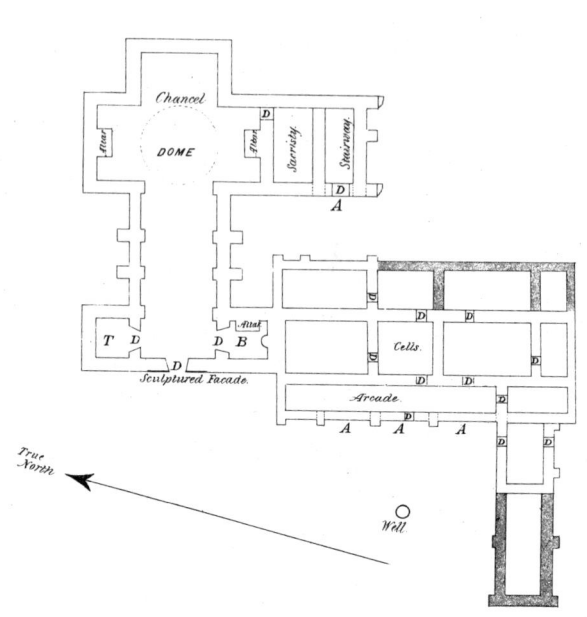

Concepcion Mission.

The shaded part is in ruins. The material is rough stone laid in mortar. B is the baptismal chamber. T is the room under the left tower. D stands for door, as A for arch. There is another room above the Sacristy.

The river is towards the west about ¼ mile.

Scale, 40 feet to the inch.

├────────────────────────┤ *1 in. on original*

In a work published in the Spanish language at Saltillo written by Esteban L. Portillo and entitled "Apuntes para la Historia Antigua de Coahuila y Texas," the author on page 305 remarks concerning the Mission Concepcion, apparently deriving his information from Mexican State Records :—"In order to guard it, the Monastery had a stone wall with three gateways, as well as two bronze cannons of an eight-ounce calibre, with a weight of 3 arrobas 8 libras," (83 lbs each). As has been said in our description of this Mission the traces of such walls are to-day hardly to be defined and these defences are not shown in the plan for fear of inaccuracy.

William Corner's plan of the church and friary of Mission Nuestra Señora de la Purísima Concepción, 1890.

second floor in the friary proper consisting of a single room. Of the several rooms of the friary, some may have been added by later tenants. Such residents did wall up the front arches of the friary and put windows in them before ca. 1890, as is shown on a photograph of that date.

Some cells of the friary were in ruins already in 1756. One of the rooms was restored in 1957. There is also a modern stairway which connects with the original stone steps leading to the tower.

The stone used in building the church was quarried a few yards from it, probably inside the square; and the spot is still discernible in the yard on the other side of Mission Road. Noteworthy are also the excellent acoustics of the interior of the church, so much so that they have been compared with those of the Mormon Temple in Salt Lake City.

Later History of the Mission

Soon after the Brothers of Mary returned the ownership of Mission Concepción and surrounding property to the bishop of San Antonio in 1911, an orphanage, called St. Peter's-St. Joseph's Home, was built on the other side of Mission Road. It is staffed by the Sisters of Charity of the Incarnate Word and takes care of 134 children.

In 1919, Bishop Arthur J. Drossaerts (who was named first archbishop of San Antonio in 1926) began building St. John's Seminary next to the old mission; and it was opened the following year. Theology courses were added in 1928; and a second building was erected in 1935. The latter was named Margil Hall, to honor the memory of Venerable Father Antonio Margil, the founder of Mission San José.

Archbishop Robert E. Lucey placed the Vincentian Fathers in charge of the seminary in 1941; and in 1947 he added the third building, St. Mary's Hall. The number of young men who are preparing themselves for the priesthood at this seminary is 137.

Thus the old mission has very appropriately fallen heir to an educational institution which trains and prepares those who in our day continue to devote themselves to that work for the spiritual good of men, regardless of race or color or language, which the padres of old commenced on this very spot more than two and a quarter centuries ago.

The old mission church of Nuestra Señora de la Purísima Concepción is the oldest church in Texas and the oldest church of the Immaculate Conception in the United States. Unlike the other mission churches in Texas it has never fallen into ruins; its walls and dome and towers never had to be reconstructed. Substantially it is the same church that was completed 212 years ago. It is a historical monument and treasure of which modern San Antonio can well be proud; and a visit to the venerable structure is an interesting and ennobling experience.

Important Dates

1716, July 7: Mission Concepción was founded near Douglass in eastern Texas.

1719, June: The mission was temporarily abandoned because of war between Spain and France.

1721, Aug. 8: The Marqués de Aguayo and his army re-established the mission at its former site.

1730, July 27: The mission was moved to the Colorado River.

1731, March 5: The mission was moved to its present site on the San Antonio River.

1755, Dec. 8: The stone church of Mission Concepción, which was begun about 1740, was completed and dedicated.

1773: The Querétaran missionaries surrendered the mission to those from the College of Zacatecas.

1794, Aug. 1: The mission was partially secularized and made a sub mission of San José soon afterwards.

1813, Mar.: The revolutionary army of Bernardo Gutiérrez had its headquarters at the mission.

1819: Divine services were no longer held in the church of Mission Concepción.

1824, Feb. 29: Concepción was completely secularized, and abandoned.

1835, Oct. 27: The Battle of Concepción was fought near the mission between the Texans and the Mexicans.

1855-1911: The mission was in the care of the Brothers of Mary of St. Mary's College in San Antonio.

1919: The building of St. John Seminary was begun at Mission Concepción.

VI

Mission San Juan Capistrano
1716-1824

The story of Mission San Juan Capistrano, or San Juan de Capistrano, like that of Concepción begins in eastern Texas, where it had the name of Mission San José de los Nazonis. After the two Querétaran missions of San Francisco and Concepción had been founded, the first Zacatecan mission was begun at Nacogdoches. The third mission of the College of Querétaro was then founded for the Nazoni and Nadaco Indians in the village of the Nazonis, seven leagues (about seventeen miles) north of Mission Concepción, on an arroyo (present Dill's Creek), near the north line of Nacogdoches County, not far from Cushing.

San José de los Nazonis

Fr. President Espinosa arrived at the Nazoni village on July 9, 1716, and Ramón on the 10th. The mission was established July 11th, and named San José de los Nazonis. In the last entries of his diary, Captain Ramón wrote:

"I passed this day (July 10) in the Mission of the Nasonis. . . . We were entertained in their towns. On the eleventh day, the first steps were taken towards the building of a church and dwelling, and I proceeded to name a Chaplain. All of the people referred to are of the same kind, very agreeable and generous. They are glad to teach their language and especially to those of the Mission."

The "chaplain" or missionary appointed by Fr. Espinosa for this mission was Fr. Benito Sánchez. Though he received a warm welcome from the Nazonis, Fr. Sánchez experienced the same difficulties and hardships at his mission as the other fathers did at theirs.

After the founding of Mission San Antonio, Governor Alarcón visited the missions in eastern Texas. He arrived at Mission San José de los Nazonis on October 31, 1718, and remained for four days, inspecting the mission, giving presents to the Nazonis, and reorganizing their pueblo, which he called San José de Ayamonte.

When the French drove the Spaniards out of eastern Texas the following year, Fr. Benito Sánchez accompanied the refugees to San Antonio, and then proceeded to Mission San Juan Bautista on the Rio Grande, to await the arrival of Aguayo's army.

However, Fr. Sánchez was back in San Antonio early in 1721, because entry number 91 in the baptismal register of Mission San Antonio has his signature. He must, therefore, have gone ahead of Aguayo, who did not reach San Antonio until April 4th. He probably brought to Fr. Margil and the other waiting missionaries the good news that Aguayo had finally reached the Rio Grande.

The Re-established Mission

The day after the re-establishment of Mission Concepción on August 8, 1721, Aguayo sent ahead to the Nazoni village Fr. Benito Sánchez and a detachment of soldiers under a lieutenant. Taking along only one company of soldiers and leaving the others in camp to rest, Aguayo set out on August 12 for the Nazonis to reestablish the third Querétaran mission. When he arrived he found that the church and padre's house had been rebuilt, and the Indians gladly welcomed him. But the formal reestablishment of Mission San José de los Nazonis took place the next day, August 13.

On that day Fr. President Espinosa sang a high Mass, during which the soldiers, who were drawn up in front of the church, fired repeated salvos. Three hundred Indians were present; and after the Mass, Aguayo addressed them through an interpreter. He urged them to congregate in the mission pueblo and to place themselves under the fatherly guidance of the missionary. He told them the Spaniards had come back to protect them against their enemies and to instruct them in the Christian Faith and the customs and practices of civilized life. With the usual ceremonies he then placed the mission and its lands in the possession of Fr. President Espinosa and the Indians.

To the chief of the Nazonis, who was to serve as governor of the mission pueblo which was to be established as soon as the crops had been gathered, Aguayo gave a suit of blue cloth and a silver-headed cane or baton as the insignia of his office. He also gave clothing to each of the 300 Indians.

Fr. Benito Sánchez continued his work as best he could, despite the lack of supplies and the failure of the Indians to congregate in the mission pueblo as they had promised, during the next six years. He then left eastern Texas; for, we find him at Mission San Antonio in 1727-1728.

Moved and Renamed

Together with Mission Concepción and Mission San Francisco, San José de los Nazonis was moved, without the Nazonis, to the Colorado in 1730, and the following year to the San Antonio River. The latter transfer was accomplished in one month and a day.

With the moveable supplies of the old mission, a new mission, called San Juan Capistrano, was founded on March 5,

Mission San Juan Capistrano. (H. L. Summerville photo; courtesy of San José Mission Friary.)

1731, at the site it now occupies, about seven miles from downtown San Antonio. It is situated on the east side of the San Antonio River, in a wooded area, at so-called Berg's Mill, which is now within the city limits of San Antonio.

The reason why the name San José de los Nazonis was changed to San Juan Capistrano was the fact that about 2½ miles north of it was the Mission San José y San Miguel de Aguayo. San Juan Capistrano (St. John Capistran, or of Capistrano), was a great Franciscan saint, who was canonized in 1724, seven years before the establishment of the mission. An eloquent preacher, he traveled all over Europe; and he played an important role in Janos Hunyady's victory over the Turks at Belgrade in 1456. He died the same year, at the age of seventy, on October 23. That day is annually observed as his feast in the Franciscan Order.

On the Site of Yanaguana

There are good reasons for believing that the site of San Juan Capistrano is near the place where Terán de los Ríos and Fr. Massanet reached the village of the Payaya tribe called Yanaguana (meaning Refreshing Waters) on June 13, 1691, and named both the river and the village for San Antonio de Padua. The "level lands without woods" which they crossed when they continued their journey would then have been the flying field of Brooks Air Force Base.

"On the 13th," Governor Terán de los Rios wrote in his diary, "we marched five leagues (12½ miles) — from the Medina River in an easterly direction — over fine country with broad plains, the most beautiful in New Spain. We camped on the banks of an arroyo (the San Antonio River), adorned by a great number of trees, cedars, willows, cypresses, osiers, oaks, and many other kinds. This I called San Antonio de Padua, because we reached it on his day.

"Here we found certain rancherías in which the Peyaye tribe live. We observed their actions, and I discovered that they were docile and affectionate, were naturally friendly, and were decidedly agreeable to us. I saw the possibility of using them to form missions, the first on the Rio Grande, at the presidio, and another at this point. Different tribes in between could be thereby influenced."

Fr. Massanet, who also kept a diary wrote on Wednesday, June 13th: "We continued northeast, a quarter east, until we passed through some low hills covered with oaks and mesquites. The country is very beautiful. We entered a stretch which was easy for travel and advanced on our easterly course. Before reaching the river (the San Antonio River) there are other small hills with large oaks.

"The river is bordered with many trees, cottonwoods, oaks, cedars, mulberries, and many vines. There are a great many fish, and upon the highlands a great number of wild chickens.

"On this day, there were so many buffaloes that the horses stampeded and forty head ran away. These were collected with the rest of the horses by hard work on the part of the soldiers.

"We found at this place the ranchería of the Indians of the Payaya tribe. This is a very large nation, and the country where they live is very fine. I called this place San Antonio de Padua, because it was his feast day. In the language of the Indians it is called Yanaguana."

The following day was the feast of Corpus Christi, and the expedition remained at Yanaguana, newly named San Antonio, to celebrate the feast in a solemn manner. "On Thursday the 14th," wrote Fr. Massanet, "we did not continue our journey because of the presence of the said Indians. I ordered a large cross set up, and in front of it built an arbor of cottonwood trees, where the altar was placed. All the priests [ten in number] said Mass. High Mass was attended by Governor Don Domingo Terán de los Ríos, Captain Don Francisco Martínez, and the rest of the soldiers, all of whom fired a great many salutes. When the Host was elevated, a salute was fired by all the guns.

"The Indians were present during these ceremonies. After Mass the Indians were given to understand through the chieftain of the Pacpul tribe, that the Mass and the salutes fired by the Spaniards were all for the honor, worship, and adoration we owed to God, our Lord, in acknowledgment of the benefits and great blessings that His Divine Majesty bestows upon us; that it was to Him that we had just offered Sacrifice [of His Body and Blood] in the form of the bread and wine which had just been elevated in the Mass.

"Then I distributed among them rosaries, pocket knives, cutlery, beads, and tobacco. I gave a horse to the chieftain. In the midst of their ranchería, that is, their pueblo, they had a tall wooden cross. They said that they knew the Christians put up crosses in their houses and settlements and had great reverence for them, because it was a thing that was very pleasing to Him Who was God and Lord of all. . . . On Wednesday, the 15th, we left San Antonio de Padua and traveled east, a quarter northeast, over level lands without woods."

To commemorate the 275th anniversary of these events and the naming of the place and the river for St. Anthony of Padua, a life-size plaque was erected by Bejar Caravan No. 56, Order of the Alhambra, at Arneson River Theatre and unveiled on Sunday, June 12, 1966.

Difficult Beginnings

By May 4, 1731, the first rude, temporary structures had been constructed at the Mission of San Juan Capistrano, and a considerable number of Coahuiltecan Indians of various tribes, Pacaos, Pajalats, and Alobjas or Pitalaques, had been gathered. But progress was slow during the first decade, because of the raids of the Apaches, the obstructionist tactics of Governor Franquis de Lugo, and the epidemic of 1739.

Though the first buildings of San Juan Capistrano were

primitive structures, the mission Indians seem to have been able to protect them with the aid of three Spanish guards; for, the Apaches did not attack the mission compound itself.

Individuals, however, who left the compound for some reason or other, were often in danger, even though they did not wander far off. Thus two Indian women of the mission were surprised and killed by an Apache band in 1736. The main objective of the Apaches seems to have been the stealing of mission cattle and horses.

It was Governor Franquis de Lugo who did more harm to the mission than the Apaches during his short term of office in 1736 and 1737. Shortly after he arrived in San Antonio on September 27, he sent a notice to Fr. Joseph Hurtado, the missionary of San Juan Capistrano, that he was withdrawing two of the three soldiers at the mission.

This was a serious blow to the struggling mission, not only because it sorely needed the protection of these guards, but also because the soldiers served as overseers and teachers of the Indians on the farm and in the shops and thus greatly aided the missionary in his work. The removal of the soldiers also had a bad effect on the mission Indians.

Encouraged by the disrespectful attitude of the governor toward the missionaries, some of the Indians felt quite safe in disregarding the padre's directions and violating the rules of mission life. Some of those at San Juan Capistrano joined others of Mission Concepción in making false depositions before the governor concerning alleged mistreatment by the missionaries.

Actually, as some of the witnesses testified later, it was the governor himself who had the depositions prepared; and the Indians and others were told that they must sign them. When Lieutenant Mateo Pérez firmly objected that the accusations were not true, the governor threatened to banish him from the Province of Texas "farther than any place he could imagine," if he did not add his signature.

It is not surprising, under these conditions, that the Indians at San Juan Capistrano no longer paid any attention to the mission bell and acted as they pleased. Orderly mission life broke down completely, and construction work came practically to a standstill.

Finally, in June, 1737, most of the more than 200 Indians at Capistrano, at least 90 of them baptized Christians, abandoned the mission and returned to their former way of life in the woods. Some of them left their wives behind. Only 20 Thelojas and 3 Orejones remained. Six months later, though attempts had been made to bring them back, about 180 had not returned. Of these about 130 were Sayopines and Venados.

Fr. Mariano Viana at Capistrano

Fr. Hurtado must have been completely discouraged. Fr. Mariano de los Dolores, who succeeded him in 1737, asked Governor Orobio y Basterra on December 3 to supply an escort of soldiers, so he could go in quest of the runaway Indians. The new governor gladly acceded to the padre's request and ordered Captain Andrés Hernández to go at once to the aid of Fr. Mariano with nine soldiers and to accompany him on his trip.

When the captain and his men arrived at San Juan Capistrano, Fr. Mariano had bad news for them. He had learned that the Apaches had suddenly swooped down on the soldiers who were stationed on Cibolo Creek with a herd of horses and had driven away a large number of the horses. Under the circumstances he thought it would be well if he postponed his trip and the captain and his men returned to the presidio. The governor might be badly in need of them.

About eight o'clock in the evening Captain Hernández was back in San Antonio and gave Fr. Mariano's message to the governor. The latter must have appreciated the missionary's concern for his needs. It was a striking example of the padres' willingness to cooperate with the civil and military authorities in as far as they possibly could.

On February 23, 1738, Fr. Mariano repeated his request for an escort, and the governor once more sent Captain Hernández and nine soldiers to him. They set out in search of the Sayopines on March 2; and 21 days later, at about five in the evening, they were back at the presidio with the Indians who had come along willingly, and reported to the governor. In the plaza the Indians were counted. There were 120 of them, men, women, and children. The governor gave them gifts; and during the night the repentant Sayopines stayed at Mission San Antonio. The next day, Fr. Mariano took them back to Mission San Juan Capistrano.

Fr. Mariano Francisco de los Dolores y Viana was one of the outstanding missionaries in Texas. He had been in charge of Mission San Antonio when Governor Franquis de Lugo began his stormy regime. The differences which ensued forced Fr. Mariano to retire to Mission Concepción, where the Fr. President resided; and San Juan Capistrano was then placed in his care. In 1739 he returned to Mission San Antonio, and continued his work there until 1769.

The Mission in 1739-1740

The name of the missionary who followed Fr. Mariano at San Juan Capistrano is not known; but he had to contend with another serious setback, when the epidemic of 1739 took its toll at this mission. The 218 Indians who were at San Juan Capistrano when Fr. Mariano left, were reduced by flight and death to a mere 66. But by the end of 1740, the number of mission Indians was increased once more to 169.

The buildings of the mission, at this time, were still only temporary structures, and the church had a straw roof. But Capistrano was better able to repel an attack of hostile

Indians than the presidio of San Antonio. The Indian dwellings were inadequate, but better quarters were being built. The construction of better buildings had to yield to the prior need of digging irrigation ditches and tilling the soil, and thus providing food for the Indians.

The fields were newly planted in the spring of 1740; and the Indians settled down to the carefree and contented routine life of the mission. They were well fed and clothed, and they had the necessary tools for their work. Once or twice a week, they received rations of corn, and occasionally allowances of sugar, beans, beads, cloth, and blankets, and when they were sick the needed medicines. Each week a sufficient number of cattle were slaughtered to provide meat.

Though the mission Indians were not overburdened with work, some of them still continued to run away. Most of them, however, were well satisfied and happy under the paternal guidance of the padre.

Report of Fr. Ortiz, 1745

When Fr. Francisco Xavier Ortiz came to inspect the Querétaran missions in 1745, he went from Mission San Antonio first of all to San Juan Capistrano to see how it was faring. The church was still merely a large hall made of brush, plastered with mud, and roofed with straw; but it was well kept and very clean, and it had a tower with two bells.

Inside the church was one altar with a carved statue of Our Lady of Sorrows, three-fourths life-size, in the center, and on the sides smaller images, about 17 inches high, of the Infant Jesus and St. Joseph. Above the altar hung an oil painting of St. John Capistran, the patron of the mission, with a gilded frame, about 33 inches square.

There was also a baptismal font of copper, a confessional and two benches, and four sets of vestments of different colors. Everything else needed for divine worship was on hand.

The friary was a modest building of stone and mortar, having two private rooms and a few others for offices. There was also a granary which may have been a stone building, and carpenter and blacksmith shops; but no mention is made of a loom for weaving cloth.

The mission farm was watered by a very good irrigation ditch. As a rule 6⅖ bushels of seed corn were planted each year, and in good years they yielded 1,280 bushels. About 2⅖ bushels of beans produced about 64 bushels, which were sufficient for the needs of the mission. The farm included a fine field of melons and watermelons. For work on the farm, 17 yokes of oxen were available; and there were ten carts. On the ranch were 865 head of cattle, 304 sheep, 270 goats, and 36 horses.

Since 1731, the number of those who had been baptized was 515; and 214 had received the sacraments before their death and had received Christian burial. In 1745 the Indians living at the mission comprised 41 families or a total of 163 persons, of whom 113 were baptized Christians and 50 were catechumens.

Second Report of Fr. Ortiz, 1756

By 1756, when Fr. Ortiz made his second inspection of San Juan Capistrano, the mission had made remarkable progress. A church, with a sacristy, had been built of stone and mortar. It was a long narrow building 24 *varas* (about 80 feet) long, and 5⅔ varas (about 19 feet) wide. Its roof consisted of good beams of hewn wood. There was also a good granary, which was a stone building.

The church furnishings included a copper baptismal font and a sculptured image of St. Francis in a glass case, set in a gilded niche above the altar. On the altar itself were three carved images, each about 33⅓ inches high: a statue of St. John Capistran, patron of the mission, in the center, and on the two sides statues of Nuestra Señora del Rosario and of St.

Joseph. On a stand which was carried about during Rosary processions was an image of Nuestra Señora del Refugio of the same size.

The *convento* or friary had been enlarged. It now had three private rooms, and three other rooms, namely an office, a refectory, and a kitchen. In the textile shop were three looms. The huts for the 265 Indians who were living in the mission formed two "streets," along the east and west walls of the square.

Eighteen pair of oxen were used to cultivate the farm, which was watered by an irrigation ditch. It included a garden in which chile and melons were grown. The Indians were very fond of melons. On the ranch there were 900 head of cattle and 4,000 sheep. The cowboys and shepherds used 79 horses; and there were 40 mares and four mules.

During the 26 years since 1731, according to the printed report, 838 Indians had been baptized, 492 received Christian burial, and 85 couples entered Christian marriages. The figure 838 must be a typographical error and probably should be 638. For Concepción in 1756 the total of baptized Indians was 653, and for Espada it was 640. The total given for Capistrano in 1762 was 847.

The Report of 1762

In 1762 there were two missionaries at San Juan Capistrano, Fr. Benito Varela and Manuel Rolán. The report which they sent to Fr. President Mariano de los Dolores y Viana showed that the mission had continued to make progress during the six years that elapsed, except that the number of cattle had been greatly reduced by the raids of the Apaches.

The church was the same, a long narrow hall, now described as being 25 varas (about 83 feet) long, with a smaller room that served as a sacristy. In the church were three altars: in the center of the sanctuary, an altar with a gilded tabernacle and a statue of St. John Capistran; on the two sides, altars (or pedestals) with statues of Jesus of Nazareth and of Nuestra Señora del Rosario. There were also several good oil paintings. In the sacristy was a statue of Our Lady of Sorrows, clothed with a costly dress and having a silver crown and sword. Here was also a baptismal font with a silver shell; and in the closets and drawers, 21 vestments of silk and damask, 2 copes, 12 surplices, and other church goods.

The friary was next to the church, and alongside it was an open gallery with graceful arches. It was in the southwestern corner of the square near the San Antonio River; and for this reason it stood at an angle, because the river's course here was from northwest to southeast. The granary, which was the next building on the south side of the square, was a large structure of stone and mortar. As many as 1,600 bushels of corn and beans could be stored in it.

The textile shop had three looms and a well equipped weaving and spinning room. Blankets and cloth were woven here with cotton from the mission farm and wool from the mission's herd of sheep. The Indian houses consisted of neat houses of adobe, having thatched roofs of grass or hay; but it was planned to build Indian houses of stone and lime. Twelve carts were on hand to transport the necessary stone.

The chief crops of the mission farm were corn, beans, chile, cotton, and various kinds of vegetables. On the ranch there were now only about 1,000 head of cattle; but the sheep numbered 3,500. The cowboys had 100 saddle horses, besides more than 400 mares in eleven droves.

Three Spanish soldiers were living at the mission; and for its defence against the Apaches, the mission had several swivel guns and 20 arquebuses with a supply of ammunition.

Since the year 1731, 847 Indians, young and old, had been baptized at Mission San Juan Capistrano; and 645 had received Christian burial. In 1762, 51 Indian families, or a

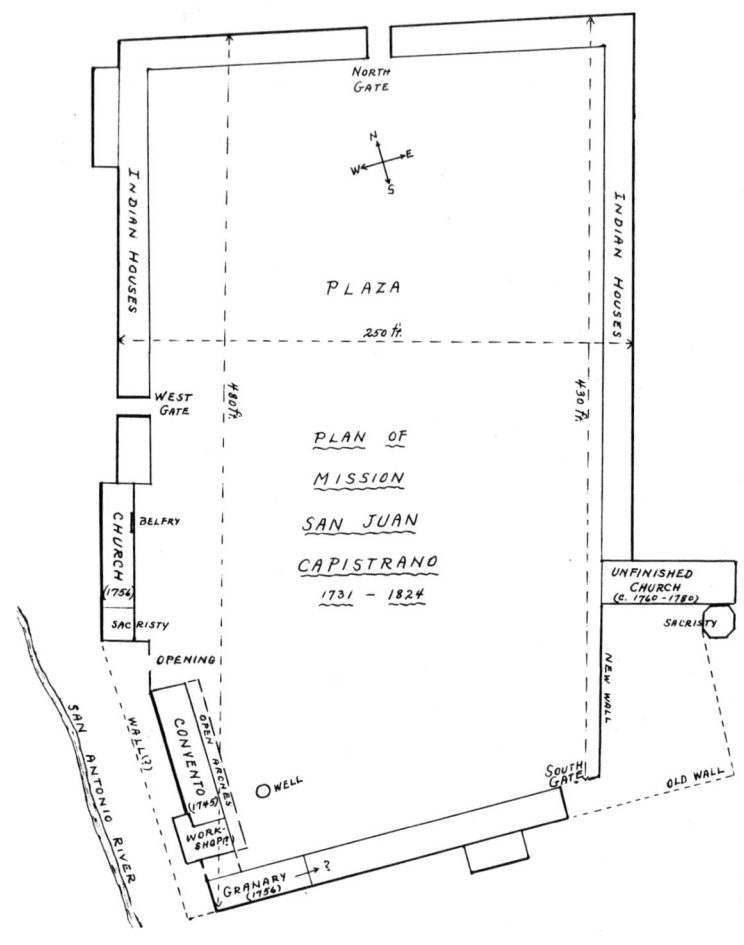

Author's diagram of the mission square of San Juan Capistrano, based in part on Corner's plan.

total of 203 persons of all ages and sexes, were living at the mission. They belonged principally to the Orejon, Sayopin, Pamaque, Piquique tribes.

A Recruiting Expedition

About a decade later, the number of Indians at San Juan Capistrano had been greatly reduced; and Fr. Andrés de San Buenaventura y Santiesteban, who was then in charge of the mission, undertook a journey to bring in new neophytes as well as runaways. With Captain Luís Antonio Menchaca of the San Antonio presidio, thirty soldiers, and some mission Indians, the padre set out on July 9, 1771, for the coast and the coastal islands. About a month later, August 7, the party returned with 107 Indian men, women, and children who had been persuaded to live in the missions. Governor Ripperdá said that for years such an expedition had not been made.

Of the 107 Indians, some had been in the missions before, but most of them were new converts. Sixty-five, of whom 18 were Christians, went to San Juan Capistrano; and the rest were assigned to Concepción and Espada.

About a year and a half later, early in 1773, the missionaries of the College of Querétaro surrendered their San Antonio missions to those of the College of Zacatecas, because they were needed in the former Jesuit missions of Pimería Alta, northern Mexico and southern Arizona. Thus all five missions in the area of the San Antonio presidio became Zacatecan missions.

Fr. Morfi's Remarks, 1777

Fr. Agustín Morfi, who visited them in 1777, does not have much to say in his *History of Texas* about Mission San Juan Capistrano. "The church," he writes, "is neat and in good order, though it does not compare with those described [the churches of missions San Antonio, Concepción, and San José] as far as the building is concerned. The friary has four rooms with a gallery, two offices, a refectory, kitchen, and workshop." Noteworthy is his statement that there was a workshop in connection with the friary.

"The pueblo or Indian quarters," continued Fr. Morfi, "do not compare with those of the preceding ones. . . . Like the others, it has steadily declined each year."

Visit of Orcoquisac Indians

The padre stationed at San Juan Capistrano in 1788 was the zealous missionary, Fr. José Mariano Reyes, who had taken an interest in the Indians of the Orcoquisac mission near the mouth of the Trinity River after it was discontinued in 1771. On September 8, 1788, a group of Indians from Orcoquisac, led by one of their chiefs, came to Capistrano, hoping to find their old friend there. But he happened to be at Espada to help his confrere who was sick. Thinking that perhaps he was in San Antonio, they went there; and after receiving gifts, which was an annual custom, they remained for four days. On the way back they stopped once more at San Juan Capistrano and found Fr. Reyes.

"Padre José," they said "you did not keep your word and come back to us, as you promised when you left. We have missed you very much. Our people actually cry for you when they are dying. The Indians on the coast are still hoping you will come back and rebuild our mission. Some even want us to take you along by force."

"You should have gone to Nacogdoches," replied Fr. Reyes. "That is much closer to your place than San Antonio. There are two fathers there for the express purpose of ministering to the Christian Indians in eastern Texas."

"We do not want to go to Nacogdoches," they objected. "We want a mission in our own country. Gil Ibarbo in Nacogdoches made many promises to us, but did not keep them."

"I would be glad to go back to your people," said Fr. Reyes, "but I cannot do so without the permission of Fr. President and the governor. You should have presented your request to them."

"We did ask Governor Cabello," the visitors answered, "but he put us off with promises. We asked Fr. President Agustín Falcon, but he did not think we were in earnest about our request."

Fr. Reyes felt convinced that they were sincere and he told them: "I will myself plead for you with the governor, and if I receive permission, which I think I can obtain, I will go with you when you come back in the spring."

That seemed to satisfy them, and their parting words were: "We will come back for you, Padre José, in the spring."

Without delay, Fr. Reyes presented the request of the Orcoquisac Indians to Governor Martínez Pacheco in San Antonio; and the governor was of the same opinion as the missionary. He replied that he would seek the consent of the Fr. President and of Comandante Juan Ugalde who was in Chihuahua. You can let the Indians know, he told Fr. Reyes, that I too will accompany them to Orcoquisac the next time they come to San Antonio.

Comandante Ugalde suggested that the sincerity of the Orcoquisacs be tested by sending Fr. Reyes to Nacogdoches in place of one of the two missionaries stationed there, and that 500 pesos be granted to him so he could procure supplies and gifts for the natives. This expenditure was authorized by the viceroy on April 15, 1789.

The Indomitable Fr. Reyes

Fr. José Rafael Oliva, the Fr. President, went to San Juan Capistrano, and Fr. Reyes got ready to visit the Orcoquisacs and to take up his residence at Nacogdoches. He received 206 pesos for work among the Orcoquisacs, and his successor at Capistrano got 200. But in the spring of 1789, the Orcoquisacs did not come to San Antonio as they had promised to do. It was a big disappointment for Fr. Reyes; and he had to admit that, because of their fickleness, his Indian friends had lost interest.

However, the long missionary career of Fr. Reyes was not yet over. In February, 1790, he was in San Antonio preparing to return to Zacatecas, when a delegation of Karankawas, Copanos, and Cujanes arrived to beg him not to leave but to establish a mission for them. The veteran missionary now undertook the task of reestablishing the two missions at La Bahía. Mission Nuestra Señora del Rosario had been closed for several years, and Mission Nuestra Señora del Espiritu Santo was now also practically abandoned. In July he reported that 45 Indians were living at Rosario, and 79 more were expected to return in October. The latter too had come back to the mission, but because of the lack of food they had left temporarily.

After he had made a good beginning, Fr. Reyes received instructions to retire to the College of Zacatecas in 1791; and Fr. José Francisco Jaudenes became his successor at Rosario, while Fr. Luís Mariano de Cárdenas was stationed at Nuestra Señora del Espiritu Santo.

Report of Fr. López, 1789

On May 5, 1789, before Fr. Reyes reestablished the Rosario Mission, Fr. President José Francisco López sent to Spain his long and detailed report on the seven missions then in Texas, including Nacogdoches. Of Mission San Juan Capistrano he wrote:

"It stands on the banks of the San Antonio River, on a small fruitful plain, covered everywhere by woods. It is square in shape, with a wall like the others. Adjoining this wall are the houses or Indians' lodgings, for the most part of the usual materials.

"Near one corner of the wall [southwest] is a large house, with sufficient space for the missionary and with rooms for the usual offices. Joined to this house is the granary [on the south side], also of ample space, and of a similar construction. Near the house [on the west side], but not joining it, is the church and sacristy now in use [the present chapel]. The structure is valued at 1,500 pesos, and its furnishings and ornaments at that same amount or more.

"Another [church] has been under construction [on the east side], but it was left about half finished; up to that time about 3,000 pesos had been spent, not counting the work of the Indians. The reason for stopping work was the same as in the case of San Antonio, that is, the lack of Indians. In addition, and more important perhaps, is the penury into which this mission has fallen. . . .

"The mission consists of:

Married couples, 21, from
    18 to 60 years of age 42
Widowers and widows, from
    20 to 70 years of age 5
Bachelors and children, from
    1 to 20 years of age 11

Total number of persons 58

"These people, for the most part, are descended from the nations of the Pamaques, Orejones, and Marahuiayos; and they usually speak their own languages. They are children of recently converted and baptized adult Indians, and are known as Marahuitos, the name given to all members of this mission."

Between 1762 and 1789, therefore, a new and larger church was begun, but it was never completed. It extended beyond the east wall, and had an octagonal sacristy on the south side. From here a wall was built to meet the south wall; but later it was moved west in line with the west wall of the rectangular square and joined a slanting wall on the south side. The irregular rectangle which was thus formed, according to Corner's measurements, was about 250 feet wide and from 430 to 480 feet long. Besides the unfinished church, several other buildings extended beyond the outer walls.

In May, 1789, according to Fr. López, San Juan Capistrano Mission had only 58 residents, while in 1762 its population was 203. Other available census figures are the following: 99 in 1783; 110 in 1786; 34 in December, 1788; 80 in December, 1789; and 21 in 1790.

Partial Secularization, 1794

Comandante Pedro de Nava's decree of April 10, 1794, which ordered the first and partial secularization of Mission San Juan Capistrano was carried out by Governor Múñoz on July 14. The padre in charge of the mission at this time was Fr. José Ramón Tejada, but he was absent just then and Fr. President José Mariano Cárdenas was substituting for him.

The mission Indians, of whom there were only 12 heads of families and hence a total of about 36, were called together; and the decree was read to them and explained. A Spaniard by the name of José Gil was presented to them as their "justice," the official who was to look after their temporal interests. He was not able to write, and had to ask his son to sign his name for him.

Pedro Huizar then immediately surveyed and subdivided the mission farm. The best land nearest the mission he divided into eight plats, each measuring 555½ by 1,111 feet. He set up markers to indicate their limits, and set them aside as the communal farm of the Indian pueblo. The income from this farm was to provide funds for the needs of orphans, widows, and the disabled and sick. Each of the twelve Indian families received a plat which was 555½ feet long and 277¾ feet wide.

Mission San Juan Capistrano. (Painting by Theodore Gentilz in the Daughters of the Republic of Texas Library at the Alamo.)

A field adjacent to the main farm, in which there were 47 rows of sugar cane, was divided into three equal sections and so marked. After the harvest, the crop was to be apportioned among the Indians; and then the three portions of the field were to be rented, and the rent received was to be used for the benefit of the pueblo. The crop produced by the $3\frac{1}{5}$ bushels of corn which had been planted on the mission farm was likewise to be divided equally at harvest time among the twelve Indian families.

The farm implements and other tools at the mission, two looms with a shuttle, spindle, and two combs, and one iron cannon with three one-pound cannon balls were then placed in the possession of the Indians. Likewise, into their hands were placed the few animals that the mission still had: one mule, one mare, two horses, four yokes of oxen, and 55 head of cattle. Of the latter there were 22 cows, 22 yearlings, and 11 calfs. Each of the twelve families took four, and the remaining three were set aside for the priest who was to have charge of the mission chapel.

This allotment of mission property to its few remaining Indians shows to what extent San Juan de Capistrano had declined as a result of the Apache raids and the confiscation of the unbranded mission cattle by the government. At one time Capistrano was the home of over 200 Indians and had 4,000 head of cattle.

A Sub Mission of Espada

But Mission San Juan Capistrano had not yet come to an end. While it lost its resident padre, the missionary residing at Mission San Francisco de la Espada took care of Capistrano as a sub mission. Twenty Indians, nine men and eleven women, were still living within the mission walls in June, 1809, when Governor Salcedo made a report on conditions.

The Spanish settlers had also begun to spread out from Villa de San Fernando and to establish homesteads, farms, and ranches at the missions and in the surrounding territory. At Capistrano, there were besides the twenty Indians, as many as 46 Spaniards, 24 men and 22 women. On the fringes of the mission lands, there were no less than fourteen large ranches in 1810; and the haciendas of some of them were almost like little villages. On the Rancho de San Bartolomé, there was a sixteen-year old servant by the name of Encarnación who had been one of the mission Indians of Capistrano.

Not all the lands of Mission San Juan Capistrano had been distributed among the Indians; some of it was being rented and cultivated by Spanish colonists. Governor Salcedo wrote that these lands extended 12½ miles east to the road connecting San Antonio with La Bahía, then 25 miles north to Pataguillos Lake, and from the headwaters of Cibolo Creek to the Rancho de San Bartolomé.

About the same time that Governor Salcedo of Texas made his report, Brigadier General Bernardo Bonavía, governor of Coahuila and coordinator of defence in Texas, met with the *junta* in San Antonio; and it was proposed that Mission San Juan Capistrano be made an organized hacienda with a rancho that would be ten miles square; and though the Indians of the mission were to be left on the parcels of land which had been given to them, the rest of the real estate should be sold at auction. The neighboring missions of San José and Espada, he suggested, should become towns. While the plan was looked upon with favor, nothing came of it; and so the mission was continued on a small scale.

Last Years as a Mission

Fr. President Bernardino Vallejo of Mission San José prepared his last report on the Texas missions at the end of 1814 and submitted it in February of the next year. He reported that at Mission San Juan Capistrano there were 15 Indians and 50 Spaniards. All of them received instructions in Christian doctrine every Sunday.

The Indians raised corn on their little farms, some of which were irrigated and others not. Though a communal farm and pasture lands were assigned to them in 1794, they had no common capital and were practically destitute. The church was in a fair condition and well provided with vestments and other church goods; but the mission lacked adequate protection against attacks of the hostile Indians of the north.

The successors of Fr. Vallejo, who returned to Zacatecas the following year, had the care, not only of San José, where they resided, but also of Concepción, Capistrano, and Espada missions.

The last missionary of these missions was Fr. José Antonio Díaz de León. In 1823 the government of independent Mexico decreed their full and complete secularization; and the following year Fr. Díaz de León surrendered the church of San Juan Capistrano and its furnishings to the acting pastor of San Fernando. Thus the mission finally ceased to exist.

After Secularization

It was not till seven years later, 1831, however, that Political Chief Músquiz of Texas was instructed to sell the remaining property of San Juan Capistrano at public auction. The population of the former mission, a year and a half earlier (March, 1829), consisted of ten families and three bachelors, a total of 42 persons.

The church or chapel of San Juan Capistrano was not included in the sale. In fact it was expressly stipulated that it should be continued in use for divine services. However, as far as records go, this was not done during the half century which followed the final secularization of the mission (1824-1873), except for an occasional visit of a priest from San Antonio during the years after 1840.

From the year 1873 on, it seems, Father Francis Bouchu, who had made his home at the Mission of San Francisco de la Espada, visited San Juan Capistrano at times. San Juan

Capistrano is mentioned now and then in the baptismal registers of Espada, beginning with the year 1873.

Visitors of the Old Mission

George Kendall, who visited San Juan Capistrano in 1841, wrote that its church was a plain and simple edifice with little ornamentation. It formed a part of one side of the square. The adjacent buildings were poor and out of repair. The granary stood by itself. In the northwest corner were the remains of a small tower; and someone was living in it.

However, as we learn from Ferdinand Roemer, the walls of the square were still standing in 1846. He wrote that the encircling walls, with Indian houses leaning against them, were almost perfectly preserved; but the church (the one on the east side which was never completed, though one half of it had been built before 1789) could be traced only by its foundations.

John R. Bartlett in 1850 was speaking of the chapel on the west side when he mentions the remains "of exceedingly rude paintings" on its walls. He adds that the earthen floor of the chapel was broken up in several places, where graves had recently been dug.

William Corner's Description

Some time before 1890 the roof of the chapel had fallen in, according to the testimony of William Corner. The minute description which he wrote of Mission San Juan Capistrano as he found it will be of interest.

"It is situated on the left or east bank of the river about six miles from San Antonio, a very picturesque locality by the San Juan ford and bridge. The settlement there is called Berg's Mill after a Scouring Mill erected some years ago. The S.A. & A.P. R.R. Depot goes by that name also.

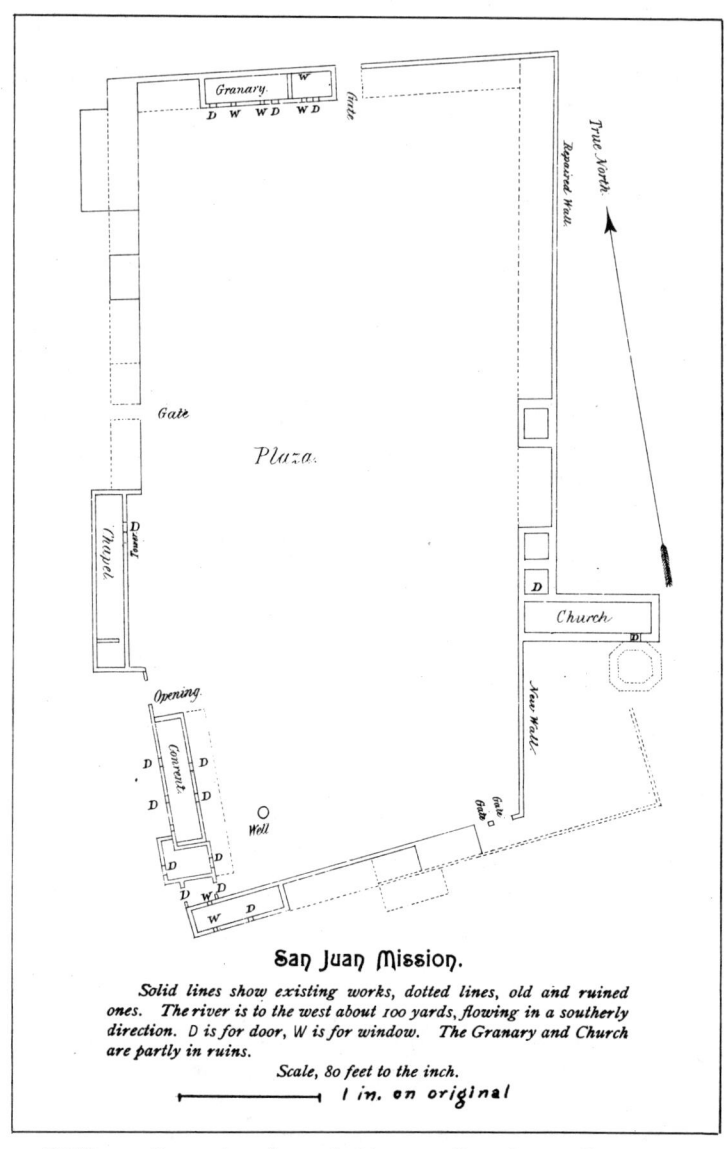

San Juan Mission.

Solid lines show existing works, dotted lines, old and ruined
ones. The river is to the west about 100 yards, flowing in a southerly
direction. D is for door, W is for window. The Granary and Church
are partly in ruins.

Scale, 80 feet to the inch.

1 in. on original

William Corner's plan of Mission San Juan Capistrano,
1890.

"About a half mile from this settlement on the right or west bank of the River is the old aqueduct [of the Espada Mission]. . . . This aqueduct takes water over the Piedra creek for the use of the Fourth Mission lands [Espada].

"Mission San Juan is less remarkable and distinguished than the other two just described [Concepción and San José], but has its points of interest. Its square is well defined, and the design of a complete Mission can be made out with less difficulty here and at the Fourth Mission than at the others.

"Its little granary, its chapel, its ruined convent or monastery which must have been a building of some importance in its day, and the foundations of a chapel which was never completed are all objects of interest. These main buildings, unlike those of the First and Second Missions, form parts of and are built into the boundary or rampart walls." It is well to point out that, according to the report of Fr. López, the friary was in the southwest corner of the square and perhaps not part of the wall.

"A number of Mexican families live here, some of the members of which possess marked Indian features. In the neighborhood of San Juan there are more traces of the Indian in faces and characteristics than anywhere else in Texas. The best time to note this is on a Sunday afternoon when they usually congregate at one of the houses near the ford for their weekly cock fight which seems to be the excitement of the community, that is among the men.

"The Chapel of San Juan is very plain and simple in construction. Just four walls—the tower being merely an elevation of a portion of the East wall with open arches in it for bells. There is still one bell left. The Chapel is roofless except for one small room at the south end which is walled off by an adobe wall and which is used as a Sacristy, vestry, and receptacle for the small remaining stock of figures, books, pictures, and other such bric-a-brac.

"The inside of the walls of the Chapel, however, will afford to such as care for that sort of thing a few minutes interesting study in rude frescoing. The frescoes are almost obliterated by exposure to the weather, and the wonder is that they have not long since been washed entirely off by heavy rains. They are a curious mixture of Old and New World ideas: detail of Moorish design, a Roman arch, an Indian figure, and pigments. 'These frescoes,' says Father Bouchu, 'I think are of later date than the completion of the Chapel; and they were probably permitted, to satisfy the Indian nature's love of color.'

"A painted rail about four feet high, running around the Chapel, first attracts the eye, then the elaborately painted Roman Arch in red and orange over the doorway. The design of this decoration is decidedly of a Moorish caste, zigzag strips and blocks of color, with corkscrew and tile work, and pillars of red and orange blocks. These pillars are about twelve feet high and support another line or rail of color; and upon this upper line are a series of figures of musicians, each playing a different instrument. The figures for some reason are much more indistinct than their instruments, the latter being accurately drawn and easy to distinguish.

"There is one of these figures over the frescoed arch of the door. It is a mandolin player. The player is indistinct, portions of his chair and instrument plainer; the latter can be made out to be of dark brown color with the finger board and keys, red. To the right of him is a violin player, the best preserved sample of all—the violin and bow are quite distinct, so are the features of the face of the figure, his hair is black, lips red, face and legs orange, feet black, the body of the violin orange, the rest of him and the bow red.

"To the right of him again is a guitar player, dressed in a bluish green color, sitting in a red chair; the instrument is quite distinct. Directly opposite this figure vis à vis is a viol player; the instrument being held by the player, finger board up, from the left shoulder across the body; head, hands, instrument, and bow being distinct, but the body of him is 'played out.' To the right of this ghostly looking viol player is a harp and a chair, but the player is either invisible or vanished.

"The lower rail, which is the more elaborate of the two, supports here and there a flower pot and flowers in incongruous colors of bluish green and dull red—carnations and roses being prime favorites, with an occasional cross on a painted pedestal or dado. . . .

"With regard to the rooms in the ramparts, it seems to have been customary at the Mission that a number of years occupation of rooms or barracks in any Mission gave some kind of title or claim to those rooms to the occupants. The Mission Government was generous to its converts and dependents. The Missions were projected for their benefit. This must explain such documents as that which may be found in the County Records dated January 28th, 1826, which relates that María de los Santos López and Barbara de los Santos López, who were then occupying three rooms in the Mission San Juan, conveyed the same to the Province of Texas for the sum of $34.00. . . . This sum was paid to them by Antonio Saucedo, then Chief Justice" (political chief, who administered the Province of Texas, under the governor of Coahuila).

In the Twentieth Century

When Father Bouchu died in 1907, the Claretian Fathers were placed in charge of San Juan Capistrano. The chapel was repaired and a new roof was put on it. On January 31, 1909, Bishop Forest reblessed it, and divine services were held at Capistrano instead of at Espada, where the chapel was temporarily closed.

In 1915 the diocesan clergy succeeded the Claretians, not only at Capistrano, but also at Espada. Father W. W. Hume had the latter chapel repaired during the previous years, so that it could be reopened. He also had further repair work done at Capistrano in 1915.

The Redemptorist Fathers began to take care of San Juan Capistrano in 1923, and continued to do so until 1956, when the diocesan priests who took up their residence at Espada started to attend Capistrano as a sub mission.

In 1967 Archbishop Lucey invited the Franciscan Fathers to return to San Francisco de la Espada; and like the diocesan priests who preceded them, two fathers living at Espada now serve also the old Mission San Juan Capistrano.

Before the arrival of the Franciscans, Archbishop Lucey had undertaken an extensive restoration of Mission San Juan Capistrano. He appointed a non-sectarian committee to assume the responsibility for this work, which is now in progress. In accordance with a recommendation of the Texas Old Missions Restoration Association, an archeological survey was conducted in and around the old mission.

The committee appointed by the archbishop hopes to raise sufficient funds to carry out an ambitious program, which includes: the restoration of the friary, porter's lodge, and granary, the raising of the enclosing walls, the rebuilding of the original fortifications of the gates, and the landscaping of the mission square and the surrounding area as park land.

All utilities will be buried underground; and all necessary facilities within the buildings will be provided for the convenience of visitors. A new access road will link the mission with the contemplated Mission Parkway; and there will be adequate but carefully screened parking facilities. The chapel will continue to serve as a house of worship for the nearby Berg's Mill community. All stone, tile, thatch, and wood work will be done by hand; and the lighting indoors and outdoors will be such that it will enhance an authentic restoration.

The Two Mission Churches

It will be well to call attention to the fact that, as the several reports concerning San Juan Capistrano from 1756 to 1789 indicate, the church on the west side of the square served as the mission's only house of worship after it was completed by 1756. It was never used as a granary.

A stone granary was constructed at the same time as this church. The granary formed a part of the south wall of the enclosure and adjoined the friary, which stood at an angle in the southwestern corner of the square but was not joined to the church. There was an opening between the two, and the friary had doors on the outside, the west side. Hence there may have been a wall between the friary and the river. On the east side, the side facing the plaza, the friary was fronted by open arches, at least by 1762.

It was planned indeed to build a larger and better church on the east side; and when there were still a large number of Indians at the mission, in the 1760's no doubt, the building was begun. But after one half of the structure was completed, the project had to be abandoned because of the lack of Indians in the mission. The ruins of this half-completed church can still be seen on the west side. It was never used as a place of worship.

The plan of the San Juan Capistrano mission square which was prepared and published by William Corner in 1890 erroneously places the granary on the north side. Otherwise the plan is correct; and it shows what was still standing in that year. It shows also that the main gate was in the southeastern corner, and that there were two other gates, one in the west wall, north of the church, and another in the middle of the north wall.

The long narrow church or chapel on the west side, therefore, which is still standing and still used, is the same as the one that was completed by 1756, except that it has been repaired several times. For more than two hundred years it

has served as a house of worship, except during the years of
the nineteenth century when it was neglected and abandoned.
It is well worth restoring.

Archeological Excavations

In 1967, archeological excavations were carried out in
several different areas on the grounds of Mission San Juan
Capistrano under the direction of Mrs. Roy Schuetz, anthro-
pology curator of Witte Museum, San Antonio. A complete
report of the findings will be published soon; and we look
forward to its publication.

Through the kindness of Dr. Curtis Tunnell, State Archeologist, the writer received a preliminary summary report after
he had completed his history of San Juan Capistrano; and so
he is able to offer the following comments. Far from adding
them in a captious spirit, we do so only in the interest of
arriving at historical accuracy. Historical research and archeological investigation are mutually helpful. If the findings of
one do not agree with those of the other, there must be an
error in the deductions or interpretations of either the historian or the archeologist.

On the basis of the excavations, it was concluded that the
west gate was probably farther north than is indicated on
William Corner's plan of 1890, that is, at the place where
Corner placed a double building. In 1890, Corner assures us,
the square was well defined, and he made careful measurements. If there was a gate farther north, it must have
antedated the one located by Corner about 35 feet north of
the present chapel.

The other "obvious west gate in the southwest corner"
apparently was not one of the regular gates of the mission
square, but a room with an open arch facing the inside of
the square and, perhaps at a later date, with a square doorway and a door on the outside. The description of Fr. López
seems to indicate that there was no "gate" here in 1789.

Buried foundations of "a possible early church," we are told, were found extending at an angle northwest from the present chapel. Whatever may have been the purpose of the structure which stood on these foundations—a building, according to the report, that was larger than any other on the grounds—we do not think it was a church. None of the five contemporary descriptions of the gradual development of Mission San Juan Capistrano make any reference whatever to such a church; and they would hardly have failed to mention a church of such dimensions. Perhaps it served as a granary at one time. Until 1745 and later, the mission had only a makeshift chapel of brush and mud, a *jacale*. By 1756 the present chapel had been built; and in 1789 this chapel was still being used as the church.

The unfinished church on the east side, according to the report, "was probably finished (although the roof may have been temporary) and served briefly as the church during the late 1760's and the 1770's. . . . It is likely that this church collapsed." The writer is of the opinion that this church was never completed and never used as a church for the following reasons. Fr. López, writing in 1789, tells us, not only that it "was left about half-finished," but also that work on this church was stopped "as in the case of San Antonio" (the Alamo church); and the reason for stopping work was the lack of Indians at the mission. The church of Mission San Antonio de Valero, now known as the Alamo, except for its sacristy and adjoining room and the dome, was not completed until this was done in 1849-1850 by the U. S. Army; the latter had to restore a part of the structure, torn down by General Cos when he made a fort of it in 1835. After 1789, the lack of Indian workers at San Juan Capistrano was even greater than before that year; and in 1794 the mission was partially secularized and then continued merely as a sub mission of Espada until 1824. Furthermore, before a building is used as a church, it is specially blessed or dedicated for that purpose;

and a half-finished building on which work has been stopped does not receive such a blessing or dedication.

After the final secularization of the mission in 1824, the unfinished church on the east side, or a part of it, may have been completed to some extent and roofed; and this structure would then have collapsed or fallen into ruins at a later date.

The presence of graves in the floor of the unfinished church cannot be adduced as proof that it was used as a church. As long as a missionary was in charge, a mission church was not used as a burial ground for the mission Indians. Their cemetery was in front of the church or near it. It was only a deceased missionary who was buried in the church, that is, in the sanctuary. The graves found in the unfinished Capistrano church may very well date from the post-mission period. In 1850 John R. Bartlett found that the earthen floor of the little church on the west side (the present chapel or church) was broken up in several places where graves had been dug recently. It should be remembered that almost a century and a half have elapsed since the mission came to an end in 1824.

At the Espada mission, it is true, a larger church was constructed and apparently completed; and then it had to be dismantled because it was poorly built and threatened to collapse. But at San Juan Capistrano all available historical evidence points to the fact that the larger church on the east side was never completed as a church and never used as a church. Anyhow we submit this as our studied opinion after a careful examination of the historical documents concerning Mission San Juan Capistrano.

Important Dates

1716, July 11: The mission was founded as San José de los Nazonis in eastern Texas near Cushing.

1719, June: The mission was temporarily abandoned because of the war with France.

1721, Aug. 13: San José de los Nazonis was re-established by Aguayo.

1730, July 27: The mission was moved to the Colorado.

1731, March 5: Moved to the present site on the San Antonio, the mission was renamed San Juan Capistrano.

1756: A long, narrow church of stone on the west side, as well as a friary and granary of stone were completed.

1760-1780: A larger and better church was started on the east side, but abandoned when it was half completed.

1773: Zacatecan missionaries took charge of the mission.

1794, July 14: The mission was partially secularized, and made a sub mission of Espada.

1824, Feb. 29: San Juan Capistrano was completely secularized.

1909, Jan. 31: Repair of the church on the west side, begun in 1907, was completed, and the church was reblessed.

1923-1956: Redemptorist Fathers of San Antonio had the care of the mission church. They were succeeded by diocesan priests.

1963: Restoration work on the walls and interior of the church was begun.

1967: Franciscans, residing at Espada, resumed the care of San Juan Capistrano. Excavations were made on the grounds, and restoration work was begun on the friary.

VII

Mission San Francisco de la Espada
1690-1824

The last in the chain of five missions at San Antonio, Texas, is the only one which does not lie within the city limits. It is just outside the southeastern boundary. Chronologically it could be put in the first place; for, it may be said to have been begun with the founding of another Mission San Francisco, the very first in the Spanish Province of Texas. It was then called Mission San Francisco de los Tejas, because it was established among the friendly Tejas Indians in eastern Texas. This was done when Alonso de León made his fifth expedition into Texas in 1690.

San Francisco de los Tejas, 1690

The founder of this mission was the energetic Fr. Damian Massanet, a member of the Apostolic College of Querétaro. He had taken along three other fathers of the same college: Fr. Miguel de Fontcuberta, Fr. Antonio Bordoy, and Fr. Francisco de Jesus Maria Casañas. They established the mission on May 24, 1690, when a temporary chapel was constructed in the principal village of the Nabedache Indians, one of the many Tejas tribes. This village was situated "on the bank of a small creek of good water," the San Pedro Creek, just northwest of present Weches in the northeastern corner of Houston County, about seven miles west of the Neches River.

A more substantial church and dwelling for the missionaries was constructed by the Spaniards and Indians of timber or logs during the week that followed: and on June 1, Fr. Massanet blessed the new church and then sang a high Mass. The following day, leaving the three missionaries in charge, with a guard of three soldiers, Fr. Massanet and De León set out on the return trip to Coahuila. Fr. Massanet now planned to erect a whole chain of missions in eastern Texas. He obtained the approval of the viceroy, Gaspar Conde de Galve; and the result was the expedition of Don Domingo Terán de los Ríos, first governor of Texas, 1691-1692.

For his project Fr. Massanet recruited nine priests and three "donados" or Franciscan brothers of the Third Order of St. Francis. One of the priests was Fr. Francisco Hidalgo, a member of the College of Querétaro. Four belonged to one of the Franciscan provinces, presumably that of the Holy Gospel or Mexico City (founded 1534), and the other four were from the Alcantarine Franciscan Province of San Diego (founded 1599).

Governor Terán de los Ríos was strangely slow and hesitant in carrying out his instructions, and he gave the missionaries little help and cooperation. The expedition ended in failure. Had Fr. Massanet succeeded, he might well have become for Texas what Fr. Junípero Serra later became for California.

From the Trinity River, where he received bad news about the Mission of San Francisco de los Tejas, Fr. Massanet hurried on ahead of the governor's party. Terán finally reached Mission San Francisco on August 4, 1691. What had happened here in the meantime? In October, 1690, Fr. Casañas had indeed founded another mission, that of Santísimo Nombre de María, on the other side of the Neches River, in southwestern Cherokee County; but a devastating epidemic of malignant fever had broken out at about that time in the villages of the Tejas. In a single month it carried off 300 victims. About 3,000 Tejas died in 1690-1691. One of the missionaries, Fr. Miguel de Fontcuberta, died after an illness of eight days on February 5, 1691. The other two had suffered much from lack of supplies.

Under the circumstances, it was not possible to found any additional missions. When Terán started out on his return trip to Mexico on January 9, 1692, six of the newly arrived fathers went back with him. Fr. Massanet, Fr. Hidalgo, and another remained with Fr. Bordoy and Fr. Casañas; and they tried desperately to make the best of the situation. Terán left few supplies with them.

A relief expedition, led by Gregorio Salinas Varona, reached Mission San Francisco on June 9, 1693; but it did not improve conditions much. When Salinas Varona departed five days later, two more missionaries went along with him. Fr. Massanet, Fr. Casañas, and Fr. Hidalgo persevered at their post. Most of the Indians grew indifferent and then positively hostile. A plot was hatched to massacre the remaining missionaries and soldiers. No alternative remained but to abandon Mission San Francisco. The other mission founded by Fr. Casañas had been destroyed by a flood in January, 1692.

Fr. Massanet had the heavier articles, like cannon and bells, buried. On October 25, 1693, after Mission San Francisco had been set on fire, the three missionaries left with heavy hearts. Of the soldiers who accompanied them, four deserted on the way. Fr. Massanet and his companions lost their way, and for forty days they wandered about aimlessly. On February 17, 1694, more than four months after leaving Mission San Francisco, the worn-out travelers finally reached Monclova, Mexico.

For Fr. Massanet it was such a disheartening blow, that he no longer devoted himself to missionary work among the Indians. Fr. Casañas was sent to the mission at Jemez, New Mexico, where the Indians murdered him in 1696. Thus he became the protomartyr of the College of Querétaro.

Fr. Hidalgo never gave up hope, and during the next two decades he did everything possible to bring about the re-establishment of missions among the Tejas. A Frenchman in Louisiana by the name of St. Denis eventually proved to be of great help in the founding of the second Mission San Francisco, as well as five other missions in eastern Texas. This was accomplished in 1716-1717 by the expedition of Domingo Ramón.

Nuestro Padre San Francisco de los Tejas, 1716

The missionaries who went with Ramón belonged to the two colleges of Querétaro and Zacatecas. Fr. Isidro Félix de Espinosa was the Fr. President or superior of the Querétaran missionaries, and Fr. Antonio Margil held the same office for the Zacatecan missionaries. One of the Querétaran missionaries was Fr. Francisco Hidalgo, who had so hopefully looked forward to this day. He was now a grey-haired veteran, but he was still full of zeal and eagerness to make good Christians of the Tejas Indians.

The first of the six missions to be established was that of Nuestro Padre San Francisco de los Tejas. It was founded on July 5, 1716, not on the site of the former Mission San Francisco, but about ten miles farther east, in the middle of the Neche Indians' village, for the Neche, Nabedache, Nacona, and Cacachau tribes, all of them Tejas who lived within a reasonable distance of each other. The site of the mission was on Bowles Creek, close to some mounds, on the east side of the Neches River, about three miles from the river crossing, and near Alto, in Cherokee County.

Fr. Hidalgo must have been a very happy man, when Fr. Espinosa placed the mission in his care, and gave him as a companion Fr. Manuel Castellanos, who was also to serve as chaplain of the presidio. The presidio had been established temporarily on the west bank of the Neches in a small clearing at the edge of a large lake. In the same year it was moved to the east side and closer to Mission San Francisco; and afterwards it was permanently erected near Mission Concepción. There Ramón remained as captain of the garrison.

Hardships of the Missionaries

The three years which followed the founding of the second mission of San Francisco proved to be a time of want and disappointment. "Almost from the beginning," Fr. Espinosa wrote in his *Crónica*, "the fathers began to maintain themselves by the bread of tears and affliction. The first trouble occurred when seven of the twenty-five soldiers who had been sent to guard the [six] missions, deserted and abandoned us, at the same time taking along some of the animals destined for the use of the friars.

"After selecting the site of each mission, the missionaries assigned to them had to construct their little thatched dwellings unaided; and, since no provisions were forwarded, abstinance commenced on the first day. Although it was not the season of Lent, the meals consisted of nothing more than a little purslane seasoned with salt and pepper. Once in a while the Indians would give us a little corn, beans of a certain kind, and some wild fruits, which served to distract rather than to appease our hunger. Rarely was a mouthful of meat available. . . .

"Chocolate, which we were wont to have with our meals, was scarce; for, we had received but fifty pounds, which had to be divided among us five friars from the Santa Cruz College [of Querétaro]. Fortunately, although all the fathers had their troubles and suffered various hardships, we were able to celebrate holy Mass every day, during which we besought the Lord most earnestly for the conversion of the Indian tribes.

"To render an account of our apostolic labors, I must remark that the Indians lived very far apart. Our main efforts, therefore, were aimed at persuading them to come together and settle down in permanent villages. Although they gave us hopes of complying with our desires at the time that they were harvesting their crops, the various difficulties that arose were so great that during the twenty years [that the Querétaran missions existed in eastern Texas] not one of the missionaries enjoyed the consolation of having all the Indians of his charge gathered together at his mission. . . .

"The fathers had to content themselves with visits from the natives. On such occasions the missionaries, who had already acquired a sufficient knowledge of the language, would endeavor to eradicate the erroneous notions of their visitors about religion, and would show them how necessary it was to receive the sacrament of baptism after they had learned and professed the truth of one God and Three Divine Persons. The poor natives, however, would appear unmoved or indifferent; for, they were so attached to what they had inherited from their forefathers, that only with the divine assistance could the absurd superstitions with which they grew up from their childhood be rooted out of their hearts. . . .

"The women manifest far greater willingness than the men to accept the truths of salvation. The happy consequence of this was that many of them had the good fortune of receiving holy baptism on their death bed, when the priest would be called to administer the sacrament. This was always postponed for want of assurance that the person, while enjoying good health, would comply with the obligations which the Christian Faith imposes.

"Among the little ones the desired fruit was gathered in abundance. Of all those who died in their infancy, only a few escaped the zealous vigilance of the missionaries and so died without baptism. So that none of the children should be deprived of the supreme happiness of dying in sanctifying grace, the fathers made out a list of the Indian huts and rancherías indicating the number of adults and children in each.

"Whenever an Indian came to visit the missionaries, they would ask him for detailed information concerning the health of his family. When they found out that anyone was ill, they would express sincere sympathy and then immediately go to visit the sick person, to give the necessary instruction to an adult and to baptize at once a child whom they found to be at the point of death. . . . By the grace of God even many adults willingly received baptism during their last illness.

"At times, sickness became general among the natives. . . . Whenever an epidemic raged, the watchful missionaries did not wait to be called. As soon as they had celebrated holy Mass, they would mount their horses and visit all the rancherías or villages and hamlets, and they would not return until they had baptized all they regarded as being in a dying condition.

"If they met with resistance, they would repeat the visit the next day, meanwhile entreating the Lord to open the spiritual eyes of the deluded Indians. The good Lord, moved by his own benignity, since these poor creatures were bought by the price of his Blood, would facilitate the administration of baptism.

"The hardships endured by the missionaries in their great zeal will be better understood, if it is borne in mind that the ranchos of the Indians lay far apart; that some of them were situated six and even seven leagues distant in every direction. Hence it was not an easy matter, even if the missionary rode his horse at a gallop, to visit the greater number of ranchos in one day, especially when he had to remain a long time to instruct the dying or to persuade those in health not to prevent the eternal salvation of the sick."

When the French drove the Spaniards out of eastern Texas in the summer of 1719, Fr. Hidalgo had to bid a last farewell to the Tejas Indians. With the rest he went to the newly founded Mission San Antonio de Valero to await the arrival of Aguayo's army; but he did not return when the missions of eastern Texas were re-established in 1721. The baptismal register of Mission San Antonio records the fact that on September 8, 1720, in accordance with an order received from the Fr. Guardian of the College of Querétaro, Fr. Diego de Alcantara, the founder of the mission, Fr. Antonio de Olivares, turned it over into the hands of Fr. Francisco Hidalgo. Entries by Fr. Hidalgo appear in the register during the next four years, showing that he was in charge of the mission until 1724.

San Francisco de los Neches, 1721

The expedition of the Marqués de Aguayo arrived in the country of the Tejas Indians on July 29, 1721, and halted on the west side of the Neches River at the same place where Ramón's first presidio had stood. The Neches River was greatly swollen at the time; and in six days Aguayo had a bridge built that was 89 feet long and 11 feet wide. "It was so well made and so durable that it was given the blessing of the Church."

However, before the bridge was completed, Aguayo sent ahead, to the site where Fr. Hidalgo's mission had been in 1716-1719, a detachment of soldiers and Fr. José Guerra to rebuild the church and priest's dwelling. This he did on August 2, and the horses of Fr. Guerra and his companions swam across the river. On August 4, after his army had crossed the river on the bridge, Aguayo sent another group of soldiers to help Fr. Guerra. The following day the re-establishment of the mission, now called San Francisco de los Neches, took place in a solemn and impressive manner.

Father Juan Antonio de la Peña, the diarist of Aguayo's expedition, has given us such an engaging picture of the ceremony that it deserves to be quoted: "Seeing that the church and the adobe of the missionaries were ready, the governor, with the entire battalion, went to reestablish the Mission of San Francisco de los Neches, vulgarly known as de los Texas. This solemn function consisted of a high Mass, sung by the Reverend Fray Antonio Margil de Jesus. During the ceremony there was a general salute by all the companies, accompanied by the pealing of bells, the blowing of trumpets, and the beating of drums.

"After the ceremony, the Indians, who also were present, knelt down at the bidding of Fray Isidro Félix de Espinosa, president of the missions of the holy College of Santa Cruz de Querétaro. In the presence of the Indians, who were congregated at the abode of the padres, and in the presence of all the captains and officers of the battalion, and in the name of our Lord and King (May God protect him!), his Lordship appointed as captain of the Neches one whom all the Indians had already unanimously acclaimed as such; and he presented him with a baton and a full suit of Spanish style. He also fitted out completely 158 men, women, and children, all of whom were extremely pleased, because they had never received as much.

"Through the Father President, who acted as interpreter, he informed them that the principal motive which actuated his coming was his Majesty's zeal for the salvation of souls, and that his Majesty received them under his royal protection and favor, in order to defend them from all their enemies.

"His Lordship showed them that the latter [the French] had given them presents only because they were interested in their chamois, bison, and horses, and especially in their wives and children, whom they wished to enslave, while our Lord the King (May God protect him!) not only made no demands on them, but as they had just seen, gave them an abundance of presents and desired solely that they enter the fold of the Church. [The governor had refused to accept so much as a single buckskin so it would not appear as if he had received anything by way of recompense.]

"He explained to them clearly his Majesty's will; and he told them that, in keeping with a practice introduced by the

Spaniards, they would have to congregate, and to establish a pueblo at the said Mission of San Francisco, which he named San Francisco de Valero. He warned them that their pueblo was to be permanent, and not merely temporary as heretofore. Finally, after they had learned all this from the said Fr. President, who is well versed in the language, all replied that they would willingly do this as soon as they had harvested their corn crop.

"That they might be able to carry out these instructions while his Lordship visited Los Adaes, they requested that the possession of the land be granted to them, as well as sufficient water for irrigation. In the name of his Majesty, his Lordship granted their request, giving them full title of possession, and left with them Fray José Guerra of Santa Cruz College. After the latter had been presented to them as missionary by the Fr. President of Santa Cruz, the governor stated that he hoped the newly appointed missionary's zeal would bring about their conversion in the shortest time possible."

The Indians were probably sincere in their promises at the time of Aguayo's visit, but they were fickle and did not keep them. They failed to settle down around Mission San Francisco and the other re-established missions. And as far as supplies for the missions were concerned, the missionaries were confronted with the same problem as before.

Fr. Espinosa tells us in his *Crónica* that "no oxen or any other livestock or implements were furnished to the missions, despite all the costly expenditures made from the royal treasury." The cost of the Aguayo expedition was over 250,000 pesos.

"It all came to this," continues Fr. Espinosa, "that we had to maintain ourselves as we had done before, by means of the annual allowance assigned by his Majesty. This the syndic [the representative and agent of the College] collected; and the College converted this alms into articles of clothing or other goods, and forwarded them to the missionaries."

We should add, however, that Aguayo and his men had to make the return trip to San Antonio on foot. Out of five thousand horses only fifty remained, and out of eight hundred mules only one hundred survived, when the expedition arrived in San Antonio on January 23, 1722.

Transfer of Mission San Francisco

The missionaries in eastern Texas carried on their work as best they could during the decade following the re-establishment of the missions. But, when Inspector Rivera closed the Presidio de los Tejas near Mission Concepción in 1729, the Querétaran friars moved their three missions in two stages to the San Antonio River. The three Zacatecan missions, with the Presidio of Los Adaes, remained; and the Zacatecan missionaries agreed to take care of the neophytes of the other missions in as far as possible.

Thus the Mission of San Francisco de los Neches, that is, its moveable property, was moved to the San Antonio and became the Mission of San Francisco de la Espada on March 5, 1731. Strange explanations for the name of "la Espada" (the Sword) have been offered. But, as in the additions to the names of the other missions, "de Valero," "de Acuña," "de Aguayo," the one added to San Francisco was probably the name of some distinguished person.

That Espada was in use as a Spanish surname is shown by the fact that a man by the name of Manuel de Espadas was captain of the presidio at La Bahía and then at Nacogdoches in the latter part of the eighteenth century.

Espada could not have derived its name from the shape of the belfry of its chapel, which some have thought resembles the hilt of a sword; for, it was called "de la Espada" before the chapel was built or even planned. Until the 1740's the Espada Mission had only temporary structures.

Mission San Francisco de la Espada. (H. L. Summerville photo; courtesy of San José Mission Friary.)

San Francisco de la Espada

The Mission of San Francisco de la Espada was established on the west side of the San Antonio River, at the place where it is now located, about nine miles from downtown San Antonio, at the end of Espada Road, just outside the southern boundary of the city, at the southeastern corner.

As in the case of the other two Querétaran missions which were "moved," the transfer amounted to the founding of a new mission. New and different Indians had to be assembled, and new supplies had to be procured. Small droves of cattle were obtained from the missions on the Rio Grande near San Juan Bautista in 1731, and several times during the years that followed up to 1737.

Since Mission San Francisco was the last in a chain of five missions, it was more exposed to the frequent raids of the Apaches. Thus, in 1736, the Apaches stole forty horses from this mission. The leader of this raid seems to have been a chief by the name of Cabellos Colorados (Red Hair), who was a particularly evil menace to the San Antonio area for several years in the 1730's until he was captured and sent as a prisoner to Mexico. Soldiers who pursued the Indians when they attacked Espada in 1736 came upon a worn-out horse which they recognized as the one Red Hair had bought a short time before from Alférez Galván in San Antonio.

The following year a band of Apaches suddenly fell upon five Indian women and two boys of San Francisco Mission who had gone to the Medina River to gather fruit. The fiends killed the women and slit open their abdomens in barbarous fashion; and they carried off the two boys as captives.

Fr. Pedro Ignacio Ysasmendi

The missionary at San Francisco at this time was Fr. Pedro Ignacio Ysasmendi. He was singled out by Governor Franquis de Lugo as a special target upon whom he vented his meanness. Not only did he remove two of the three soldiers who were at Mission San Francisco, but on one occasion when an Apache attack was expected he sent orders to Fr. Ysasmendi at midnight, requiring the one remaining soldier to come to the presidio at once since he was needed there. For eight days the mission was without a single guard and that at a time when his absence was most felt.

The accusations which the governor concocted against Fr. Ysasmendi were so patently false that they are not worth mentioning or answering. But the disrespectful attitude of the governor toward Fr. Ysasmendi encouraged the Indians to act in like manner.

In a letter which this missionary wrote in January, 1737, to Fr. Sevillano, the president of the missions on the Rio Grande, he reported that one day when it became necessary to punish one of the mission Indians for violating the rules of the mission, the culprit refused to submit and the others openly threatened the father with violence. Nothing could be done but to leave the guilty Indian go scot free.

The fickle Tacame Indians, who had previously been at Mission San José, were the first to abandon Mission San Francisco. On April 12, 1737, Fr. Fernández, the president of the Querétaran missions who resided at Mission Concepción, informed Captain Urrutia at the presidio that these Indians had run away, and asked for an escort of two or three soldiers to go along with Fr. Ysasmendi who wished to go in quest of the Tacames. Urrutia regretfully replied that he had orders from the governor not to furnish a single man to the missions; and he found it necessary to write a special letter to the viceroy explaining his refusal.

On June 8, Fr. Ysasmendi wrote to Fr. President that all the other Indians of Mission San Francisco had followed the example of the Tacames on the day before and had gone off to live in the woods. Of the 230 Indians who had been at Espada, all of them Christians, not a single one remained. A

few days before their departure, certain neophytes had killed
some mission cattle without permission and committed other
excesses. Not to make matters worse, Fr. Ysasmendi had
contented himself with merely reprimanding them and letting
the incident pass. But even a scolding was now too much for
these Indians, who had become emboldened by the governor's
conduct.

In Quest of Deserters

After Franquis de Lugo had been removed from office, Fr.
Ysasmendi sent a letter on November 4 to Governor Orobio y
Basterra, who restored the three soldiers to Mission San
Francisco. The missionary related that shortly after June 7, he
sent a messenger to the runaway Indians to tell them that they
should come back and all would be forgiven. A few days later
the messenger returned with only five adults and two children.
He sent a second Indian messenger, and he failed to come
back. He tried a third time, but in vain. An escort was
requested of Governor Franquis, and he refused. The crops
were ready for the harvest and would be lost during the rainy
season if the Indians did not come back. What caused the
missionary the greatest concern, however, was the fact that
the Indians who had gone away were Christians.

The new governor immediately instructed Captain Gabriel
Costales of La Bahía to send ten men who were to accompany
Fr. Ysasmendi on a trip to the land of the Apaches to which
the apostate Indians of Espada had gone. On December 23,
Sergeant Miguel Olivares reported to the governor that he and
his nine men had gone with Fr. Ysasmendi in quest of the
Pacao and Arcahomo Indians of Espada. After a search that
lasted twenty-one days, they had found the runaways.

The Indians were told that the soldiers would do them no
harm. On the contrary they would protect them against the
Apaches. The missionary succeeded in bringing back to the
mission 108 Indians, of whom 87 were married and 21 were

children. Only 24 who were on the mission's roster, not
counting the Tacames, were still missing. Thus the evil effects
of Franquis de Lugo's administration were in some measure
repaired at Mission San Francisco.

The Epidemic of 1739

However, in 1739, a dreadful epidemic of smallpox and
measles afflicted the Indians of Mission San Francisco. It was
"a time-honored custom" among them to abandon the sick
even if they belonged to their tribe; and so, many of them
sought safety in flight.

Of the 120 Indians who were at Espada at the time, only
50 remained after the plague had spent itself. The others had
died or run away. Heedless of danger to himself, Fr. Ysasmendi attended the sick and dying without stint. He too fell a
victim of the epidemic, and died a martyr of charity.

His successor (we do not know his name) once more
persuaded the runaways to return and made new converts;
and by the end of 1740, Mission San Francisco once more had
a total of 120 mission Indians. Already in the spring of that
year the fields had been planted. The Indians settled down,
and they seemed to be contented.

Report of Fr. Ortiz, 1745

By the middle of 1745, Fr. Francisco Xavier Ortiz was able
to report that remarkable progress had been made at Mission
San Francisco. A new church of stone and mortar had been
started. Its sacristy had been completed and was being used as
a chapel while the church was building.

Above the altar in the chapel was a carved statue of St.
Francis, about 33 inches high. On each side a picture, about
33 inches square, hung on the wall, one of San Bernardino and
one of San Juan Capistrano. There was also a carved image of
Our Lady of Sorrows (Nuestra Señora de los Dolores), about

25 inches high, and several additional pictures of various saints. The chapel was supplied with the needed church goods, including sacred vessels of silver, five sets of vestments of different colors and of new material. There was a baptismal font; and the chapel even had two rugs.

The friary was a two-story house of stone and mortar, with two rooms on each floor, those on the first floor serving as offices. The granary too had been constructed of stone. But the Indian houses grouped about the church were still for the most part *jacales,* huts of brush, mud, and straw.

The Espada Ditch and Aqueduct

The mission farm was irrigated by means of a canal which led water from the San Antonio River at a dam that was about two miles to the north and transported it across an aqueduct that was built over Piedra Creek. This aqueduct, which is about a mile north of the mission, on the east side of the road, has become famous. The aqueduct is still standing, and water still flows over it. Built of tufa from the Concepción quarry, it has two arches.

Fr. Hoermann, who was at Mission San José in the 1860's tells us, that the lower section between the arches at one time became detached from the foundation, but the structure remained standing. Having been covered with a crust of lime, it formed a solid mass that has remained in place. The construction of the aqueduct probably took place between 1740 and 1745.

In 1930 the De Zavala Chapter of the Daughters and Sons of the Heroes and Pioneers of the Republic of Texas set up a plaque at the road beside the aqueduct supplying the following information: "Aqueduct over Piedra Creek. Built by the Franciscan Fathers. Part of ancient irrigating system to convey water from the San Antonio River to the mission below."

The aqueduct of Mission San Francisco de la Espada over Piedra Creek. (H. L. Summerville photo; courtesy of San José Mission Friary.)

In 1965 the aqueduct was declared to be a National Historic Landmark. The marker put up at the time has the following inscription: "Espada Aqueduct has been designated a Registered National Historic Landmark, under the provisions of the Historic Sites Act of August 21, 1935. This site possesses exceptional value in commemorating and illustrating the history of the United States. U.S. Department of the Interior, National Park Service, 1965." Beside this marker is also a medallion of the State Historical Survey Committee of Texas.

Espada Mission in 1745

In the irrigated fields of Mission San Francisco, according to the report of Fr. Ortiz in 1745, eight bushels of corn were planted and these produced 1,600 bushels; also 3⅕ bushels of beans, which yielded about 64 bushels. There was also a field of cotton and several patches of melons and pumpkins.

The livestock included 1,150 head of cattle, for which the mission had its distinctive branding iron, 740 sheep, 90 goats, 81 horses used by the Indian cowboys, and 16 yokes of oxen for work on the farm.

Besides carpentry and bricklaying tools, there were on hand 20 hoes, 9 handbars, 15 adzes, and 30 axes. The household utensils of the Indians included pots, pans, *metates* for grinding corn, and *comales* or flat pieces of iron used to make tortillas.

Any surplus corn was sent to the presidio; and the payment received for this, together with the annual allowance granted to the missionary, was expended by the College of Querétaro to purchase implements for the mission farm and such items for the Indians as woolen and cotton cloth, blankets, shirts, hats, rosaries, knives, salt, and tobacco. Every year a Franciscan brother of the college conducted a train of such supplies to the missions.

Since its establishment on the San Antonio River in 1731, as the records of Mission San Francisco showed, 393 Indians had been baptized and 213 had received Christian burial. The total number of mission Indians at Espada in 1745 was 204, of whom 180 were baptized Christians and 24 were under instruction. Periodically the missionary made trips to induce new Indians to come to the mission, sometimes to distant tribes who had never seen a mission.

Second Report of Fr. Ortiz, 1756

When Fr. Ortiz visited San Francisco de la Espada for the second time in 1756, the construction of the church which had been started before 1745 was completed. It was about 39 feet long and 15½ feet wide, built of lime and stone and having a ceiling of hewn beams. This was no doubt the present (restored) chapel.

The altar in the church was a walnut chest with four locked drawers in which the vestments were kept. On top of the altar were shelves on which stood a carved image of St. Francis, less than 33 inches high, and some vases from Guadalajara. In the church were also a small statue of Christ with a baldaquin, a good picture of Nuestra Señora de Passaviense, a portable stand with an image of Nuestra Señora de los Dolores which was carried about in processions during which the Rosary was recited or sung, and a baptismal font of copper.

The friary was the same as in 1745, a two story building with four rooms; also the granary. The mission now had three looms, operated by the Indians to weave various kinds of cloth.

Fifty Indian families, a total of 200 persons, were living in the mission. Their dwellings were still only huts (*jacales*), but a beginning had been made in the building of stone houses.

The cattle on the ranch had been reduced to 700 head, but the sheep had increased to 1,950. There were also 50 horses and 52 mares.

Since 1731, the number of Indians of all ages who had been baptized was 640; and there had been 200 Christian marriages and 372 funerals.

Fr. García's Manual

Though the numerous tribes who were represented in the five San Antonio missions spoke different dialects, the missionaries succeeded in reducing them to "one language which is common or uniform in meaning and differs only in the greater or less stress of speed with which some Indians, called Bozales, because they use and understand very little Spanish, are being instructed" (Fr. José Francisco López in 1789).

This common language was Coahuiltecan. During his sojourn at Espada, Fr. Bartolomé García, who was the assistant of Fr. Acisclos Valverde in 1756, wrote a manual in Coahuiltecan for the use of the missionaries of the San Antonio area in the administration of the sacraments.

The manual was printed in 1760 in Mexico with the title: *Manual para Administrar los Sacramentos;* and besides being very helpful to the missionaries during the rest of the mission period, it has preserved the basic or common language of the nomad Indians who once roamed through the region extending from the San Antonio area to the coast and across the Rio Grande into Coahuila. Dr. Castañeda wrote of Fr. García's manual that it has been aptly called the first textbook of Texas.

The Report of 1762

In 1762 there were likewise two missionaries at Mission San Francisco, Fr. José Ignacio María Alegre and Fr. Tomás Arcayos. In that year, because the Franciscan commissary general of the missions had requested it, these missionaries sent a report to Fr. President Mariano Francisco de los Dolores y Viana, who in turn forwarded it on March 6 with the reports of the other Querétaran missions in Texas.

A new and larger church had been begun, but it had not been completed because of the lack of laborers and materials. The Indians had to be coached with much patience. They were averse to systematic work and sustained effort; and they worked slowly and irregularly. As far as materials were concerned, a new quarry had recently been discovered near Espada, and work on the church had been resumed. It was to be completed as soon as possible.

In the meantime a large room at the friary was being used as a chapel. In this little church (the one which was begun before 1745 and completed by 1756, and is still used) were two altars, one of St. Francis and one of Our Lady of the Rosary, and two confessionals as well as several benches. The altar of St. Francis, patron of the mission, had a carved and gilded tabernacle, also a statue of the saint and other carved and painted images. In the sacristy, adjoining the chapel were closets and drawers containing the articles needed for divine services.

The friary had been enlarged and now had three rooms on the ground floor and four on the second floor. The building was flanked by an arcade. In one of the rooms of the friary on the ground floor were three looms as well as spinning wheels and all the accessories required for weaving cloth.

The granary was a large and spacious building of stone. It contained over 1,600 bushels of corn, about 82 bushels of beans, and a supply of chile, salt, cotton, and wool.

The Indian houses too were built of stone and mortar and formed three rows on three sides of the mission square, an irregular rectangle. Each home was fitted out with the necessary furniture and household utensils. The number of Indian families living in the mission in 1762 was 52, and the total number of persons was 207. For its defence the mission had two swivel guns and sixteen firearms with a supply of ammunition.

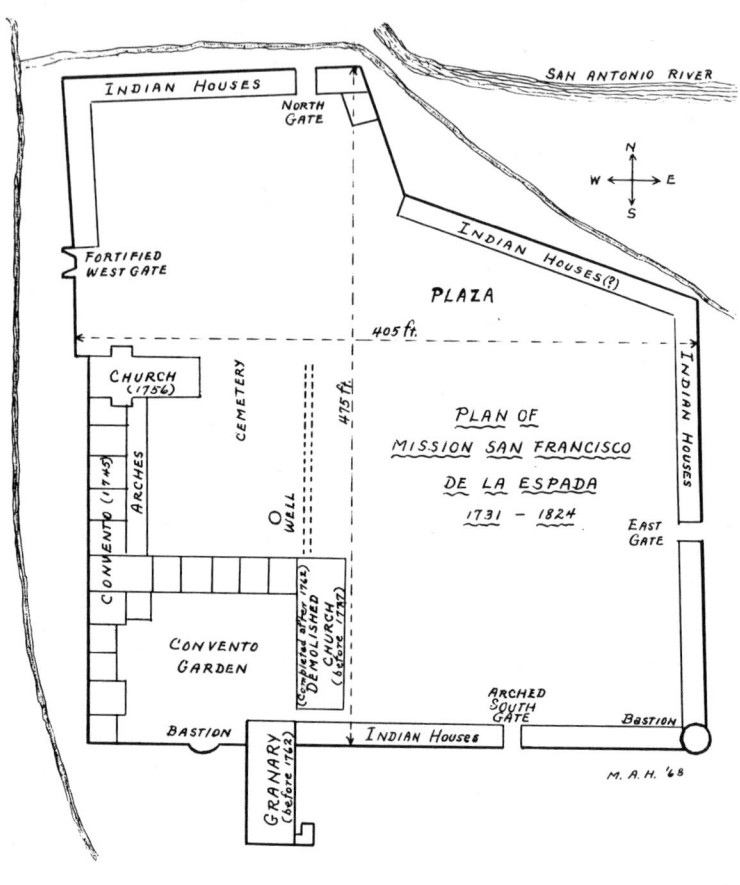

SAN ANTONIO RIVER

INDIAN HOUSES

NORTH
GATE

N
W ← → E
S

FORTIFIED
WEST GATE

INDIAN HOUSES (?)

PLAZA

405 ft.

CHURCH
(1756)

CEMETERY

415 ft.

INDIAN HOUSES

PLAN OF
MISSION SAN FRANCISCO
DE LA ESPADA
1731 - 1824

CONVENTO (1745)

ARCHES

O
WELL

EAST
GATE

(Completed after 1745)
DEMOLISHED
CHURCH
(before 1777)

CONVENTO
GARDEN

BASTION

ARCHED
SOUTH
GATE

BASTION

INDIAN HOUSES

GRANARY
(before 1762)

M. A. H. '68

Author's diagram of the mission square of San Francisco de la Espada.

The mission was supplied with carpenter, mason, blacksmith, and farm tools. The latter included, besides the plows, 40 harrows, 58 hoes, 46 axes, 10 scythes, and 16 bars. Thirty-seven yokes of oxen were used as beasts of burden and for work on the farm.

The ranch was situated at some distance from the mission and had a good stone house where the cowboys and shepherds could live comfortably. The stock comprised 1,262 head of cattle, 4,000 sheep, 145 saddle horses, 11 droves of mares, and 9 donkeys.

During the three decades since 1731, 815 Indians had been baptized and 513 had received Christian burial. The Indians of the mission belonged to the Pacao, Barrado, and Mesquite tribes. In 1762, therefore, Mission San Francisco de Espada was in a very flourishing condition.

New Recruits and a New Church

Accompanied by Captain Menchaca and thirty soldiers of the presidio, the missionary of San Juan Capistrano made a month-long journey to the coast in 1771 to gather runaway Indians and new converts for all the San Antonio missions. He came back with 107 men, women, and children; and of these Mission San Francisco received 26. The missionary in charge of the Espada mission at this time was Fr. Antonio Ramos.

Two years later, the missionaries of the College of Querétaro regretfully left the missions on the San Antonio River, because they were needed in Pimería Alta; and San Francisco de la Espada received a missionary of the College of Zacatecas.

Some time before 1777, at the end of which Fr. Morfi visited the San Antonio area with Teodoro de Croix, the church which had been in the process of construction at Mission San Francisco for a long time seems to have been completed; but it was poorly built and had to be torn down because it was in danger of collapsing.

In his *History of Texas,* Fr. Morfi wrote: "The church was demolished because it threatened to fall down, and services are being held in an ample room [the church of 1756] that has a choir and a sacristy, all very neat."

"The friary," continues Fr. Morfi, "is laid out on a straight line with four rooms on the second floor and three on the first, galleries, workshop, and a good-sized granary, all made of stone, but ill-arranged and plain. The pueblo, or Indian quarters, consists of three rows of houses that form a square with the friary, a wall, likewise of stone, closing a portion of the enclosure where there are no houses. This mission was founded for the Pacaos, Borrados, and Mariquitas. . . . Today [at the end of 1777] there are forty families with 133 persons."

In 1783, the number of mission Indians was 96. It rose once more to 144 in 1786; but in 1788 it dropped to 46. In 1789, the number of Indians living in Mission San Francisco de la Espada was 57.

Report of Fr. López, 1789

In his report of that year, Fr. José Francisco López wrote of the Espada Mission: "It lies between three and a fourth and four leagues down the river from San Antonio and the royal presidio, on a plain that is on the watershed and is thickly covered with woods. The mission is square in shape and is surrounded by a stone and mud wall. Contiguous to these walls are the houses, mostly of stone and mud, where the Indians live.

"The missionary's house, the church, and the sacristy, which adjoin each other, take up half of the west side. They are of stone and lime and have sufficient room for all purposes. The church and sacristy, on account of their superior construction and their ornaments and furnishings, are valued at three or four thousand pesos. On the south side

*Mission San Francisco de la Espada. (Painting by Theodore
Gentilz in the Daughters of the Republic of Texas Library
at the Alamo.)*

stands the granary, which is of stone and mud, but which has enough room to meet its requirements.

"This mission, like the others, was very populous; but . . . its population has fallen very much, as will be shown by the list of the persons now living in it:

Married couples, 14, from
   40 to 80 years of age 28
Widowers and widows, from
   40 to 80 years of age 13
Bachelors and children, from
   1 to 15 years of age 16
Total number of persons 57

"These are descendants of the Pacao tribe (which was fairly numerous when the mission was founded for its benefit, their language being the one most commonly used) and the Barrados and Marhuitos. Many of the latter were brought from the south coast, to which some returned and died, while others of this nation died in the mission during the small pox epidemic in the recent year of 1780. No small number have died and are dying of buboes."

Partial Secularization, 1794

Mission San Francisco was the first at which the decree of partial secularization was carried out in 1794. On July 11, Governor Múñoz personally went to the mission to put the decree into effect. Fr. Pedro Noreña, who was the missionary in charge at the time, called together the mission Indians, of whom there were only fifteen heads of families, and hence a total of about 45. Of the fifteen men, three were old and disabled. To the governor it was quite evident that they would not be able to administer, much less to increase, the property that was to be given to them; but he proceeded with the secularization.

The decree of the commandant general was read and explained to them; and José Lazaro de los Santos was presented to them as their "justice," who would henceforth look after their temporal interests instead of the missionary.

The next day Pedro Huizar surveyed the mission farm, and the distribution of the land took place. Eight plats, each measuring 1,111 by 555½ feet, were set aside as the communal lands of the pueblo; and fifteen plats, each of them 850 by 555½ feet, were given to the fifteen heads of families. One plat was also reserved for the diocesan priest who was to be appointed the pastor of the pueblo; but none was appointed and Fr. Noreña, who had been at Espada since 1778, continued to take care of the mission. That is why it was only a partial secularization.

The list of animals and tools which were given to the Indians shows that the mission had been reduced to a state of poverty. There was only one cow with a calf, one mare, three horses, three mules, eight yokes of oxen, but 1,150 head of sheep.

Of the sheep, 207 with their lambs were not distributed among the Indians but left in the care of one Joaquín Lerma, who was to be paid for his services after the sheep had been sheared. His monthly pay was to consist of eight pesos, one *fanega* (1.60 bushels) of corn, and 1½ pesos worth of cigarettes.

The list of the tools and other articles which were placed into the hands of the Indians follows. There were not enough to be distributed, and so the Indians must have shared the use of them:

5 axes	9 sets of harness	1 English saw
4 bits	9 harrows	1 handsaw
1 compass	4 hoes with	1 pair of beam scales
3 crowbars	handles	1 brass scale
1 small brass frame	11 plows	15 pairs of shears
	1 bucksaw	

Materials turned over to the Indians consisted of 25 pounds of iron, 3 pounds of steel, and 875 pounds of wood. They also received two looms with combs, cards, spinning wheels, and shuttles. Likewise, two canons weighing 256 pounds, and enough lead to make 98 one-pound cannon balls.

Last Years as a Mission

After the secularization, Fr. Pedro Noreña continued to reside at Mission San Francisco de la Espada and to exercise the sacred ministry at both this mission and San Juan Capistrano, at least until 1799. On January of that year he sent to Governor Múñoz, for approval, the results of the elections for the Indian *gobernador* in the two pueblos of Espada and Capistrano.

How much longer Fr. Noreña remained, we do not know; but Fr. Bernardino Vallejo's report of December 31, 1804, shows that there was still a resident missionary at Mission San Francisco. The total population of Espada at this time was 94, of whom 37 were Indians (21 men and 16 women) and 57 were Spaniards (33 men and 24 women).

The number of Indians at Espada was reduced to 24 (14 men and 10 women) by 1809. On April 17 of that year, Brigadier General Bernardo Bonavía, governor of Durango and coordinator of defence in Texas, arrived in San Antonio; and he suggested that Espada be made a town. The home government approved of the idea and offered free land to the first fifty families who would settle there; but nothing came of the plan.

By 1813, it seems there was only one missionary, residing at San José, who took care of all four missions; and thus Espada became a sub mission or mission station. Fr. Bernardino Vallejo began to make entries for Mission San Francisco in the records of San José.

During the years 1813-1815 Fr. Vallejo assisted at eight funerals which were held at Espada. One of them was that of Victor Jaime, husband of Vicenta Dias, also of Espada, who died as a result of wounds inflicted on him by the Comanches. Fr. Vallejo recorded the fact that Jaime received the last sacraments except Holy Communion because his wounds rendered this physically impossible. The burial took place on February 27, 1815.

The previous year, hostile Indians had attacked the ranch of Ignacio Calvillo, which was a few miles distant from Espada. They killed Calvillo and drove away his cattle; but ten to twelve survivors, including several women and children, managed to escape and reach the mission.

Private ranchos had been established on the confines of the land that belonged to Mission San Francisco. The mission lands extended north to the dam in the San Antonio River and south to Atascoso Creek; on the west it extended as far as the ranch of Luís Pérez, and on the east as far as the property of one Delgado.

Fr. Vallejo's report of 1815 indicates that the number of Spaniards who had settled at Espada had increased considerably. There were 72 Spaniards and 27 Indians, a total of 99 persons.

The "justice" of Espada in that year, now called Spanish *alcalde*, was José Antonio Bustillos. On December 28, 1817, Manuel Díaz was appointed his successor.

Fr. Bernardino Vallejo's successor, Fr. Manuel Fellechea, conducted two funerals of residents of Espada in 1817; and the next missionary of San José, Fr. President Francisco Frexes, had one such funeral in 1818. He was succeeded by Fr. Miguel Muro in 1819; but it was Fr. Antonio de Jesús Anzar, of the mission at La Bahía, who conducted a funeral at Espada on June 13, 1820.

A School at Espada

Among the letters which have been preserved in the Béxar Archives is one written on April 22, 1820, by the Spanish *alcalde* of Espada, Manuel Díaz, to Governor Antonio Martínez. He tells the governor that the services of a teacher had been obtained for the children at Espada. The teacher's pay consisted of a small amount of corn that was planted for him by the people.

But lately a new teacher had appeared on the scene uninvited. He was not qualified for the work; and Díaz asks Martínez, whether force could be used to compel the children to remain with the old teacher and to attend his classes. With his letter Díaz enclosed samples of the writing of some of the children who were pupils of the old teacher.

Later the same year, on July 25, Díaz wrote to Governor Manuel Antonio Cordero, about a fire that had broken out in the tower (bastion) at Mission San Francisco. The fire started when someone lit a cigarette in the tower.

At the same time Díaz asked permission to travel. His successor as Spanish *alcalde* at Espada was Josef Nicolas Paez y Tolmo, who in 1823 sent to José Antonio Saucedo, political chief of Texas, a list of the Indians at Espada who had a claim to the land which was distributed in 1794.

The successor of Fr. Muro and the last missionary of the four missions of San José, Concepción, Espada, and Capistrano was Fr. President José Antonio Díaz de León. He conducted six funerals and administered two baptisms at Espada during the years 1820 to 1824; and when he made entries for these in the records of San José, he expressly stated, he was the missionary in charge of the Espada mission. The last funeral, which took place on February 25, 1824, was that of María del Pilar, an Indian widow about 45 years old.

The dam in the San Antonio River, on the grounds of Mission Burial Park, where the irrigation ditch of Mission Espada begins. (H. L. Summerville photo; courtesy of San José Mission Friary.)

Final Secularization, 1824

Four days later, February 29, 1824, Fr. Díaz de León signed the inventory he had made of Mission San Francisco de la Espada, and surrendered its church and furnishings to the acting pastor of San Fernando and representative of the bishop of Monterrey.

The mission was thus finally completely secularized, and came to an end — 135 years after the first San Francisco Mission was founded in eastern Texas, 108 years after the Espada Mission was founded as Nuestro Padre San Francisco de los Tejas, and 93 years after it was transferred to the San Antonio River.

During the years which followed the secularization of the mission, though people continued to live there, the church was completely neglected. In the spring of 1826, a band of Comanches made an attack on Espada, wounding several men. They killed the stock and stole the green corn in the fields. Commandant General Mateo Ahumada then sent an entire company of soldiers under Captain Candido Arcos from Coahuila to protect the settlers at the former missions.

Later, the same year, a fire broke out in the kitchen of a section of the mission square at Espada, which had been occupied by a lieutenant of dragoons. The fire spread and destroyed a good part of the buildings, but the flames did not reach the chapel.

In September, 1831, the governor of Coahuila and Texas, José María Letona, sent orders to Ramón Músquiz, political chief of Texas, that all mission property except the churches be sold at a public auction and that the money received be held until further notice by the city treasurer of San Fernando.

During the war of independence, James Bowie and James W. Fannin Jr. made the Espada Mission their headquarters, when they arrived with about 100 Americans on October 22, 1835. They had no trouble taking possession of the mission square. Only a few Mexican soldiers were stationed there at the time, and they fled before the arrival of the Texans. Three days later, as recorded by Ammon Underwood, a force of about 200 Mexicans made an attack; but the walls of the mission could not be stormed, and they soon retreated.

Five years later, when Father John Odin came to San Antonio in the summer of 1840, he found both San Francisco de la Espada and San Juan Capistrano to be a mass of ruins.

The following year, George Wilkins Kendall, a journalist of New Orleans who took part in the Texan Santa Fe Expedition, visited Mission San Francisco de la Espada. In his *Narrative* he wrote that the church, a simple edifice with little ornamentation, which formed a part of one side of the square, lay in ruins, and the adjacent buildings were poor and out of repair; but the place was still inhabited. Two sides of the square consisted merely of walls; and the other sides were composed of dwellings. The granary was an isolated building. On the northwest corner there were remains of a little tower.

Father Francis Bouchu

There would probably be no Mission San Francisco de la Espada today, if it had not been for Father Francis Bouchu, who lived and worked at this mission during the latter half of the nineteenth century.

Born in France in 1829, he came to the United States as a young man, and was ordained a priest in Galveston on March 19, 1855, at the age of twenty-six. He was then assigned to the Church of San Fernando in San Antonio as an assistant pastor for the Spanish-speaking parishioners.

He took a special interest in San Francisco de la Espada, and began his work there as early as 1858. Later, if not then, he established his residence at the old mission. He preferred to live alone, and even in his old age he did not want anyone to wait on him.

In 1858, he found only the façade and the rear wall of the church or chapel still standing. With his own hands he rebuilt the side walls on the old foundations, and then plastered and whitewashed them. He put a tin roof on the chapel, and placed doors at the entrances. Inside the chapel he laid a wooden floor, built a choir loft, set up a sanctuary railing, and installed simple but sturdy pews (benches and kneelers). There were still some old statues on hand of St. Francis, the Blessed Virgin, and Christ Crucified. These he regilded and put on the altar in the sanctuary.

The people living in the vicinity spoke the Spanish language. Father Bouchu instructed them in this language; but he needed a catechism, especially for the children. Since none was available, he wrote one himself and printed several thousand copies on a simple, old-fashioned printing press, doing most of the work himself. The first printing appeared in 1872. By 1897, four editions had made their appearance. The previous year Bishop John A. Forest had made it the official catechism for the Spanish-speaking people of the diocese of San Antonio. It was used also in other parts of Texas and in New Mexico for a long time.

The Records of Father Bouchu

The records of baptisms, marriages, funerals, and confirmations, which are still kept at San Francisco de la Espada, begin with the year 1873. This may indicate that Father Bouchu began to reside at the mission in that year. One volume, marked "Book A," records the baptisms administered from 1873 to 1876, and the marriages, funerals, and confirmations from 1874 to 1876. It shows that Father Bouchu extended his priestly work also to the two old missions north of Espada, namely San Juan Capistrano and San José; and for the year 1873 there are some entries in the register of baptisms which were made by two Jesuits who assisted Father Bouchu, Fathers Tomás Mas and José María Bordas.

Supplementary to "Book A" is a separate volume which

records 241 funerals from March 15, 1876, to March 19, 1907, all of them conducted by Father Bouchu. The same volume has a record of marriages from 1876 to 1906, all of them blessed by Father Bouchu.

"Book B" is Father Bouchu's baptismal register from 1875 to 1907. He made the first entry in French on July 11, 1875; but the second, on May 13, 1876, he wrote in Spanish. His last entry is number 1,074, on June 23, 1907.

For almost a half century Father Bouchu bestowed loving care on Mission San Francisco de la Espada. When a storm destroyed the roof of the chapel in 1883, he replaced it. Living alone, without a companion or a housekeeper, he continued to exercise the sacred ministry among the residents of the area until a week before his death. He was then taken to Santa Rosa Hospital; and there he died on August 19, 1907, at the age of 78 years.

William Corner's Account

William Corner, who visited and described Mission San Francisco in 1890, wrote of Father Bouchu, that he "is wonderfully active and persevering. He knows something of many subjects, which he has practically proved here at the Mission. 'Padre Francisco' is Priest, lawyer, bricklayer, stone mason, photographer, historian, printer.

"His little pamphlets in Spanish would be credit to an office of much larger pretensions. He has lived in this community for many years and is well versed in information pertaining to the history of the Missions; and being himself one of those Priests who join with their vocation a knowledge of practical handicraft, he enters into the spirit of the founders with more than ordinary keenness. He is simple, unaffected, and garrulous, and meets the wants of the little settlement.

"He has built with his own hands, upon the ruin of the old Convent and arcade, a comfortable Priest house. Under his rule the Mission Chapel has been almost entirely renewed, the front only retaining a portion of its ancient work.

"The Chapel is in the form of a cross. The front is the belfry tower. . . . Its three bells clang out three times a day, and would be startling on the still country air to one who was ignorant of the vicinity of the Mission. It is said that some of the Mission bells were cast in San Antonio in its earliest days. So there is no knowing what these old Missionaries did not come prepared to do.

There are several pretty little bits of wrought iron work in this and the other Missions. Here is another artistic accomplishment to be added to the list of those possessed by the fathers. The entrance door of the Chapel is unmistakably Moorish, having the true Alhambra shape and lines.

"Sebastian Tejada, the Mission's oldest resident [born at Espada in 1813], maintains that there was still another place of worship on the inside of the South wall by the road [the larger church which was completed after 1762 but had to be torn down before 1777 because it threatened to fall down].

"Here was the old main South entrance, and the Granary was built projecting lengthwise outside the walls by the same entrance. Only the bare foundation of these two buildings now exist. Opposite the old Convent is the well, which was never forgotten in the building of a Mission. The Convent, its yard (which form now the Padre's residence), and the Chapel or Church are built into and form portions of the western ramparts."

The mission square, of which Corner published a plan, is described by him in 1890 as follows:

"Parts of the ramparts or enclosing walls of this Mission are pretty well preserved, others are in total ruins; but the foundations of the limits can be clearly made out all around, except at points facing the banks of the River [on the north and northeast sides, the latter forming two obtuse angles]. The Square is of irregular shape. . . .

"In the southeast corner is an object of much interest. Projecting from the angle of the walls outwardly, is a small round tower of quite a feudal character. It is in a state of fine preservation; and its three dressed-stone, round cannon holes near the base, and its seven musket holes about eight feet from the ground, lend it quite a menacing presence.

"The interior of it is in equally good repair; and one cannot refrain from conjuring up vivid scenes of fights with Indians in those early days of the Mission struggles with the red man—of women handing out the loaded muskets from the secure chambers to the right and left rear, of the unerring marksmen making it very hot for the attacking hostile, with an occasional lull in which is run out a small brass swivel gun to the diminutive embrasure, which makes the Apache or Comanche wish he were safe home in his fastness among the hills of Bandera.

"And it might have been that the recent remembrance of the total destruction of the San Sabá Mission and the massacre of its inmates in 1758 [an Apache mission destroyed by the Comanches and other northern tribes] lent some zest in these encounters. For, while these old Missionary pioneers were ever anxious to deal tenderly with any hostile, yet unfortunately there were occasions when sternness was necessary, 'that they might feel, the velvet scabbard held a sword of steel.'

"There was another of these 'baluartes' or bastions on the south wall by the road [beyond the granary], west of this one; but no trace of it is to be found. The chambers to the west of the existing 'baluarte' have, looking out upon the square, alternate doors and arches, and one of the wide arched entrances [south entrance] still exists.

"The rooms to the north have been fitted up for a school by Rev. Father Bouchu. . . . Several Mexican families still reside in tumble-down huts on the lines of the Mission Square."

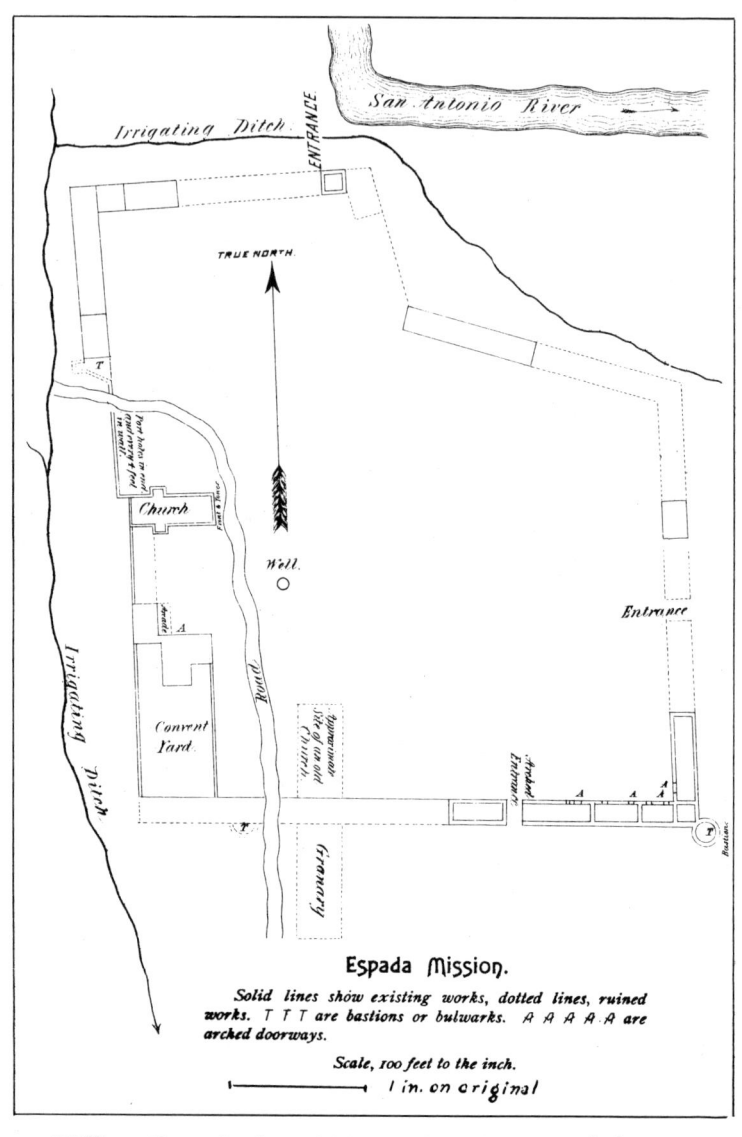

Espada Mission.

Solid lines show existing works, dotted lines, ruined works. T T T are bastions or bulwarks. A A A A A are arched doorways.

Scale, 100 feet to the inch.

1 in. on original

William Corner's plan of Mission San Francisco de la Espada, 1890.

Besides the south entrance—perhaps two south entrances, namely the arched entrance mentioned by Corner, and what he calls the old main south entrance beside the second bastion in the south wall—the mission also had a fortified entrance on the west side just north of the chapel, and, it seems, also an entrance on the north side, and another on the east side.

Espada in the Twentieth Century

"Book C" in the archives of Mission San Francisco de la Espada is a continuation of the baptismal register by the successors of Father Bouchu during the years 1908 to 1932. From it we learn that the chapel of this mission was closed on January 31, 1909. During the next six years the chapel of San Juan Capistrano was used instead of the Espada chapel. The Capistrano chapel, which was larger, had been repaired, and Bishop John A. Forest solemnly blessed it on the same day that the Espada chapel was temporarily closed. The Claretian Fathers had been placed in charge of San Francisco de la Espada on the death of Father Bouchu, and they continued to serve San Juan Capistrano until 1915.

In 1911, through the efforts of Father W. W. Hume, another restoration of the chapel of San Francisco was undertaken. A wooden ceiling and a new roof was put on the building; and new doors and windows were substituted for the old ones. The interior received a brick floor. Originally the chapel had two transepts; and Father Bouchu rebuilt both of them. In 1911 the north transept was not restored; and it was not rebuilt until 1962.

The restored chapel of Espada was reopened for divine services in 1915; and during the next eight years many diocesan priests took turns attending the chapel regularly on Sundays. During the years 1916 to 1917, some Josephite Fathers from Mexico also conducted divine services at Espada. Among the diocesan priests whose signatures are found in "Book C," besides that of Father Hume, we find — to mention only a few — those of Fathers M. S. Garriga, M. J. Gilbert, Manuel Villar, J. P. Vervaeke, R. Klyn, Paul P. Kaspar, L. J. Fitzsimon.

A school was also opened in 1915 in one of the old buildings of Espada that had been repaired; and the Sisters of the Incarnate Word took charge of it. Later a nearby home was acquired and converted into a sisters' convent; additional clasrooms were also built. But in 1967 the school was discontinued.

From 1923 to 1956, the Redemptorist Fathers of San Antonio regularly attended San Francisco de la Espada on Sundays. The chapel was then placed in the care of the diocesan clergy once more. The rooms adjoining the chapel were made habitable, and two priests resided there to take care not only of Espada, but also of Capistrano and other rural parishes.

In 1967 the Franciscans accepted the invitation of Archbishop Robert E. Lucey and returned to Mission San Francisco de la Espada. Two fathers now reside there; and like the diocesan priests who preceded them, they have the care also of Mission San Juan Capistrano and the country churches of Southton and Villa Coronado. Among the articles in the friary which have survived from the mission days of the eighteenth century are four items of silver: two cruets, a pyx, and an oil stock.

It will be of interest to add that during the centennial year of 1936 more than 6,500 persons visited the mission and signed a visitors' book. Among the signatures is that of President Franklin D. Roosevelt, made on June 11.

Considerable restoration work was done at Espada in 1930-1932, and from June, 1955, to October, 1956. During the latter period the archdiocese spent the sum of $12,000 for this purpose. Further work of this kind is contemplated; and eventually, according to plans, so-called Mission Road, which connects the five old missions of San Antonio, will be repaired, improved, and beautified.

Important Dates

1690, May 24: The first San Francisco de los Tejas Mission was founded in eastern Texas near Weches. The site is now a State Park.

1716, July 3: The second mission, Nuestro Padre San Francisco de los Tejas, was founded in eastern Texas near Alto.

1721, Aug. 5: The mission was re-established as San Francisco de los Neches, after having been temporarily abandoned in 1719.

1730, July 27: The mission was moved to the Colorado.

1731, March 5: Moved to the San Antonio River, the mission received the name San Francisco de la Espada.

1739: Fr. Pedro Ignacio Ysasmendi, missionary of Espada, died during an epidemic.

1745: A friary of stone was completed. Also an aqueduct of stone across Piedra Creek, as part of the mission's irrigation system.

1756: A small church of stone, the present restored church, was completed.

1777: A larger church, begun before 1762, had to be torn down after it had been completed because it threatened to fall.

1794, July 12: The Espada Mission was partially secularized, but a missionary remained in residence.

1820: A primary school was conducted at Espada.

1824, Feb. 29: The Espada Mission was completely secularized.

1858-1907: The Rev. Francis Bouchu served as the pastor of the former mission. He was followed by the Claretian Fathers till 1909. From 1909 till 1915, they used the Capistrano church.

1909-1915: Temporarily closed, the church of Espada was repaired and reopened in 1915. In 1915, diocesan priests followed the Claretian Fathers, and a school was opened. In 1967 this school had to be closed.

1923-1956: Redemptorist Fathers of San Antonio had the care of Espada.

1956-1967: Diocesan priests served both Espada and Capistrano, and further restoration work was done in 1962.

1965: The Espada Aqueduct was designated a National Historic Landmark.

1967: Franciscan Fathers began to reside at Espada and to serve this and the Capistrano Mission.

VIII

The Missionaries

The names of no less than 93 missionaries, members of one of the two apostolic colleges of Querétaro and Zacatecas, who were stationed or lived at the five San Antonio missions for longer or shorter periods, are found in the extant records.

There were, of course, others who passed through the San Antonio area and stopped at one or more of these missions on their way to or from their assignments to northeastern or southeastern Texas. It will be of interest and also personalize the story of the San Antonio missions, if we present an alphabetical roster of these 93 missionaries with a few biographical facts. The apostolic college to which each one belonged will be indicated by the letters "Q" and "Z" after their names.

Fr. Juan José Aguilar (Z) was the missionary in charge of Mission Nuestra Señora del Espíritu Santo at La Bahía (Goliad) from 1794 to 1800; but he spent about five months at Mission San José in 1798 as an assistant. During this time he administered three baptisms, and officiated at two marriages and seven funerals. From 1801 to 1804, he was one of the consultors of the College of Zacatecas.

Fr. José Guadalupe Alcivia (Q), as the missionary of San Juan Capistrano, endorsed the plan of Fr. President Mariano Viana to move Mission San Francisco Xavier from the San Marcos River to the Guadalupe, which was submitted to all the fathers in the Querétaran missions of Texas by the Fr. Visitor Ortiz in 1756. At this time the College of Zacatecas had among its members a friar with exactly the same uncommon name. He had become a Franciscan in the Province of the Holy Gospel as Fray José Fernández de Alcivia, and was still a seminarian when he joined the College of Zacatecas in 1724.

On this occasion he changed his name to Fray José Guadalupe Alcivia. In 1732, with a companion, he preached a series of parish missions throughout the present states of Campeche and Tabasco, which lasted a year and five months. From 1756 to 1759 he was the Fr. Guardian of the College of Zacatecas.

Fr. José Ignacio María Alegre (Q) was stationed at Mission San Juan Capistrano in 1759, and at San Francisco de la Espada in 1762.

Fr. Juan Salvador de Amaya (Q) served Mission San Antonio de Valero at least from 1728 to 1733. He had been a member of the Franciscan Province of Jalisco before he joined the College of Querétaro in 1728. In the same year he went to Texas and remained as a missionary for twenty-four years until his death on November 17, 1752.

Fr. Antonio de Jesús Anzar (Z) was at Mission San José for a short time in 1820, and performed a baptism at Espada, then a sub mission, on June 13. He was placed in charge of Mission Espíritu Santo shortly afterwards, but remained at most for a few years before returning to Zacatecas.

Fr. Francisco Aparicio (Q) was stationed at Mission Concepción in 1759 and 1760, and perhaps longer.

Fr. Francisco Cayetano del Aponte y Lis (Q) was one of the builders of the stone church of Mission Concepción, which is still standing. A native of Pontevedra, in the archdiocese of Santiago, Spain, he joined the Franciscan Order in his home town. In 1730 he went to New Spain and became a member of the Franciscan Province of Michoacán. Ten years later he joined the College of Querétaro. He was a Querétaran missionary for 51 years, ten of which he spent in Texas, all of them at Mission Concepción, 1748 to 1757. The new church was under construction when he arrived, and it was completed by December 8, 1755. He made 22 entries in the mission's marriage record in 1748-1753 and three more in 1757. Three years later he was the superior of the College's hospice in the city of Puebla de los Angeles. When he died at Querétaro on May 25, 1781, he was 93 years old.

Fr. Miguel Aranda (Q) was the assistant of Fr. Aponte y Lis at least from 1753 to 1758. The marriage record of Concepción shows that he officiated at 29 marriages during these years.

Fr. Tomás Antonio Arcayos (Q) was the companion of Fr. Alegre at Mission San Francisco de la Espada in 1762, and a missionary at San Antonio de Valero in 1771. Fr. Manuel Arcayos, who was elected guardian of the Zacatecas College, September 13, 1777, and died soon afterwards, may have been his brother.

Fr. Juan Domingo de Arricivita (Q) a missionary at San Antonio de Valero in 1750, later wrote a voluminous chronicle of the College of Querétaro, which was a continuation of Fr. Espinosa's *Crónica*. This work was published in Mexico City in 1792.

Fr. Joseph Cosmé Borruel (Z) assisted Fr. Núñez at Mission San José in 1736-1737, and then went to Mission Espíritu Santo, which was on the Guadalupe River at that time. The name of the missionary who is known to have taken his place at San José in 1737 has not been recorded. Before Fr. Borruel became a Franciscan at the College of Zacatecas, he had been a diocesan priest and held the office of rector as well as professor of philosophy and theology at the seminary in Guadalajara.

Brother Francisco Bustamente (Q) was at San Antonio de Valero in January 1731; and in April of the same year he was at the Hospice of San Fernando in Mexico City. The names of most of the lay brothers who served the missions as conductors of supplies, infirmarians, and in other ways are not mentioned in existing records and reports; we know the names of three who were at Mission San Antonio.

Fr. Ventura Bustamente (Z) came to assist Fr. Díaz at San José and the three neighboring missions in 1822, but he did not remain long in Texas.

Fr. Joaquín Camargo de Santa Ana (Q) was the companion of Fr. President Fernández at Mission Concepción from 1738 to 1743, during which time he made six entries in the marriage record.

Fr. Josef María de Jesús Camarena (Z) was the last resident missionary who had the care of Mission Concepción. He was in charge of the mission from 1787 to 1794, when it was partially secularized and made a sub mission of San José. In November and December, 1794, he made two entries in the baptismal register of San José. We find him again at San José in 1797, substituting for Fr. President Cárdenas and officiating at the funeral of a Lipan Apache woman. Once more he was at San José and baptized two persons in 1812. He was a missionary in Texas for 25 years. Returning to Zacatecas, he held the office of a *discreto* or consultor at the College for two terms, 1816-1819 and 1825-1828.

Fr. Juan de Diós Camberos (Z) had the care of San José at least from 1762 to 1764, and he may have been the Fr. President of the Zacatecan missions at this time. Born about 1720, he entered the Franciscan Order at the College of Zacatecas in 1738 and was ordained a priest about 1749. He was at La Bahía (Goliad) in 1754, and in that year journeyed all the way to Mexico City to obtain approval for the establishment of Mission Nuestra Señora del Rosario. Returning, he founded this mission in November, the same year, with the aid of private donations. He was still at the Rosario Mission in 1758. Shortly after he had granted asylum to Captain Martínez Pacheco at San José, he died on November 7, 1764, only about 44 years old.

Fr. José Mariano de Cárdenas (Z) was the missionary of Capistrano in 1778, and of Espíritu Santo in 1790. The marriage record of San José shows he was at San José with Fr. Pedrajo in 1792. Two years later he succeeded Fr. López as Fr. President of the Texas missions and supervised the partial secularization of San José and its three neighboring missions.

He resided at San José and attended Concepción from there, 1794 to 1799, during which time he baptized 39 persons and conducted the funerals of ten. He probably returned to Zacatecas at the close of his term as *presidente,* and was succeeded by Fr. Vallejo in 1800. From 1804 to 1807 he served as vicar of the college. For at least 22 years he was a missionary in Texas.

Fr. Manuel Carrasco (Q) was stationed at Mission San Antonio in 1772 and 1773.

Fr. Francisco Xavier Castellanos (Q) was a missionary at San Antonio de Valero in 1727. He was a native of Mexico City and a member of the Franciscan Province of Santo Evangelio before he joined the College of Querétaro. There he held the offices of master of novices for two terms, and of Fr. Guardian after 1848. He died at the College on February 12, 1759, 59 years old.

Fr. Manuel Castellanos (Q) was assigned in 1716 to the second Mission San Francisco in eastern Texas as the companion of Fr. Hidalgo and chaplain of the presidio. As one of the refugees from eastern Texas, he made an entry in the baptismal register of San Antonio de Valero on October 19, 1719. He died in Texas before August, 1728.

Fr. Ignacio Antonio Ciprián (Z) was at Mission San Antonio in 1731 and in that year administered the first baptism in the new Villa de San Fernando with the permission of its parish priest. In 1749 he was the missionary of Mission Espíritu Santo, which in that year was moved from the Guadalupe to the San Antonio River. Apparently he was also the Fr. President of the Zacatecan missions in Texas; for, in the same year, he wrote a report concerning them. He says he was an eyewitness of what he relates about Mission San José.

Fr. José María Delgadillo (Z) was a young priest who came to San José in 1799 to assist Fr. Cárdenas and then Fr. Vallejo. In 1804 he wrote a letter to the commandant general, requesting permission to re-establish the Orcoquisac mission at the mouth of the Trinity, the cost of which he expected to cover with donations from friends in Mexico. No doubt he did this with the knowledge and approval of Fr. President Vallejo but his petition was not granted.

Fr. José Antonio Díaz de León (Z) was the last missionary of San José, Concepción, Capistrano, and Espada, the last Fr. President and the last Zacatecan missionary in Texas. He began his missionary career in Tamaulipas, then called Nuevo Santander, and came to Texas in 1817, when he was assigned to Mission Nuestra Señora del Refugio. Three years later he was appointed Fr. President of the Texas missions and took up his residence at San José in the fall of 1820. He attended this and the other three neighboring missions until their final secularization in February, 1824. In the fall of 1825, he left San Antonio for Mission Espíritu Santo and tried to save this mission and Refugio until they too were secularized in February, 1830. Later that year, he took up his duties as pastor of Nacogdoches, including San Augustine and Liberty. Returning from a pastoral visit that he made to the Trinity River, he was shot to death by a bigoted frontiersman, about a mile east of Sandy Creek, on November 3, 1834.

Fr. Francisco Dura (Q) was a missionary at Concepción in 1771 and 1772, and at San Antonio de Valero in 1772.

Fr. Isidro Félix de Espinosa (Q) was the founder and Fr. President of the three Querétaran missions in eastern Texas, which were later moved to the San Antonio River. Born at Querétaro in 1679, he became a Franciscan at the College when he was seventeen. After completing his studies for the priesthood in the Franciscan Province of Michoacán, he was ordained a priest in 1703. A few years later he was doing missionary work on the Rio Grande in the missions at and near San Juan Bautista. With Fr. Guardian Olivares and Captain Aguirre he made an expedition into Texas as far as the Colorado in 1709. He led the Querétaran missionaries to eastern Texas in 1716, and did missionary work at Mission Concepción until 1719. Driven out by the French, he followed his fellow missionaries to San Antonio, and then went on to Coahuila and Mexico City. With Aguayo he returned in 1721 for the re-establishment of the missions in eastern Texas; but on October 25 of that year he was elected guardian of the College and was back at Querétaro at the end of March, 1722. Soon after completing his term of office he was named chronicler of the College; and in the years that followed, although suffering much from poor health, he became the author of several published and unpublished works. The principal one was the voluminous *Crónica* of the apostolic colleges, which was completed by 1744, and printed in 1746-1747. In 1731 he founded the Hospice of San Fernando in Mexico City, which became a college like that of Querétaro two years later. In the meantime Fr. Espinosa returned to Querétaro and filled out the term of Fr. Guardian Pérez de Mezquía, 1732 to 1733. He was working on a chronicle of the Province of Michoacan, to which he had belonged for a short time as a seminarian, when he died on February 14, 1755, at the age of 75 years.

Fr. Josef Agustín Falcón Mariano (Z) was the Fr. President of the Texas missions at least in 1784 and 1785, with headquarters at Mission San José. Ten entries in San José's baptismal register, one in the marriage record, and eleven in the record of burials have his signature. In 1785, as mentioned in Concepción's marriage record, he made an official visitation of the missions, for which Fr. Francisco de Jesús María Hervaez served as his secretary. He seems to have been the president of the Texas missions till 1788.

Fr. Manuel María Fellechea (Z) was Fr. Vallejo's successor at San José in 1816 and 1817, and may also have been the Fr. President.

Fr. Benito Francisco Fernández de Santa Ana (Q) was the missionary of San Antonio de Valero for three years before he was named Fr. President of the Querétaran missions in 1733 and took up his residence at Concepción. He had charge of this mission during the next sixteen years and made 57 of the 89 entries in the mission's marriage record; the others were made by successive assistants. In 1749 he went to Mexico City to plead the cause of the new missions on the San Xavier (San Gabriel) River, and remained there for three years. He did not return to Texas.

Fr. Manuel del Fillagra (Z) was the missionary of Mission Concepción in 1785, as shown by two entries he made in the marriage record.

Fr. Francisco Frexes (Z) was Fr. President and missionary of San José and its three neighboring missions from 1817 to 1819. They were not a pleasant year and a half for him. He received no allowance from the government, and the Indians rendered no service to him. He was falsely accused of theft by the Indians, and the governor believed them. But he could not have been the kind of person that the governor made him out to be. After Fr. Frexes left, the governor invited him to come back. For three-year terms each, Fr. Frexes was chosen vicar of the College of Zacatecas twice in 1825 and 1831, guardian once in 1837, and *discreto* or consultor three times in 1834, 1846, and 1851. He was also an author and the chronicler of his college.

Fr. Francisco Frias (Q) was a missionary at San Antonio de Valero in 1736.

Fr. Joseph Francisco de Ganzabal (Q) was the assistant of Fr. President Fernández at Concepción, 1744-1747. He rewrote the earlier entries of the mission's marriage record in his neat handwriting and has thus preserved them for posterity. In 1748 he was sent to Mexico City to present the plan of the San Xavier missions to the viceroy, but was opposed by Governor Barrio of Texas. Returning to Texas he became the first regular missionary of San Ildefonso, which was founded December 27, 1748, and took permanent form February 25,

1749. It was situated two and a half miles east of Mission San Francisco Xavier on the south side of the San Gabriel River. He died at Mission Candelaria, the third San Xavier mission, on May 11, 1752, when an Indian shot him through the heart, at the instigation, as it seems, of Captain Felipe de Rábago y Terán.

Fr. Bartolomé García (Q) was with Fr. Valverde at Espada in 1756. Previously both had been at the San Xavier missions. While at Espada, Fr. Bartolomé García wrote a manual in the Coahuiltecan language, *Manual para Administrar Sacramentos,* which was printed in Mexico in 1760 and used by the missionaries of the San Antonio missions.

Fr. Diego Martín García (Q) made entries in the baptismal register of San Antonio de Valero in 1721, 1749, and 1754. In 1745 he wrote an unpublished work, *Breve y Legal Noticia,* on the customs of the Indians in Texas and the method employed by the missionaries to civilize and Christianize them. He had become a Franciscan at the College of Querétaro on January 5, 1733, when Fr. Espinosa was its Father Guardian.

Fr. Joseph María García (Z) was a missionary at Concepción in 1787. He came to Texas in 1782.

Fr. Juan Bautista García de Suares (Z) the last portion of whose name is sometimes given as Resuárez, was at San Antonio de Valero in 1729. Earlier the same year, that is, on July 20, he was one of the missionaries in east Texas. Later in 1750-1755, he was an untiring and very successful missionary in the new missions on the lower Rio Grande. Escandón wrote of him in 1753: "Had I found half a dozen like him, the conversion of the natives would be much farther along."

Fr. Josef Francisco Mariano de la Garza (Z) was Fr. President of the Texas missions and the missionary of San José in 1782 and 1783. Born at Linares about 1740, he studied for the priesthood at the seminary in Guadalajara. Soon after his ordination he entered the Franciscan Order at the College of

Zacatecas in 1765. He went to Texas in 1772 and became the first Zacatecan missionary of San Antonio de Valero. Assigned to the Bucareli settlement on the Trinity River in 1776, he accompanied the settlers to Nacogdoches in January, 1779, and became one of the founders of the present city. From Mission San José he returned to the College in 1783, but came back to Texas in 1791 as the companion of Fr. Manuel de Silva and helped him to found the Refugio Mission in 1793. The same year, he returned to Zacatecas. He died in Sonora, August 15, 1807.

Fr. Joseph Manuel Gonz (Z) was stationed at Concepción 1775-1777, and at San José in 1786.

Fr. Luís Gonzaga Gómez (Z) was at Mission San José in 1786.

Fr. Joseph Antonio González (Q) was the assistant of Fr. Hidalgo at San Antonio de Valero, 1721-1724, and his successor for two more years. He took care of Mission San Francisco Xavier de Nájera as a sub mission, 1722-1726. In his eagerness to establish a peace pact with the Apaches, he became involved in an unfortunate disagreement with Captain Flores Valdez of the San Antonio presidio. He perished on the road from San Antonio to San Juan Bautista on the Rio Grande some time before August, 1728. Another Queretaran missionary by the same name of Fr. Joseph González did missionary work on the Rio Grande. A Zacatecan was at La Bahía, 1747-1753.

Fr. José de Guerra (Z/Q), a member of the College of Querétaro, succeeded Fr. Margil as guardian of the new College of Zacatecas for two terms, 1713 to 1717, and then returned to Querétaro. He was at the San Antonio mission in 1720 when Fr. Margil founded Mission San José, and represented the Querétaro College at the founding ceremony. With Aguayo he went to eastern Texas and was placed in charge of the re-established Mission San Francisco in 1721.

Fr. Francisco Hidalgo (Q), went to the first San Francisco mission in eastern Texas with Fr. Massanet in 1691 and remained there until the mission had to be abandoned in 1693. During the years that followed, as a missionary on the Rio Grande and as guardian of the College of Querétaro from 1701 to 1703, he left no stone unturned to bring about the reestablishment of missions in eastern Texas. His hopes were realized in 1716, when he was appointed the first missionary of the second mission of San Francisco. Compelled to retreat to Mission San Antonio in 1719, he was placed in charge of that mission as the successor of Fr. Olivares, 1720-1724. Two years later, on November 6, 1726, he died at San Juan Bautista, 67 years old.

Fr. José María Huerta de Jesús (Z) was stationed at Nacogdoches when he was falsely accused of disloyal political activities and retired to Mission San José to spend some time there in 1811. He held the office of a *discreto* or consultor at the College of Zacatecas for two terms from 1819 to 1825.

Fr. Joseph Hurtado de Jesús María (Q) was at Mission San Antonio in 1725 and 1726, and at Capistrano in 1736 and 1737. Subsequently he was elected Fr. Guardian of the College of Querétaro for one term, 1742-1745.

Fr. Pedro Ignacio Isasi Isasmendi (Ysasmendi) (Q), was the padre in charge of Mission San Francisco de la Espada in 1736-1739. He had been admitted to the College of Querétaro as a novice when Fr. Espinosa was its Fr. Guardian, 1724-1726. A victim of the epidemic of 1739, he died at Espada in that year.

Fr. José Francisco Jaudenes (Z), was the successor of Fr. Reyes at the Rosario Mission, 1791-1797; but in 1794 he came to San José for about a month to receive medical treatment, and Fr. Pedrajo took his place at Rosario.

Fr. Ignacio María José Lanuza (Z) was stationed at the Rosario mission when Fr. Solís came to inspect the Zacatecan missions in Texas in 1768, and he was chosen as the secretary of the Fr. Visitor. In 1770-1772, while Fr. President Ramírez was absent on business in eastern Texas, Fr. Lanuza had charge of Mission San José. He held the office of a *discreto* at the College from 1780 to 1783.

Fr. José López (Q) was the companion of Fr. President Mariano Viana at San Antonio de Valero and resided at this mission in 1756 and at Concepción in 1764. A native of Santiago de Galicia in Spain, he came to New Spain and joined the College of Querétaro in 1730 when he was 31 years old. At the college he held the offices of master of novices and of a *discreto*. In Texas he was a missionary for fifteen years; and for a time he was also the Querétaran Fr. President, probably in 1760 when Fr. Mariano Viana made a trip to Mexico City. He seems also to have been the latter's successor from 1763 to 1766, and hence the predecessor of Fr. President Valverde. Returning to the College, he made use of his skill in calligraphy, even after passing his eightieth year, writing breviary books for the choir. He died on November 22, 1788, at the age of 89 years, of which he had spent 72 in the Franciscan Order and 58 in the priesthood.

Fr. José Francisco López (Z) was the missionary of Espíritu Santo mission when Fr. Solís visited this mission in 1768. From 1773 to 1783 he had the care of Mission Concepción; and when Fr. Ramírez died in 1781, he held the office of interim *presidente* until Fr. Garza received his appointment in 1782. In 1783 Fr. López was placed in charge of San Antonio de Valero; and he continued to reside at this mission also after he was appointed to the office of *presidente* as the successor of Fr. Oliva. In 1789 he wrote an important report about the seven remaining missions in Texas and the reasons for their decline. He was still *presidente* in 1793 when Mission San Antonio was suppressed, and seems to have returned to Zacatecas not long afterwards. He was a missionary in Texas for at least 26 years.

Brother Juan de Los Angeles (Q) was stationed at San Antonio de Valero with Fr. Mariano Viana and Fr. José Francisco López in 1762. Brother Juan seems also to have visited the other three Querétaran missions regularly to look after the sick Indians.

Fr. José Francisco Lozano (Z) was the companion of Fr. José Francisco López at San Antonio de Valero when it was completely secularized in 1793.

Brother Pedro Maleta (Q) helped Fr. Olivares to found Mission San Antonio in 1718. On June 5, 1719, he baptized a dying Jarame child at this mission. Born in Spain, he joined the Franciscan Province of Burgos; and coming to New Spain, he became a member of the Province of Zacatecas and later joined the College of Querétaro.

Fr. Antonio Margil de Jesus (Q/Z), the saintly Apostle of New Spain, was a missionary in Texas for about six years, 1716-1722. As the *presidente* of the Zacatecan missionaries, he founded Mission San José and four other missions in Texas. Born in Spain in 1657, he came to New Spain with Fr. Llinás for the founding of the College of Querétaro. For eighteen years he was a very successful missionary in the several countries of Central America. He served as the Fr. Guardian of the College of Querétaro, of the College which he founded in Guatemala, and for three terms of the College of Zacatecas. He died in Mexico City on August 6, 1726, not quite 69 years old. Regarded as a saint by all, he was honored with the title of "Venerable" by Pope Gregory XVI in 1836, the year of Texas Independence. Of the many biographies of Fr. Margil which have been published in Spanish, the best is the one by Eduardo Enrique Rios, translated into English by Fr. Benedict Leutenegger.

Fr. Ildefonso José Marmolejo (Z) was a missionary in eastern Texas in 1737. After serving as the Fr. Guardian of the College of Zacatecas from 1750 to 1753, he returned to Texas as the missionary of San José and probably also as Fr. President of the Zacatecan missions. His work at San José was highly praised by Governor Barrios in 1758. His successor at San José in 1762-1764 was Fr. Camberos.

Fr. Pedro Múñoz (Q), a native of Morelia, Mexico, was the Fr. President of the San Juan Bautista missions on the Rio Grande when Fr. Olivares founded San Antonio de Valero in 1718. The same year, Fr. Múñoz conducted a new train of supplies into Texas for the eastern missions; and the next year he came to the aid of Fr. Olivares when he broke his leg. After Fr. Olivares had recovered and moved the mission to the east bank, Fr. Múñoz again visited him and brought along an assistant for him, in the person of Fr. Rodríguez. After he had been an Indian missionary for over twenty years, Fr. Múñoz was elected Fr. Guardian of the College of Querétaro, 1734-1737. He died July 22, 1740, 67 years old.

Fr. Miguel Muro (Z), co-worker of Fr. Díaz, was one of the last two missionaries of the Zacatecas College in Texas. Born about 1790, he joined the Franciscans of the Province of Zacatecas when he was seventeen. While still a seminarian he entered the College of Zacatecas, and was ordained a priest in 1816. The following year he went to Texas and took charge of Mission Espíritu Santo. He succeeded Fr. Frexes at San José in the summer of 1819, and in the fall of the next year exchanged places with Fr. Díaz at Mission Refugio. As this mission's last missionary he served it as best he could until it was secularized in February, 1830. During the three years that followed he was chaplain of the presidio at La Bahía, renamed Goliad in 1829, and pastor of the townspeople. During these years he also conducted an elementary school. Recalled to the College in 1833, he held the offices of master of novices and a *discreto*, 1834-1837. Four years later he went to California, where he had the care of another San José Mission, 1842-1845, and of Mission San Francisco or Dolores for a while longer. He died at the College in Zacatecas on June 20, 1848, at the age of 58 years.

Fr. Pedro Noreña (Z) was the missionary of San Francisco de la Espada for many years, at least twenty, from 1778 to 1799, with the exception of a half year in 1786 (February 5 to

July 26) when he was at Mission San José. At the latter mission he baptized 13 persons. From 1794 to 1799, Fr. Noreña also attended San Juan Capistrano.

Fr. Miguel Núñez de Haro (Z) came to Texas for the first time in 1717 when he conducted supplies for the eastern missions as far as the Trinity. He was present at the founding of San Antonio de Valero, performed the first baptism there the same day, two more on December 10, 1719, and four between October 23 and December 9, 1727. Appointed to the new Mission San José when it was founded by Fr. Margil in 1720, he served this mission during its first 32 years, moved it before 1727 from the east to the west bank, and in 1740 to the present site. There he built its first permanent structures, and died on December 2, 1752. His remains were taken later to Zacatecas.

Fr. José Rafael Oliva (Z) was at Concepción in 1788 and at San Juan Capistrano in 1789. He was then Fr. President.

Fr. Antonio de San Buenaventura y Olivares (Q), at first a missionary of the Province of Zacatecas (says Espinosa) or of Jalisco, joined the College of Querétaro about 1699, and the same year went to Coahuila. In 1700 he established Mission San Juan Bautista on the west side of the Rio Grande not far from Eagle Pass, Texas. It was also due to him that the Presidio of San Juan Bautista was founded the same year. In 1700 Fr. Olivares also founded another mission in this area, San Francisco Solano. From 1706 to 1709 he was the Fr. Guardian of the College of Querétaro; and during the last year of his term of office he made an expedition into Texas as far as the Colorado with Fr. Espinosa and Captain Aguirre. In 1716 he went to Mexico City to obtain the viceroy's approval for the transfer of his Mission of San Francisco Solano to the San Antonio River near San Pedro Springs and the founding of a presidio and villa at the same place. Thus he became the founder of the City of San Antonio. He founded Mission San Antonio de Valero on May 1, 1718, and the following year moved it from the west to the east bank. In 1720 he was succeeded by Fr. Hidalgo and returned to Querétaro. He died at the College on June 7, 1722.

Fr. Francisco Xavier Ortiz (Q) twice visited the Querétaran missions in Texas as their official inspector, the first time in 1745 and the second time in 1756. Each time he prepared a detailed report concerning them. He was the Fr. Guardian of the College of Querétaro in 1762, when Fr. President Mariano Viana and his fellow missionaries in Texas sent him a third detailed report.

Fr. Manuel de Ortuño y Velasco (Q) entered the College of Querétaro when Fr. Espinosa was its Fr. Guardian, 1722-1724. He was a missionary at San Antonio de Valero in 1729. Earlier the same year, that is, on July 20, he was one of the missionaries in east Texas.

Fr. Pedro Parras (Q) was stationed at Mission Concepción for at least seven years, 1758-1765. During this time he made all the entries in the mission's marriage record except four, a total of fifty.

Fr. Augustín Patrón y Guzmán (Z) accompanied Fr. Margil to eastern Texas in 1716; and when Fr. Margil founded Mission San Miguel de Linares near present Robeline, Louisiana, in March, 1717, he placed it in the care of Fr. Patrón and a Franciscan brother. With the other refugees from eastern Texas, Fr. Patrón arrived at Mission San Antonio in October, 1719; and when Fr. Margil founded San José in February of the following year, he appointed Fr. Patrón and Fr. Núñez as its first missionaries. In March of the very next year, however, Fr. Margil sent Fr. Patrón with Captain Ramón to Lavaca Bay to prepare the way for the founding of Mission Nuestra Señora del Espíritu Santo, which was done officially a year later. Two young priests who were Fr. Patrón's assistants at this mission in 1725 died in that year; and the next year Fr. Patrón moved the mission to the Guadalupe River, south of present Victoria. About a year later Fr. Anda y Altamirano came to take his place, and Fr. Patrón returned to Zacatecas. Here he was subsequently elected Fr. Guardian of the College, 1732-1735. Like Fr. Margil, Fr. Patrón had the reputation of being a very saintly friar and priest.

Fr. José Manuel Pedrajo (Z) was a very successful missionary at Mission San José for five years, 1789 to 1794. Born at Ojocaliente, Mexico, in 1761, he became a Franciscan in 1781, and was ordained a priest in 1783. During his sojourn at San José, he built a flour mill at the irrigation ditch outside the north walls of the square. In 1794, after the partial secularization of San José, he took the place of Fr. Jaudenes at the Rosario Mission for a short time, and then joined Fr. Silva at the Refugio Mission. He made a trip back to San Antonio and San José the next year; but because of poor health he left Refugio soon afterwards and returned to Zacatecas.

Fr. Pedro Portugal (Z) was a missionary in eastern Texas when he suffered a nervous breakdown in 1797. He was taken to Mission San José for rest and treatment for a while, and then probably to Zacatecas.

Fr. José María de Jesús Puelles (Z) was not only a missionary in Texas but also a cartographer and scholar, who was commissioned by the government to study the question of the boundary between Texas and Louisiana. He was at Mission San Antonio in 1805 and at San José in 1807. Returning to Zacatecas, he was elected for three-year terms to the office of a *discreto* four times, in 1816, 1819, 1837, and 1840, and to that of Fr. Guardian of the College in 1825.

Fr. Pedro Ramírez de Arellano (Z) had a long and distinguished missionary career in Texas of at least thirty years. He was in eastern Texas in 1751, then at San José from 1759 to 1762, and at Espíritu Santo from 1762 to 1764. Returning to Mission San José after the death of Fr. Camberos, he continued to reside at this mission until 1781, except for about two years that he spent in eastern Texas, 1770-1772. When Fr. Solís visited San José in 1768, Fr. Ramírez was the

Fr. President of the Zacatecan missions, a position he held until his death. In 1773, when the Querétaran missionaries left Texas and turned over their missions to the Zacatecan friars, Fr. Ramírez became the *presidente* of all the Texas missions. In this capacity, he received the extraordinary faculty of administering the sacrament of confirmation throughout the Province of Texas in 1778. The new stone church which he began to build at San José in 1768 was practically completed when he died on September 30, 1781. He was buried the same day in the sacristy, which was then still being used as a church, because the sanctuary of the new church was not quite ready. Fr. Ramírez was a contemporary of Fr. Junípero Serra, the founder and Fr. President of the first nine California missions, who died August 28, 1784.

Fr. Joseph Guadalupe Ramírez de Prado (Q) was a missionary in Texas for 27 years. In 1738 he was at San Antonio de Valero. Born in 1705 at the Mission of Las Palmas in the Sierra Gorda, Mexico, he entered the Franciscan Order in the Province of Michoacán and taught philosophy for three years and Canon Law for six years before he joined the College of Querétaro. He wrote several learned but unpublished books. On August 19, 1777, he died at the College, in the 73rd year of his life.

Fr. Antonio Ramos (Q) was at Mission San Francisco de Espada in 1771.

Fr. José Mariano Reyes (Z), a former member of the Holy Gospel Province, came to Texas in 1782. He was at Nacogdoches in 1785, and at Mission Rosario in 1786. In 1788-1789 when he was at San Juan Capistrano some Orcoquisac Indians visited him and begged him to reestablish the former mission, and for a time the matter was given serious consideration. In 1789-1790, Fr. Reyes revived the Mission of Espíritu Santo and reopened the Rosario Mission which had been temporarily abandoned. Recalled to Zacatecas in 1791, he went to Tarahumara in 1792 and died there May 29, 1808.

Fr. Joseph Andrés Rodríguez de Jesús María (Z) came to San Antonio de Valero in the summer of 1719 and assisted Fr. Olivares until Aguayo arrived in the spring of 1721. He then went along to eastern Texas, and Fr. Margil placed in his care the re-established Mission of Nuestra Señora de Guadalupe at Nacogdoches on August 18, 1721.

Fr. Manuel Rolán (Q) was the companion of Fr. Varela at San Juan Capistrano in 1762.

Fr. José Mariano Roxo (Z) was an assistant at Concepción in 1790 and at San José in 1790-1792. He was especially adept in teaching the Indians music and singing. He then returned to Zacatecas and held the office of vicar of the College for two terms, 1792-1795 and 1798-1801.

Fr. Juan Joseph Sáenz de Gumiel (Q) was stationed at Concepción from 1765 to 1770. His birthplace was Villa de Mendavia in Spain, and he entered the Franciscan Order in the Province of Burgos. As a member of the College of Querétaro, he spent eight years in the missions of Texas, and twice he held the office of Fr. Guardian of the College. After spending a little less than sixty years in the sacred ministry, he died at the College in his 84th year on March 11, 1807.

Brother Estevan Sáenz Monge (Q) was at San Antonio de Valero in 1731.

Fr. José María de Salas de Santa Gertrudis (Z) was the missionary in charge of San Antonio de Valero from 1777 to 1783, and of Mission San José from 1783 to 1790. He died at San José on June 17, 1790, and was buried the same day in the sanctuary of the new stone church.

Fr. Esteban de Salazar (Q) was at Concepción Mission in 1766.

Fr. Benito Sánchez (Q) had the care of Mission of San José de los Nazonis in eastern Texas from 1716 to 1719 and from 1721 to 1727. From 1727 to 1728 he was stationed at San Antonio de Valero.

Fr. Nicolás de San José y Sandi (Q), who had been a *discreto* of the College of Querétaro in 1728, was at San

Antonio de Valero in 1729. He was a companion of Fr. Espinosa at the new Hospice of San Fernando in 1731; and the next year he traveled to Spain to obtain approval for the elevation of the hospice to the rank of the independent College of San Fernando. The document he sought was issued October 15, 1733.

Fr. Andrés de San Buenaventura y Santesteban (Q) was a missionary at Concepción from 1768 to 1770, at San Antonio de Valero in 1770, and at San Juan de Capistrano in 1771.

Fr. Juan María Sepulveda (Z) was stationed at San José in 1811 and 1813.

Fr. Miguel Sevillano de Paredes (Q) was the Fr. President of the Querétaran missions in Texas in 1726-1727 with headquarters at San Antonio de Valero. In 1727 he was elected Fr. Guardian of the College of Querétaro; and after the expiration of his three-year term, he returned to the San Juan Bautista missions on the Rio Grande as the Fr. President of these missions. He was still the *presidente* there in 1736-1737, when Governor Franquis de Lugo was in San Antonio. Fr. Sevillano defended the missionaries of the San Antonio missions, and as a result was ignobly ridiculed by the retiring governor when he was removed from office. The governor's removal was brought about by a memorial which Fr. Sevillano had written and which was presented in April, 1737, to the viceroy by the Fr. Guardian of the College of Querétaro Pedro Múñoz.

Fr. José Gaspar de Solís (Z) made an official inspection of the seven Zacatecan missions of Texas in 1768 and described each of them in the diary which he kept during his journey. Previously he had been the Fr. Guardian of the College of Zacatecas for two terms, 1753 to 1756, and 1762 to 1765.

Fr. Mariano Sosa (Z), like Fr. Huerta de Jesus, was stationed at Nacogdoches when he was falsely accused of aiding the revolutionaries. He stayed at San José for a while in 1812. Later he was elected a *discreto* of the College of Zacatecas for one term in 1822, and Fr. Guardian in 1834.

Fr. José Ramón Tejada (Z) was the missionary of San Juan Capistrano at the time it was partially secularized in 1794; but he happened to be absent when the formal secularization took place and Fr. President Cárdenas substituted for him. Fr. Tejada was a *discreto* of the College of Zacatecas, 1801-1804.

Fr. Bernardino Vallejo (Z) was San José's outstanding missionary during the period following its partial secularization. He resided at this mission from 1800 to 1816, taking care also of Concepción and exercising the office of Fr. President. Twice during these years he was elected a *discreto* of the College, but permitted to remain at his post. However, shortly after he returned to Zacatecas in 1816, he was elected Fr. Guardian; and later, 1831 to 1834, he had a second term. During the intervening years he was twice chosen to be a *discreto,* in 1822 and in 1825.

Fr. Asisclos Valverde (Q) was the last Fr. President of the Querétaran missions in Texas. A native of the town of Villa de Torre in the diocese of Córdoba, Spain, he became a member of the College of Querétaro in 1743. At the College he held the offices of master of novices, *discreto,* and vicar. For some 23 years he was a missionary in Texas, first in the missions on the San Gabriel River, then at Espada at least from 1756 to 1759, then at Concepción in 1766 (as this mission's marriage record shows), and lastly at San Antonio de Valero as late as 1773, when the Querétaran missionaries left Texas. He appears to have been appointed Fr. President when he moved from Espada to Concepción, and to have exercised this office till 1773. It has been claimed that Fr. Diego Jiménez, who was the *presidente* of the San Juan Bautista missions during these years, exercised this office also for the San Antonio missions. Fr. Jiménez was appointed the successor of Fr. Alonso Giraldo Terreros after the latter was killed by the Comanches at the San Sabá Mission in 1758; and while his jurisdiction extended to the two new Apache missions he founded in 1762 on the Nueces River, the boundary between the provinces of Texas and Coahuila, it hardly included the San Antonio missions. Fr. Valverde returned to Querétaro in 1773 and died there on December 3, 1775, at the age of 60 years, of which he spent 44 in the Franciscan Order.

Fr. Benito Varela (Q) was at San Antonio de Valero in 1755.

Fr. Mariano Antonio Vasconcelos (Z) was stationed at Concepción, 1780-1781, and at San José in 1781-1783 and 1786. He was the vicar of the College of Zacatecas, 1789-1792.

Fr. Gabriel de Vergara (Q) was the companion of Fr. Espinosa at Mission Concepción in eastern Texas in 1716-1719 and again in 1721. After Fr. Espinosa was recalled to Querétaro, Fr. Vergara continued to have the care of Concepción until it was moved to the San Antonio River in 1731, and there too he had charge of the mission until 1733. At the time of the removal of the missions Fr. Vergara was the Fr. President of the Querétaran missions, and he exercised that office also at their new location. He seems to have returned to Querétaro in 1733; and in 1737 he was elected Fr. Guardian of the College. Going to Mexico City on business in 1739, he took sick at San Juan del Rio on February 6 and died the next day. He was buried in the local Dominican *convento;* but about seven months later his body was exhumed at the request of a countryman who was an official of Querétaro, and it was found to be still wholly incorrupt and flexible. It was then placed in a new sepulchre, and 41 years later, only the skeleton was found. These facts were related by Fr. Bringas de Manzaneda.

Fr. Mariano Francisco de los Dolores y Viana (Q) probably spent more years in Texas as a missionary than any of the others, no less than 35 years. He came to Texas in 1733, and his entries in the baptismal register of San Antonio begin in 1736. Forced to leave by Governor Franquis de Lugo, he took care of San Juan Capistrano from 1737 to 1739, and then went back to San Antonio. He continued to reside there until 1769, except in 1760 when he made a trip to Mexico City. In the establishment of the San Xavier missions and the Apache missions he played an important role. From 1750 until 1763, he was the Fr. President of the Querétaran missions in Texas. In 1752 Fr. Alonso Giraldo de Terreros, the *presidente* at San Juan Bautista, was instructed to exchange places with Fr. Viana; but the change was not made because of developments on the San Gabriel River and the murder of Fr. Ganzabal. Fr. Viana was still in San Antonio in 1769, when he must have been more than sixty years old; and probably he retired to the College shortly afterwards.

Fr. Joseph Zarate (Q) was a missionary at San Antonio de Valero from 1766 to 1769.

The names of other missionaries who served one or more of the five missions of San Antonio as well as additional information concerning those whose names we know may yet be found. We have presented only what we could find at the present time; but the fragmentary data that we have been able to gather suffice to demonstrate that these were men of heroic stature, sturdy pioneers of civilized life on the Texas frontier, noble messengers of the Christian Faith in a new land, and therefore men whose lives are still an inspiration today and whose memory deserves to be held in honor.

IX

Old Cathedral of San Fernando
1749-1968

The church and parish of the Villa San Fernando which, together with the Presidio of San Antonio de Béxar and the Mission of San Antonio de Valero, occupied what is now the center of the City of San Antonio in colonial times, was not a mission in the strict sense of the word. But its story is closely related to that of the five old missions, and hence it is not out of place to add a brief account of the Old Cathedral of San Fernando. Not only will it be of interest, but it will help to complete the picture of the mission days.

On the ninth day of March in the year 1731 a group of fifty-five weary travelers arrived at the Presidio and Villa of San Antonio de Béxar. They were the members of fifteen families who had come all the way from the Canary Islands to establish the first civil settlement in the Spanish Province of Texas. Until they could build their own homes, they were lodged in the best houses of the soldiers of the presidio.

A villa or town had been established near the San Pedro Springs by the governor of Texas, Don Martín de Alarcón, thirteen years earlier, at the same time that he founded the Presidio of San Antonio de Béxar. It consisted of the families of those soldiers who were married, about thirty in number. Both villa and presidio had been moved in 1722 to the west bank of the San Antonio River, opposite the Mission of San

Antonio de Valero, which then stood on or near the spot where old St. Joseph Church is now situated.

Villa San Fernando de Béxar, 1731

The new town of 1731 was named San Fernando de Béxar. Villa de San Antonio de Casafuerte, the name of the viceroy, was the first name proposed; but the Marquis of Casafuerte declined the honor in favor of Don Fernando, Prince of Asturias, second son of King Philip V, who succeeded his father as King Ferdinand VI in 1746 and ruled the Spanish Empire until 1759. The old name Béxar honored the memory of the Duke of Béxar, who died defending Budapest in the war against the Turks, 1716-1718. He was the brother of the Marqués de Valero, the viceroy of New Spain in 1718.

The Villa of San Fernando de Béxar was not laid out until the summer, July 2 to 6. The place chosen for the church and plaza was to the east of the presidio "at a distance of a musket shot"; but the first church was not completed until twenty years later. During these two decades the settlers used the wretched and inadequate barracks chapel.

The first parish priest assigned to the town of San Fernando by the bishop of Guadalajara was Father José de la Garza (1731-1734). He seems to have been a member of the Oratory of the Oblate Clerics of San Carlos. But the first baptism recorded in the baptismal register was administered by Fr. Ignacio Antonio Ciprián, a missionary of the Franciscan Apostolic College of Zacatecas — the same who in 1749 wrote a detailed report about the Zacatecan missions in Texas. In the presidio chapel, with the permission of the pastor, he baptized Ignacia Agustina, born on August 27, 1731, daughter of the Spanish settlers, Don Miguel Núñez y Murillo and Josefa Flores y Valdes, the godparents being Alberto López and Juan Jiménez.

The lands assigned to the colony comprised an area, bounded on the east by the San Antonio River, on the south by those of Mission San José and the Paso de los Nogalitos, on the west by the Arroyo de León, and on the north by the Arroyo Salado.

According to the original order of King Philip V, dated February 4, 1729, the first group of settlers were to be followed by others until 200 families, or about 1,000 persons, had emigrated from the Canary Islands to the new frontier town; but the first 55 settlers were the only ones who came. Seven years after their arrival, the settlement was far from being in a prosperous condition. The people were poor and had little more than the bare necessities of life.

The Building of a Parish Church, 1734-1749

The second pastor, Father Juan Recio de León, (1734-1743) wrote in 1738 that the small, unadorned, and unsightly presidio chapel was unfit for the administration of the sacraments. On February 18, the same year, a drive was launched to collect funds for the building of a church. A week later, a total of 642 pesos had been contributed.

Governor Orobio y Basterra gave 200 pesos; Captain Joseph de Urrutia of the presidio gave 100; Captain Gabriel Costales of the La Bahía presidio, 25 pesos; Father Recio de León, 25 pesos; and the other 292 pesos came from the settlers and soldiers. That was all they could afford. Money was scarce, and some made their contributions in kind. An additional 22 pesos was added to the fund later.

On May 11, 1738, the cornerstone of the parish church was laid. Plans called for a stone building that would be similar to the adobe church of Mission San Antonio de Valero. It was to be 30 *varas* (83⅓ feet) long and 6 *varas* (16⅔ feet) wide, with a sacristy and a baptistery. Its location was on the west side of the town plaza, with its main entrance facing east. Our Lady of the Purification (Candelaria, Candlemas) and of Guadalupe was chosen as the heavenly patroness of the church.

About a month later the governor informed the viceroy that a beginning had finally been made in the construction of the church, but the contributed funds covered only one-fourth of the estimated cost; and he made an appeal for the promised grant of royal aid. The viceroy authorized the expenditure of 12,000 pesos on April 7, 1740; but none of this was paid out during the next eight years.

By October 2, 1745, the work on the church was practically abandoned. Not only was there a lack of funds, but also a lack of workers. A part of the presidio chapel had fallen down, and it was dangerous to use what remained. The *alcalde* of the Villa de San Fernando issued an order requiring a certain number of days of work from each citizen; those who failed to render this service would be punished with a fine of 25 pesos and fifteen days in jail.

Two years later, when the church was about half completed, Vicente Alvárez Travieso of San Fernando traveled all the way to Mexico City to obtain the necessary funds from the viceroy; and in the spring of 1748, the 12,000 pesos were at long last supplied.

The church could now be completed; and on November 6, 1749, or according to Castañeda a year or two later, the Church of Nuestra Señora de la Candelaria y Guadalupe in the Villa Real de San Fernando de Béxar was solemnly dedicated. It had a transept, dome, and tower, and in 1757, it was described as "perfect and harmonious in every detail." The cost of constructing it was 7,000 pesos. This did not include the furnishings. The wages given to the workers seem ridiculously small to us today. The master masons received two pesos a day and board; the masons, eighteen pesos a month with board; and their helpers fifty centavos a day without board.

In the Eighteenth Century

Toward the close of 1759, the first bishop who came to the Spanish Province of Texas, Bishop Martínez y Tejada of Guadalajara, visited the Villa de San Fernando, and administered the sacrament of confirmation in the parish church. He informed the viceroy that he found only about sixty families in the town, and all of them were poor people.

Captain Luís Antonio Menchaca of the presidio reported to the viceroy in May, 1763, that the Villa de San Fernando and the surrounding territory within a radius of some sixty miles had a total of about one hundred men, including the aged, infirm, invalids, and vagrants. Not more than 25 men could be mustered from their ranks to help the presidio soldiers, should the need arise. At the presidio there were besides himself only one sergeant and five soldiers. Three soldiers were stationed at each of the five missions in the San Antonio area. However, by 1770, the population of San Fernando de Béxar and the surrounding area had risen to 870. When Zebulon Pike visited San Antonio in 1808, he says its population was about 2,000. His estimate no doubt included the missions.

When Mission San Antonio de Valero was suppressed in 1793, the mission chapel and its furnishings were surrendered to the pastor of San Fernando, Father José Clemente Arocha. The mission chapel was not used for divine services again until 1803, when the Flying Squadron of El Alamo came from Parras, Mexico, and established itself at the former mission.

At the close of the century the parish of San Fernando had a distinguished orator as its pastor, the Reverend Father Gabino Valdez. In September, 1800, he went all the way to Saltillo to preach the sermon on a special occasion. While he was absent, the military chaplain of the presidio took his place at the Church of San Fernando, as it seems to have been called at this time. Besides Our Lady of Guadalupe, San

262   *The Alamo Chain*

Fernando and San Antonio were also regarded as patrons of the church.

Since the completion of the church about 1750, the ground adjoining the church was used as a cemetery. The last burial here took place in 1808; and a new cemetery was then opened on the land where Santa Rosa Hospital now stands.

For the latter part of the eighteenth century we have some detailed and exact statistics for the Villa de San Fernando. In 1778, the number of persons living in the whole area, including the missions, was 2,060. In the Villa de San Fernando and the Presidio de San Antonio, in 1783, there were 1,248 persons, including 21 slaves. In 1786 the population had dropped to 975; but in 1789 it rose again to 1,279, of whom 961 were Spaniards. In the latter year, the pastor of San Fernando served also as chaplain of the presidio; and in the five missions there were six Franciscan missionaries. The next year (1790) the total rose again to 1,001, of whom 780 were Spaniards. In 1792, there were 31 foreigners in the villa.

In the Nineteenth Century

Stirring events occurred in the shadow of San Fernando Church during the first part of the nineteenth century. After the Casas Rebellion in 1811, the town was rewarded for its loyalty by being raised to the rank of a "ciudad," a city; and it received a coat of arms and a *cabildo* or city council of six members. In 1819, the city suffered considerable damage as a result of a flood. The church, including some of its records, was damaged by a fire in 1828. In fact, there were several fires in the church on different occasions.

Early in 1822, after Mexico had gained its independence, the pastor of San Fernando, the Rev. Refugio de la Garza, went to the National Congress as a delegate. Until November of that year, when the military chaplain Father Francisco Maynes arrived, Fr. Antonio Díaz de León, the last missionary of the remaining four missions, San José, Concepción, Espada, and Capistrano, took care also of the parish of San Fernando. When these missions were secularized in 1824, Fr. Díaz de León surrendered their churches and furnishings into the hands of Father Maynes.

The next year, after Father Refugio de la Garza returned, the first vicar forane of the Department of Texas, Father Juan Nepomuceno de la Peña came to San Fernando and conducted an official visitation or inspection of the parish of the town. He seems to have been succeeded in his office the following year by Father Maynes.

An interesting entry in the marriage records of San Fernando, made by Father Refugio de la Garza, is that of James Bowie's wedding in 1831. After the banns had been read three times, on April 11, 17, and 24, Don Santiago Bowie, a native of Louisiana, son of Raymond Bowie and Albina Yons, contracted marriage, during a nuptial Mass in San Fernando Church, with Ursula de Veramendi, a native of San Antonio, daughter of Don Juan Martín de Veramendi and Doña Maria Josefa Navarro, on April 25, 1831. The witnesses were Don José Angel Navarro and Don Juan Francisco Bueno.

After the Texans had won the Battle of Concepción on December 12, 1835, Frank W. Johnson raised the flag of victory in the tower of San Fernando Church. But only a few months later. Santa Ana had the flag of "no quarter" hoisted in the same place at the siege and fall of the Alamo.

Burial Place of the Alamo Heroes

Were the ashes of the heroes of the Alamo buried in the church of San Fernando? The question has been debated to and fro, because of Dr. John Sutherland's statement that they were buried in a peach orchard, and that of J. M. Rodríguez which declared they were placed "beneath the sod." The claim that the church was the final resting place of the remains of the Alamo heroes is based on the following known facts.

The Texans had held Santa Anna's army at bay for ten days, when the Alamo fell on March 6, 1836, following an attack that lasted three hours. Besides more than thirty women, children, and slaves, there were only five men who survived. The latter were shot by order of Santa Anna. The number of the defenders of the Alamo who lost their lives was 183. Santa Anna ordered their bodies and those of the Mexicans who had died to be burned. That same afternoon three funeral pyres, consisting alternately of layers of wood and corpses, were set on fire, and they burned for two days.

After the Battle of San Jacinto, that is early in February, 1837, General Sam Houston instructed Colonel Juan N. Seguín to have the ashes and remains of the heroes buried with military honors. Seguín declared he did this on February 25. According to a published account, he placed the remains in a large coffin, took them first to the church of San Fernando, then to the sites of the three pyres where a salute was fired, and finally he buried them.

In 1889, when he was in his eighties, Colonel Seguín was asked where the burial took place, and he replied that he had buried the casket containing the remains outside the sanctuary railing, near the steps, in the old San Fernando Church.

Workmen, doing some repair work in the cathedral in 1936, were digging in this very spot when they came upon a box containing charred bones, particles of coal, rusty nails, shreds of military uniforms, buttons, and crushed skulls. Many distinguished persons examined what had been found, and all were convinced that here were the remains of the heroes of the Alamo. They are still kept in a place of honor in the cathedral.

Neglect and Restoration of the Old Church

Before and after the battle of the Alamo, the old church of San Fernando was permitted to fall into a sad state of neglect. At this time Father Refugio de la Garza was serving as pastor, and Father José Antonio Valdez was his assistant. They were still in San Antonio after Texas gained its independence in 1836. Nominally, the Republic of Texas still belonged to the diocese of Monterrey, Mexico.

When San Antonio was founded in 1718, the Spanish Province of Texas formed a part of the vast diocese of Guadalajara. But a new diocese, including Coahuila and Texas, namely that of Nuevo Reyno de León, was created in 1777, with Linares as the episcopal city; and in 1791, the see was transferred to Monterrey. It was only in 1839 that Texas was made a separate prefecture apostolic, and two years later a vicariate apostolic. Finally, in 1847 the diocese of Galveston, comprising all of Texas, was established.

In 1839, before his appointment as prefect apostolic of Texas, Father John Timon reported that the church of San Fernando was almost in ruins, but the fine old building still had an estimated worth of $15,000. In San Antonio, the former Real Ciudad de San Fernando, he said, there were about 1,500 Mexicans and 150 Americans; and of the latter 100 were Protestants and 50 were Catholics.

The following year Father John M. Odin came to San Antonio as vice-prefect, and undertook to repair the old church. With the approval of the trustees of the parish, he sold some broken silver plate belonging to the church in order to buy materials for its restoration. For the same purpose the trustees purchased loose stones from the ruins of the friary at Mission Concepción at the cost of twenty-five cents (in Texan money) a cartload.

The church was quickly renovated and made to look as it had in former days. The two old Mexican priests, Fathers Garza and Valdez, were relieved of their duties; and Father Michael Calvo, the zealous companion of Father Odin, was installed as pastor of San Fernando and also of the old mission churches as "Mass stations."

The population of San Antonio grew by leaps and bounds during the decades that followed. In 1846, according to available statistics, the town had a population of only 800; but in 1850, it skyrocketed to 3,448; in 1860, it more than doubled, reaching a total of 8,235; in 1870, it was 12,256; in 1880, it reached 20,550; and in 1890, San Antonio was a "big" city with 37,673.

The New San Fernando Church

In 1868, more than a hundred years after the old church had been completed, it was decided to enlarge it and to build "the new San Fernando church," the old cathedral of today. The cornerstone was laid on September 27, 1868. The architect's plans and specifications were furnished by F. Giraud, who was the mayor of San Antonio when the new church was opened in 1873.

The heavy tower and front part of the old church with the choir loft and baptistery were torn down, and the new structure was added. In 1872, before the new church was completed, the original dome collapsed and the present one was constructed. Thus the present sanctuary still has the walls of the original church of about 1750.

On October 6, 1873, the remodeled and enlarged church was completed, except that it had only one tower. The original plans provided for two identical towers with 25-foot superstructures of wood surmounting the masonry. The latter were never added. The second tower was constructed after 1890. An old photograph of that year still shows the cathedral with only one tower.

The new church of San Fernando became a cathedral the very next year, when the diocese of San Antonio was erected, with Bishop A. D. Pellicer as its first bishop. By a decree of August 27, 1874, which was effective on September 3, Pope Pius IX separated the territory lying between the Colorado and the Nueces rivers from the diocese of Galveston to which it had belonged and thus created the new diocese of San Antonio. It was raised to the rank of an archdiocese on August 3, 1926, with the Most Rev. Arthur J. Drossaerts as the first archbishop.

As bishop of Galveston, Bishop Odin had purchased the ground for San Fernando Cemetery Number One in 1855, the third of the parish; and in 1921, Archbishop Drossaerts acquired the land for San Fernando Cemetery Number 2. Father Camilo Torrente tells us that by 1927 the number of those buried in these two cemeteries was 5,039, all Spanish or Mexican except 100 others.

From him we also learn that the records of San Fernando Church and Cathedral for the 196 years from 1731 to 1927 show that there were 56,433 baptisms, 7,405 marriages, and 22,911 burials. The records are not complete, because some of them were destroyed by fire. During this same period, San Fernando had 32 pastors. By 1949 the number of baptisms had risen to over 71,000; and those confirmed to 32,000+.

The Vincentian Fathers who were placed in charge of the church in 1840 were later followed by Oblates of Mary Immaculate for a short time and then by diocesan priests. Among the latter was Father Claude Dubuis, who became bishop of Galveston in 1862, and Father John C. Neraz, who was the second bishop of San Antonio, 1881-1894.

The Claretian Fathers

The Claretian Fathers, so named after their founder, St. Anthony Claret, have been the pastors of the Cathedral of San Fernando since 1902. The previous year some Claretians had come from Mexico City to conduct parish missions in the vicariate apostolic of Brownsville. Impressed by the good work they were doing, Bishop John A. Forest, the third of San Antonio (1895-1911), invited them to preach a Spanish mission also in the Cathedral of San Fernando and then entrusted into their care the cathedral parish on September 17, 1902.

The extent of the work of the Claretians at the cathedral is indicated in some measure by the fact that during the first 25 years of their pastoral activities a total of 15,105 persons received the sacrament of confirmation. In 1927 the parishioners numbered 9,457; and the pupils in the parochial school (which opened in 1888 with one teacher, a Brother of Mary) were 515 in number. During the four decades which have elapsed since then, the Claretians have continued and expanded their pastoral work at the cathedral; and as the city increased in extent and population many new churches were built.

The Archdiocese of San Antonio

The members of the little parish of 1731 would indeed be amazed to see that today it has grown into a large archdiocese having a total of 143 parishes (of which 55 are in the city of San Antonio), with 506,084 Catholics in a population of 1,234,814.

The shepherd of this flock for over a quarter century has been the Most Rev. Robert E. Lucey. Consecrated bishop of Amarillo in 1934, he succeeded Archbishop Drossaerts on January 23, 1941, as archbishop of San Antonio. In 1956 he received an auxiliary in the person of Bishop Stephen A. Leven.

Working under the direction of Archbishop Lucey, there are, at the present writing, 450 diocesan and religious priests, 175 religious brothers, and 1,142 sisters. In a single year (1966-1967), the baptisms administered were 17,654 in number.

The little Villa de San Fernando de Béxar has become a big modern city, including an area, some sixteen miles from north to south, and about eleven and a half miles from east to west. Within this area are five independent smaller municipalities, a large international airport, Stinson Field, Fort Sam Houston, and two Air Force bases. In 1959 the official population of the city was 408,400; today it is close to 700,000.

Important Dates

1731, Mar. 9: Forty-five Canary Islanders arrived at San Antonio de Béxar to found the town of San Fernando.

1731, Aug. 27: First baptism of the parish of San Fernando was administered by Franciscan missionary, Fr. Ignacio Antonio Ciprián.

1738, Mar. 11: Cornerstone of the church of San Fernando was laid.

1749 (1750?), Nov. 6: Church of San Fernando was completed.

1793, Apr. 12: Mission San Antonio de Valero was secularized and became a part of the parish of San Fernando.

1811: The town of San Fernando was raised to the rank of a city.

1824, Feb. 29: Missions Concepción, San José, Capistrano, and Espada were secularized and made a part of the parish of San Fernando.

1828: Church of San Fernando was damaged by fire.

1831, Apr. 25: Wedding of James Bowie in the church of San Fernando.

1835, Dec. 12: Battle of Concepción was won by the Texans.

1836, Mar. 6: Fall of the Alamo.

1837: Ashes of the heroes of the Alamo and Mexican soldiers were buried in San Fernando church by Colonel Seguin.

1840: Father John M. Odin repaired San Fernando church and appointed Father Michael Calvo pastor.

1868, Sept. 27: Cornerstone of the new San Fernando church was laid.

1873, Oct. 6: The new church, retaining part of the old as its sanctuary, was completed.

1874, Aug. 27: Diocese of San Antonio, with San Fernando as its cathedral, was erected (143rd anniversary of the first baptism).

1902: Claretian Fathers were placed in charge of the cathedral.

1926, Aug. 3: Diocese of San Antonio was raised to the rank of an archdiocese.

1941, Jan. 23: Archbishop Robert E. Lucey succeeded the first archbishop, Arthur J. Drossaerts.

APPENDIX

I

Comparative Statistics
Indians in the San Antonio Missions

Year	San Antonio	San José	Con-cepción	Cap-istrano	Es-pada
1721	240	227			
1738	300+	c.300	250	218	120
1739	184	49	120	66	50
1740 (Feb.)		95			
1740 (Dec.)	238	249	210	169	121
1745	311		207	163	204
1750		220			
1756	328		247	265	200
1758		281			
1762	275		207	203	207
1768		350			
1777	42	c.300	c.170	c.155	133
1783 (Dec.)	144	128	76	99	96
1786 (Dec.)	126	189	104	110	144
1788 (Dec.)	45	114	51	34	46
1789 (May)	52	138	71	58	57
1789 (Dec.)	121	198	74	80	46
1790 (Dec.)	48	144	47	21	93
1791		106			
1793	39	114			
1794 (Jul.)		93	38	c. 30	c.40
1804 (Dec.)		57	27	28	37
1809 (Dec.)		55	21	20	24
1815 (Jan.)		49	16	15	27

II
Principal Indian Tribes

The following are the principal Indian tribes that were represented in the five San Antonio missions. They are mentioned in the reports concerning these missions. Not included are the tribes for whom the three Querétaran missions were founded in eastern Texas. The following abbreviations are used: A—Mission San Antonio; P—Purísima Concepción; J—San José; C—San Juan Capistrano; E—San Francisco de la Espada. For a more complete list, see the 36 tribes compiled from the marriage record of Concepción and the 103 from the record of burials of Mission San Antonio, by Richard Santos, in *Texas Libraries*, vol. 28, no. 4 (Winter 1966-1967), pp. 157-159.

Aguasallas J
(Aguastallas)

Alobjas C

Apaches A
(Lipanes and
Ypanis,
Ypandis,
Yprandes)

Arcahomos E

Borrados P, E, J
(Barrados)

Bozales E

Canamas J

Canas J
(Cannas)

Cocos A

Jarames A

Jaranames A
(Aranames,
Xaranames)

Karankawas A
(Carancaguaces)

Kiowas A

Manos de Perro P

Marahuitos C, E
(Marahuiayos,
Mariquitas,
Marhitas)

Mesquites P

Orejones C

Pacaos P, C, E

Pajalaches P, C
(Pajalates,
Pajalats,
Pajalotes,
Paxalaches)

Pamagues C
(Pamaques)

Pampopas J
(Pampoas)

Pastías P

Pataguas A

Payayas A
(Payayes,
Payatas,
Peyayes)

Piquiques C

Pitalaques C

Postitos J

Sanas A
(Samas
Zanas)

Sanipaos P

Sayopines C
(Saipones,
Chayopines)

Scipxames A

Sciquipiles P

Tacames A, P, J, E

Tamiques A

Thelojas C

Tops A
(Tovs)

Venados C

Xaunaes J

Yierbipiames A
(Ervipiames,
Hierbipiames)

Yutas A

III

The Presidents of the Missions

An exact and complete list of the Father Presidents of the Querétaran and Zacatecan missions in Texas can not be compiled from available sources. The two tentative lists which follow contain what is found or indicated in them.

Querétaran Missions

1716-1722: Fr. Isidro Félix de Espinosa
1726-1727: Fr. Miguel Sevillano de Paredes
1728-1731: Fr. Gabriel de Vergara
1731-1750: Fr. Benito de Santa Ana Fernández
1750-1763: Fr. Mariano de los Dolores y Viana
1763-1766: Fr. José López
1766-1773: Fr. Asisclos Valverde
1752-1758: Fr. Alonso Giraldo de Terreros President of the missions on the Rio Grande (Coahuila), including the Apache Mission of San Sabá which was in the Province of Coahuila.
1759-1773: Fr. Diego Jiménez Successor of Fr. Terreros. His jurisdiction extended to the two Apache missions on the Nueces, 1762-1769.

Fr. Terreros was instructed on February 18, 1752, to exchange places with Fr. Mariano Viana; but the change was not made because of developments at the San Xavier Missions on the San Gabriel River.

Zacatecan Missions

1716-1722: Fr. Antonio de Jesús Margil
 ? -1747: Fr. Francisco Vallejo. He was elected Father Guardian of the College in 1747, after having been in eastern Texas since 1724. In 1750 he returned to eastern Texas.
1747-1749: Fr. Ignacio Antonio Ciprián (?)
1753-1759: Fr. Ildefonso José Marmolejo (?)
1762-1764: Fr. Juan de Dios Camberos (?)

1764-1781: Fr. Pedro Ramírez de Arellano. President at least since 1768. In 1773 he became the Father President of all the missions in Texas.

1768:   Fr. Miguel de Santa María de los Dolores. He was a missionary on the lower Rio Grande, 1754 to at least 1757. In 1768 Fr. Solís appointed him president of the Zacatecan missions in eastern Texas, which were abandoned in 1773.

1781-1782: Fr. José Francisco López. Interim president after the death of Fr. Ramírez.

1782-1783: Fr. Joseph Francisco María de la Garza

1784-1788: Fr. Joseph Agustín Falcón Mariano

1788-1789: Fr. José Rafael Oliva

1789-1793: Fr. José Francisco López. He was president in 1789, and on April 12, 1793, when Mission San Antonio was secularized.

1794-1800: Fr. José Mariano de Cárdenas

1800-1816: Fr. Bernardino Vallejo

1816-1817: Fr. Manuel María Fellechea

1817-1819: Fr. Francisco Frexes

1820-1830: Fr. José Antonio Díaz de León

BIBLIOGRAPHY

The sources for the history of the five missions of San Antonio and their missionaries are listed under three captions: I. Manuscript Sources; II. Printed Sources; III. Printed Works and Studies. The first includes only those documents which have not appeared in printed form. Primary sources which have been printed in Spanish or an English translation are listed under Printed Sources. Printed Works and Studies is a list of secondary sources.

Originals or copies (transcripts or photostats) of most of the documentary material are in the University of Texas Library. To indicate the location of the original manuscripts or copies of them, the following abbreviations are used:

ACQ. Archivo del Colegio de Querétaro, at Celaya, Mexico. About one fourth of these archives has been lost. A few of its documents are in the Archives of Mission Santa Barbara, Santa Barbara, Calif.; and some are in the General Archives of the Franciscan Order in Rome. Transcripts of some, by Dr. W. E. Dunn, are in the U. of Tex. Libr. Microfilms of a considerable part (53 rolls, 200 feet of film), made by the author, are in the Bancroft Library, Berkeley, Calif.

ACZ. Archivo del Colegio de Zacatecas, at Zacatecas, Mexico. The greater part has been lost, but some important documents are still at Zacatecas. See Alcocer, *Bosquejo* (Printed Sources).

AGI. Archivo General de Indias, in Seville, Spain. Most of the documents pertaining to Texas have been transcribed by Dr. W. E. Dunn for the U. of Tex. Libr.

AGN. Archivo General y Publico de la Nación, Mexico City. Copies of many of the Texas documents are in the U. of Tex. Libr.

ASFC. Archives of the Cathedral of San Fernando, San Antonio, Texas.

ASFG. Archives of San Francisco el Grande, the principal Franciscan friary in Mexico City during colonial times, now in the Biblioteca Nacional. Photostatic copies of about 10,000 pages, pertaining to Texas, were made by C. E. Castañeda, and are now in the U. of Tex. Library.

BA. Béxar Archives, now at the University of Texas.

BN. Biblioteca Nacional, of the Universidad Nacional de Mexico, in Mexico City.

CA. Catholic Archives of Texas, at the Chancery Office, Austin, Texas.

DRT Libr. Daughters of the Republic of Texas Library at the Alamo, San Antonio, Texas.

NA. Nacogdoches Archives of Nacogdoches, Texas.

SA. Biblioteca del Estado de Coahuila, Saltillo, Mexico. About 13,000 pages, photostated by C. E. Castañeda, are in the U. of Tex. Libr.

SAT. State Archives of Texas, Austin, Texas.

I. MANUSCRIPT SOURCES

Aguayo, Marqués San Miguel de
    Decree for the founding of Mission San José, Jan. 22, 1720, in Testimonio de la possón. y Missón de Sn. Joseph (also containing Letter of Fr. Margil to Aguayo, Dec. 26, 1719, and Account of the founding of Mission San José by Captain Juan Valdez on Feb. 23, 1720). *AGI, Aud. de Guadalajara,* 67-3-11. Dunn Transcripts, 1718-1738, U. of Tex. Libr.

Aguilar, Fr. Juan José, 5 letters from Mission Espíritu Santo, 1794-1797, *BA:* to Gov. Múñoz, Sept. 26, 1794; Feb. 23, & Jul. 30, 1795; to Commandant Gen. Nava, Jan. 26, 1797; To Gov. Elguezábal, May 11, 1797.

Barrios y Jáuregui, Gov. Jacinto
    Informe del gobernador sobre la misión de San José, May 28, 1758. *ASFG* in *BN.* Cast. Phot. in U. of Tex. Libr., vol. 12, pp. 62-63.

Camarena, Fr. Josef María de Jesús
    Report on Mission Concepción, Aug. 2, 1794. *BA.* Letter to Gov. Múñoz, from Mission Concepción, Sept. 1, 1794. *BA.*

Cárdenas, Fr. José Mariano de, 26 letters, 1788-1799, *BA:*
to Gov. Martínez Pacheco, from La Bahía, Jul. 15, 1788; to
Capt. Espadas, from La Bahía, Aug. 20, 1790; to Gov. Múñoz,
from La Bahía, Mar. 11, Aug. 17, & Dec. 15, 1791, Apr. 12 &
Oct. 31, 1793; May 9 & Jul. 4, 1794; to Gov. Múñoz, from San
José, Sept. 2, Sept. 13, Oct. 1, Oct. 9, Oct. 13, & Oct. 16, 1794;
to Gabriel Gutiérrez, from San José, Oct. 20, Oct. 21, & Oct.
29, 1794; to Gov. Múñoz, from San José, May 13 & Dec. 24,
1795; Jan. 1, 1796; Jan. 1 & Je. 5, 1797; to Gov. Múñoz,
from La Bahía, Sept. 14, 1797; to Gov. Múñoz from San José,
Jan. 1, 1798; Jan. 14, 1799.

Census reports, *BA:* Jan. 31, 1784 (Texas missions); June 30, 1787
(Texas); Dec. 31, 1790 (Texas missions); Dec. 26, 1791
(Béxar); Nov. 23, 1793 (San José and Espada missions); Dec.
31, 1796 (Espada Mission); Aug. 26, 1803 (Texas missions,
by Fr. Vallejo); Aug. 31, 1803 (Texas missions, by Gov. El-
guezábal); Dec. 31, 1803 (Espada Mission); Jan. 31, 1805
(Concepción Mission); Jan. 31, 1805 (San José Mission, by
Alcalde Hernandes); Dec. 31, 1808 (Capistrano Mission);
Dec. 31, 1808 (Espada Mission); Je. 19, 1809 (4 San Antonio
missions, by Gov. Salcedo); Feb. 27, 1815 (Espada Mission,
by Alcalde Bustillos); Feb. 27, 1815 (San José Mission, by
Alcalde Huisar); Feb. 27, 1815 (Concepción Mission, by Al-
calde Bustillos); Feb. 27, 1815 (Espada Mission, by Alcalde
Bustillos); Feb. 27, 1815 (Capistrano Mission, by Alcalde
Gil); Je. 13, 1815 (Capistrano Mission, by Alcalde Bustillos);
Je. 16, 1817 (San José Mission, by Alcalde Huisar); 1819
(Espada and Capistrano missions); Dec. 20, 1820 (San José,
by Alcalde León).

Ciprián, Fr. Ignacio Antonio
Report on the Zacatecan missions in Texas, to the Franciscan
Commissary General of New Spain, Oct. 27, 1749. *ASFG* in
BN. Cast. Phot. in U. of Tex. Libr., vol. 5, pp. 41-17.

Colegio de Querétaro, Discretorio del
Relación de 1722 (11 large pages). *ACQ,* Letra N, Leg. 1,
num. 18. The author has a contemporary duplicate copy. Relación de 1728 (24 pages). *ACQ.,* Letra C, Leg. 1, num. 1. The
author has a photocopy. This Relación, also marked "Frutos de
el Colegio de la Sma. Cruz," was sent to the general chapter of
the Franciscan Order held in Milan in 1729.

Colegio de Zacatecas, Discretorio del
  Carta Informe de los PP. del Colegio Ap.co de propaganda fide
  de N.ra S.ra de Guadalupe de Zacatecas al Rey de España,
  Jan. 15, 1750. *BN*, Caja 6, Num. 133. The author has a micro-
  film and a photocopy of this document of 15 pp. Representa-
  ción de los PP. del Col.o de Guadalupe de Zacatecas al
  Comis.o Gen.l de Yndias Fr. Mathias de Velasco, Jan. 15, 1750.
  BN, Caja 6, Num. 133. The author has a microfilm and photo-
  copy of this document of 5 pp. Informe de los padres del
  Colegio de Zacatecas, May 25, 1757. *ASFG* in *BN*. Cast. Phot.
  in U. of Tex. Libr., vol. 6, pp. 112-116. Petición al Commte.
  G.r.al Theodoro de Croix . . . Jan. 13, 1780. *SA*. Cast. Phot. in
  U. of Tex. Libr., vol. 5, pp. 2-4
Delgadillo, Fr. José Antonio, 4 letters to Gov. Cordero, 1806, *BA:*
  from Espíritu Santo Mission, Jan. 1 & Feb. 22, 1806; from
  Béxar, May 5, 1806; from La Bahía, Jul. 27, 1806.
Diaz de León, Fr. José Antonio, 19 letters, 1819-1823, *BA:* to Capt.
  Alderete, from La Bahía, Oct. 17, 1819; to Gov. Martínez,
  from Refugio, Je. 5, 1820; from Béxar, Dec. 13, 1820; from
  San José, Feb. 23, 1821; to Capt. García, from La Bahía, Mar.
  17, 1821; to Gov. Martínez, from La Bahía, Jul. 8, 1821; from
  San José, Jul. 20 & Aug. 5, 1821; from San José, Jan. 28, 1822;
  from Béxar, Mar. 28 & Aug. 23, 1822; to the Ayuntamiento,
  from Béxar, Aug. 29 & Sept. 18, 1822; to Gov. Trespalacios,
  from Béxar, Dec. 18, 1822; to Political Chief Saucedo, from
  San José, Oct. 25, 1823; from Béxar, Oct. 29, 1823; from San
  José, Nov. 3 & Nov. 21, 1823.
Díaz, Manuel, Spanish Alcalde of Espada Mission, 2 letters, 1820,
  BA: to Gov. Martínez, Apr. 22, 1820; & . . . 1820; to Gov.
  Cordero of Coahuila, Jul. 25, 1820.
Fellner, Fr. Felix, of St. Vincent's Archabbey, Latrobe, Pa., to Ernst
  F. Schuchard, Nov. 10, 1935. Copy at Mission San José.
Frexes, Fr. Francisco, 9 letters, 1818-1820, *BA:* to Gov. Martínez,
  from San José, Jan. 1, Jan. 2, Jan. 6, Aug. 8, Oct. 16, 1818;
  Jan. 4, 1819; from Béxar, Jul. 21, 1819 (2); from Boca de
  Leones, Apr. 22, 1820.
García, Fr. Diego Martín
  Breve y legal noticia de las calidades y costumbres de los
  indios: metodo que han de observar. . . . Año de 1745. Bolton
  had a typewritten transcript, and Castañeda used a photostatic
  copy of the latter. This work describes the customs of the
  Texas Indians and the method employed by the missionaries to
  Christianize them.

Guadiana, Capt. José María, of Nacogdoches, to Gov. Múñoz, May 9, 1797, *BA*.

Gutiérrez, Gabriel, Factor de Abilitacion, Béxar, to Gov. Múñoz, Aug. 29, 1794-Oct. 25, 1794. *BA*.

Hernandes, José from Mission Concepción, to Benito Hernular, Mar. 13, 1814.

Herrera, José, Justicia de San José, Lista de las Raciones dadas a los Indios del Pueblo de S.or S.n José desde lo de Octubre de 1794 hasta 3 de D.re del mismo (15 pp). *BA*.

Huerta de Jesus, Fr. José Maria, 4 letters, 1804-1810, *BA:* to Gov. Elguezábal, from Refugio Mission, Aug. 26, 1804; to Gov. Cordero, from Refugio Mission, Feb. 15, 1807; to Gov. Salcedo, from Nacogdoches, May 3, 1810; from Béxar, Jul. 23, 1810.

Huisar, José Antonio, Spanish Alcalde of San José, to Gov. Martínez, 5 letters, *BA:* from San José and Espada, Dec. 28, 1817, & Mar. 22, 1818; from Concepción, Apr. 16, 1818; from San José, Jul. 3, & Jul. 7, 1818.

Jaudenes, Fr. José Francisco, 23 letters, 1791-1797, *BA:* to Gov. Múñoz, from Rosario Mission, Mar. 4 & 11, 1791; from La Bahía, Apr. 7, 1791; from Rosario, Jul. 20, Aug. 1, Sept. 9, Oct. 13, Oct. 21, Nov. 1, Nov. 5, Nov. 30, Dec. 2, 1791; to Sierra Gorda, from Rosario, Je. 4, 1792; to Gov. Múñoz, from Rosario, Oct. 19 & Oct. 24, 1792; Jan. 19 & Feb. 20, 1793; to Comandante Nava, from Rosario, Nov. 17, 1793; to Capt. Vásquez, from Rosario, Aug. 11, 1794; to Gov. Múñoz, from Rosario, Sept. 26, 1794; Sept. 9, 1796; Oct. 23, 1796; to Capt. Cortes, from Rosario, Apr. 5, 1797.

Lanuza, Fr. Ignacio María
Letters to Gov. Ripperdá, from San José, Aug. 2 & 4, 1771. *AGN, Prov. Int.,* vol. 100, pt. 1, pp. 206 & 193-196.

León, Tomás de, Spanish Alcalde of San José, to Gov. Martinez, Dec. 13, 1819. *BA*.

Lista de Religiosos Ap.cos de N.ra S.ra de Guadalupe de Zacatecas. . . . 1797. *ACZ*. Partially transcribed by Oberste, *History of Refugio Mission,* Appendix, p. 385.

López, Fr. José Francisco, 5 letters, 1789-1794, *BA:* to Gov. Martínez Pacheco, from Mission San Antonio, Nov. 14, 1789; to Gov. Múñoz, from San Antonio, Nov. 14, 1789 and Apr. 11, 1793; from San Fernando Parish Church, Dec. 31, 1793; Jan. 4, 1794.

Margil, Fr. Antonio
Letter, to the Marqués de Aguayo, from Mission San Antonio,
Dec. 26, 1719. *AGI* (see Aguayo).
Marmolejo, Fr. Ildefonso Joseph, & Fr. Juan Cipriano Martínez
Testimonial concerning eastern Texas, June 17, 1737. *AGN*,
Hist., vol. 524, pt. 3, pp. 725-729.
Marmolejo, Fr. Yldephonzo Joseph
Letter to Capt. Ortiz Parilla et al., from San José, Jan. 6, 1757.
Transcript in *CA*, 5 pp. The author has a copy.
Martínez Pacheco, Capt. Rafael
Ynforme echo al Ex.mo Senor Virrey por el Capitan Pacheco,
Nov. 8, 1772. *AGI, Aud. de Guad.*, 104-6-20. Dunn Transc.,
1767-1772, pp. 121-129, in U. of Tex. Libr.
Martínez, Gov. Antonio, to Spanish Alcaldes of San José, Capistra-
no, and Espada, Jan. 28, 1820. *BA.*
Massanet, Fr. Damian
Letter to the viceroy, June 14, 1693. *AGI, Aud. de Guad.*, 67-4-
11. Dunn Transc., 1694, pp. 61-68, in U. of Tex. Libr. Letter
to the viceroy, Feb. 17, 1694, in Prosiguen los autos de la
retirada de los religiosos misioneros. *AGI, Aud. de Guad.*, 67-4-
11. Photostat in St. Edward's Univ. Libr., Austin.
Menchaca, Capt. Luís Antonio
Report to the viceroy, May 11, 1763, in Testimonio de los
autos formados a representación de Don Toribio de Urrutia.
AGI, Aud. de Mex., 92-6-22. Dunn Transc., 1748-1763, pt. 2,
pp. 191-204, in U. of Tex. Libr.
Morfi, Fr. Juan Agustín
Provincias de los Tejas o Nuevas Filipinas. Plano que manifiesta
el numero de Vasallos que tiene el Rey en esta Provincia . . .
Chihuahua, 26 de Septiembre de 1778. El Caballero de Croix.
DRT Libr.
Muro, Fr. Miguel, 20 letters, 1820-1824, *BA:* to Gov. Martínez,
from San José, Feb. 10, Mar. 12, & Mar. 13, 1820; to Gov.
Martínez, from Refugio, Apr. 14 & May 18, 1820; Jan. 20 &
Feb. 16, 1821; to Gov. Martínez, from La Bahía, Mar. 17,
1821; to Gov. Martínez, from Refugio, May 12, 1821; to
Guadalupe de los Santos, from Refugio, Je. 16, 1821; to Gov.
Martínez, from Refugio, Je. 18, Jul. 8, Jul. 20, & Oct. 24, 1821;
to Gov. Martínez, from La Bahía, Nov. 23, 1821; to Gov.
Martínez, from Refugio, Jan. 15, 1822; to Fr. Antonio Anzar,
from Refugio, Feb. 12, 1822; to Gov. Martínez, from Béxar,
Apr. 6, 1822; to Fr. Díaz de León, from La Bahía, Mar. 12,

1824; to Political Chief Saucedo, from La Bahía, Mar. 31, 1824.

Navarro, Angel

Expediente promovido por D.n Angel Navarro s.bre cantidad de pesos que demanda a la Mis.on de S.n Josse. Ano de 1795 (Apr. 21, 1795-Jan. 15, 1796). *BA.*

Noreña, Fr. Pedro, 4 letters to Gov. Múñoz, from Espada, 1791-1799, *BA:* Jul. 7, 1791; Je. 1, 1792; Dec. 31, 1793; Jan. 1. 1799.

Nuestra Señora de la Purísima Concepción de los Aynais Mission, Auto de fundación, Aug. 8, 1721. *AGI, Aud. de Mex.,* 61-2-2. Dunn Transc., 1713-1722, in U. of Tex. Libr.

Nuestra Señora de la Purísima Concepción de Acuña,

Libro de Casamientos de Esta Missión de la Purísima Concepción Pueblo de Acuña, 1733-1790, *ASFC.* Ynventario de los bienes de Temporalidad de la Misión de la Purísima Concepción. Año de 1794. *SA.* Cast. Photost., vol. 6, in U. of Tex. Libr.

Núñez de Haro, Fr. Miguel

Testimony given at San Antonio de Valero, Je. 14, 1724. *AGN, Prov. Int.,* vol. 32, pt. 2.

Olivares, Fr. Antonio de San Buenaventura

Seven memorials addressed to the viceroy in 1716: *AGI, Aud. de Mex.,* 61-6-35; Dunn Transcr., Gulf Region, 1713-1721, pp. 169-177, 210-214, in U. of Tex. Libr. (four memorials). *AGN, Prov. Int.,* vol. 181, pt. 1, pp. 131-134, 214 (two memorials). *ASFG* in *BN;* Cast. Photost. vol. 8 in U. of Tex. Libr. (one memorial). Letter to Francisco Antonio Solorzano, Je. 5, 1717. *AGI, Aud. de Mex.,* 61-6-35. Dunn Transcr., 1713-1721, pp. 18-19, in U. of Tex. Libr. Letter to Alarcón, Je. 5, 1717. *AGI, Aud. de Mex.,* 61-6-35. Dunn Transcr., 1713-1721, pp. 19-22, in U. of Tex. Libr. Letter to the viceroy, Je. 22, 1718. *ASFG* in *BN.* Cast. Photost., vol. 8, pp. 205-212, in U. of Tex. Libr. Oposición a la fundación de la Missión de San Joseph del rio de San Antonio, año de 1720. *ACQ.* Dunn Transcr., 1716-1749, in U. of Tex. Libr. A petition, signed by Fr. Olivares and the alcalde and cabildo of Béxar, addressed to Capt. Juan Valdez, Feb. 23, 1720.

Ortiz, Fr. Francisco Xavier

Visita de las misiones . . . 1745. *ACQ.* Dunn Transcr., 1729-1758, pp. 7-41, in U. of Tex. Libr. Questions for the examination of witnesses, June 22, 1745. *ASFG* in *BN.* Cast. Photost., vol. 3, pp. 80-82, in U. of Tex. Libr.

Palacio, Fr. Luís del Refugio de
Provincias y Colegios de los PP. Franciscanos en Mexico, Zapopan, 9 de Marzo de 1936. Ms. of 65 pages in the possession of the author.

Patrón y Guzmán, Fr. Agustín
Letter to Aguayo, Apr. 8, 1722. *AGI, Aud. de Guad.*, 67-3-11. Dunn Transcr., 1710-1738, in the U. of Tex. Libr.

Pedrajo, Fr. José Manuel, 9 letters, 1791-1795, *BA:* to Gov. Múñoz, from San José, May 8 & Je. 8, 1791; Aug. 28, Sept. 10, & Dec. 3, 1793; Je. 14 & Je. 15, 1794; to Gov. Múñoz, from Béxar, Je. 12, 1795; to Gov. Múñoz, from Refugio, Je. 28, 1795. Relación de las cantidades que debe la Misión de S.or San José, San Antonio de Béxar, Je. 5, 1795, on fol. 7r of Navarro, Expediente (see above). *BA.* Relación de lo que adeudan a este Mission de S.or S.n José, Je. 5, 1795. *SA.* Cast. Photost., vol. 6, pp. 209-214, in U. of Tex. Libr.

Puelles, Fr. José M., 11 letters, 1797-1818, *BA:* to Gov. Múñoz, from Rosario Mission, Nov. 6, 1797; to Gov. Elguezábal, from Nacogdoches, Nov. 30, 1803; Je. 4, 1804; Sept. 17 & Dec. 4, 1805; to Gov. Cordero, from Nacogdoches, Je. 4, 1807; to F. Viana, from Nacogdoches, Je. 25 & Jul. 26, 1807; to Gov. Cordero, from San José, Aug. 18, 1807; from Zacatecas, Mar. 8, 1809; to Gov. Martínez, from Zacatecas, Nov. 19, 1818. A facsimile of one of Fr. Puelles' letters is in E. W. Winkler, *Manuscript Letters and Documents of Early Texans, 1821-1845*, p. 72. Mapa geografica de las provincias septentrionales de esta Nueva Espana, 1807. (The author has not been able to locate the map.)

Ramírez de Arellano, Fr. Pedro
Testimony concerning eastern Texas missions, Nov. 6, 1751. *ASFG* in *BN.* Cast. Photost. vol. 14, pp. 95-99, in U. of Tex. Libr. Letter to Gov. Ripperdá, from San José, Jul. 6, 1776. *BA.* Letter to Teodoro de Croix, Apr. 27, 1777. *AGN Hist.*, vol. 51, pp. 359-365. Letter to Gov. Cabello, Jan. (Mar. ?) 22, 1778. *AGN Hist.*, vol. 51, pp. 410-411.

Reyes, Fr. José Mariano, 7 letters, 1788-1791, *BA:* to Gov. Martínez Pacheco, from Capistrano Mission, Sept. 13, 1788; to all officials in behalf of Indians going to Mexico, May 1, 1790; to Gov. Múñoz, from Rosario, Nov. 18, Dec. 23, & Dec. 29, 1790; Jan. 1, 1791; from Zacatecas, Je. 14, 1791.

Ripperdá, Gov., to Fr. Lanuza at San José, Aug. 1 & 3. *AGN, Prov. Int.*, vol. 100, pt. 1, pp. 202-204 and 206-207.

Rivera, Brig. Gen.Pedro de
Proyecto mandado . . . la Visita hecho por el Brigadier D.n Pedro de Rivera, Mar. 23, 1728. *AGN, Prov. Int.*, vol. 29. Copy in *ASFG* in *BN;* Cast. Photost., vol. 2, pp. 11-253. Letter to the viceroy, Sept. 30, 1730. *AGN, Prov. Int.*, vol. 236, pt. 1, pp. 54-57.
Roxo, Fr. José Mariano, to Gov. Múñoz, from San José, Je. 23 & Nov. 29, 1791. *BA*.
Saenz, Fr. José María, to Gov. Múñoz, Apr. 7, 1796; to Gov. Salcedo, from Zacatecas, Jul. 21, 1810. *BA*.
San Antonio Conservation Society Records, San Antonio, Tex.
San Antonio de Valero Mission
Libro de Bautismos, 1703-1783. *ASFC*.
Libro de Casamientos, 1709-1825. *ASFC*.
Libro de Entierros, 1703-1782. *ASFC*.
San Francisco de la Espada Mission
Ynventario de los bienes de Temporalidad de la Misión de Sn. Fran.co. de la Espada. Año de 1794. *SA*. Cast. Photost., vol. 6, in the U. of Tex. Libr. Four record books of Espada Mission: (1) Funerals, 1876-1907, & Marriages, 1876-1906; (2) Book A. Baptisms, Marriages, Funerals, Confirmations, 1873-1876; (3) Book B. Baptisms, 1875-1907; (4) Book C. Baptisms, 1908-1932. All, except Book C, are the records of Father Bouchu.
San Francisco de los Neches Mission
Auto de fundación, Aug. 5, 1721. *AGI, Aud. de Mex.*, 61-2-2. Dunn Transcr., 1713-1722, in the U. of Tex. Libr.
San Francisco Solano Mission
Auto de fundación. *AGN, Prov. Int.* vol. 28, pp. 70-77.
San Francisco Xavier de Nájera Mission
Auto de posesión, Mar. 12, 1722. *AGI, Aud. de Guad.*, 67-3-11. Dunn Transcr., 1710-1738, in the U. of Tex. Libr.
San José y San Miguel de Aguayo Mission
Testimonio de la possessión y Missión de San Joseph. *AGI, Aud. de. Guad.*, 67-3-11. Dunn Transcr., 1710-1738, in the U. of Tex. Libr. Ynventario de los bienes de Temporalidad de la Misión de S. S. José. Año de 1794. *SA*. Cast. Photost. in the U. of Tex. Libr. Copy in *CA*. Libro de Bautismos, Casamientos, y Entierros perteneciente a la Missión de Señor San Josef, 1777-1824. *ASFC*.
San José de los Nazonis Mission
Auto de fundación, Aug. 13, 1721. *AGI, Aud.de Mex.*, 61-2-2. Dunn Transcr., 1713-1722, in the U. of Tex. Libr.

San José y Santiago del Alamo Pueblo
 Libro en que se asient.n los Batismos del Pueblo de San Josef y
 Santiago del Alamo, 1788-1825. *ASFC.*
San José Mission Friary, Archives and Chronicle (since 1931).
San Juan Capistrano Mission
 Ynventario de los bienes de temporalidad de la Misión de S.n
 Juan Capistrano. Ano de 1794. *SA.* Cast. Photost. in the Univ.
 of Texas Libr.
Sevillano de Paredes, Fr. Miguel
 Representación . . . Presidente de las Miss. del Rio Grande al
 Muy Reu.o Padre Fray Pedro Mezquía (Guardian of
 Querétaro College), Jan. 1726. *ACQ.* Dunn Transcr., 1716-
 1749, in the U. of Tex. Libr. Representación, to the King, Aug.
 25, 1728. *AGI.* Aud. *de Mex.*, 62-2-29. Dunn Transcr., 1723-
 1729, in the U. of Tex. Libr.
Sosa, Fr. Mariano, 7 letters, 1805-1811, *BA:*
 to Gov. Cordero, from Nacogdoches, Dec. 4, 1805; to Gov.
 Salcedo, from Villa Salcedo, May 1, 1810; from Nacogdoches,
 May 3, May 12, & May 26, 1810; Je. 4, 1811; to the Junta,
 from Nacogdoches, Je. 4, 1811.
State of the Missions of the College of Zacatecas in Texas, Jul. 30,
 1802. *AGN, Prov. Int.*, Misiones 13, p. 286. Ramsdell Trans-
 cripts, cited by Oberste, *History of Refugio Mission*, Appendix,
 p. 385.
Tamarón, Pedro, Bishop of Durango
 Noticia general y descripción . . . 1759-1765, *AGI, Aud. de
 Guad.*, 104-7-30. Dunn Transcr., pp. 246-254, in the U. of
 Tex. Libr.
Urrutia, Capt. Toribio, to the viceroy, Dec. 17, 1740. *AGN, Prov.
 Int.*, vol. 32, pp. 89-98.
Vallejo, Fr. Bernardino, 24 letters, 1760-1816, *BA:* to Gov. Martos
 y Navarrete, from Nacogdoches, Je. 10, 1760; to Capt. Gua-
 diana, from Nacogdoches, Feb. 20, 1797; to Gov. Elguezábal,
 from San José, Apr. 19 & Aug. 26, 1803; to Gov. Cordero,
 from San José, Jul. 1 & Dec. 13, 1806; Dec. 4, 1807 (2); Jul.
 18, 1808 (4); to Gov. Salcedo, from San José, Dec. 11, 1808;
 Jan. 12, 1809; Jul. 21 (2), Aug. 8, Oct. 29, & Nov. 5, 1810; to
 Juan Maria Sambrana, from San José, Mar. 5, 1811; to Gov.
 Herrera, from San José, Oct. 5, 1811; to Gov. Salcedo, from
 San José, Jan. 6, 1812; to Gov. Armiñan, from San José, Feb.
 11, 1815; to Gov. Pérez, from Zacatecas, Je. 6, 1816; Reports
 on the Texas missions, Aug. 26, 1803; Dec. 31, 1804; Jan. 16,

1806. *BA.* Report on the Texas missions, Feb. 11, 1815. *SAT & NA.*

Varela, Gov. Mariano, to the Spanish Alcaldes of San José, Capistrano, and Espada, from Béxar, May 31, 1816. *BA.*

Valverde, Fr. Acisclos
to the viceroy, Jan. 18, 1764. *ASFG* in *BN.* Cast. Photost., vol. 13, pp. 97-101; to Gov. Ripperdá, Sept. 3, 1770. *AGN, Prov Int.,* vol. 100, pt. 1, pp. 68-69.

Vergara, Fr. Gabriel de, et al. Representación de los Religiosos . . . July 20, 1729. (Protest against the suppression of the Presidio de los Tejas, signed by the following six missionaries in the east Texas missions: Fr. Gabriel de Vergara, Presidente, Fr. Joseph Andrés Rodríguez de Jesus María, Fr. Juan Bautista Garzía de Suarez, Fr. Alonso Giraldo de Terreros, Fr. Manuel de Ortúño, and Fr. Joseph de San Antonio y Estrada.) *ASFG* in *BN.* Cast. Photost., vol. 3, pp. 4-6.

Viana, Fr. Mariano Francisco de los Dolores y
35 memorials, reports, and letters, now in various archives (*AGI, Aud. de Mex.; AGN, Hist.; ASFG* in *BN; ACQ;* & *NA),* listed by Castañeda, *Our Cath. Heritage in Tex.,* III, 420-421, & IV, 365. Report on the murder of Fr. Ganzabal, "Escrito de Indicios—1752." *ACQ.* A duplicate eighteenth-century copy of this 14-page document is in the possession of the author.

Ysasmendi (Isasi Isasmendi), Fr. Pedro de
Letter to Fr. Sevillano, from Espada, Jan. 11, 1737. *AGN, Misiones,* vol. 21, pt. 1, pp. 172-174. Report concerning Espada Mission, Feb. 23, 1739. *NA,* vol. 1, pp. 47-48.

To this list of manuscript sources may be added the following unpublished material:

Batz, Richard. *The Acquisition and Restoration of the San José Mission Granary by the San Antonio Conservation Society, 1924-1933.* Dissertation of 39 pp., submitted in partial fulfillment for the requirements of Historical Methods, Dr. Donald Everett professor. Copy in the archives of the San Antonio Conservation Society, San Antonio, Texas. Contains transcripts and translations of ten letters in the *BA,* 1806-1824, pertaining to the acquisition and ownership of San José Mission's granary by José Antonio Huisar.

Camiade, E. B. *Development of the Texas State Park System* (1923-1963). 4 pp., mimeographed. From the Texas State Parks and Wildlife Department.

Czibesz, P. L. *Unknown Facts about Technical History in San Antonio.* Mimeographed paper, San Antonio, 1955. Copy at Mission San José.

Historic American Buildings Survey (more than 26,000 sheets of drawings of floor plans, elevations, details, and 30,000 photographs, made in 1934-1936, as WPA Official Project no. 265-6907) in the custody of the Library of Congress, Prints and Photographs Division. A catalog with 6,000 entries, *Measured Drawings and Photographs of the Survey,* was printed in Washington, 1941. The collection contains 15 photos of the Alamo (Mission San Antonio de Valero), 33 photos and 6 sheets of drawings of San José, 14 photos and 5 sheets of Concepción, 20 photos and 4 sheets of Espada, and 17 photos and 2 sheets of Capistrano. Copies can be obtained from the Chief, Photo-duplication Service, Library of Congress.

Prospectus of a Plan for the Restoration of Mission San Juan Capistrano, San Antonio, Texas. A copy at Mission San José.

Rotchford, W. P., et al. Map of the *acequias* and farm lands of the Presidio of San Antonio de Béxar, the town of San Fernando, and the five San Antonio missions. Project of the Texas CWA. The map is now at Mission San José.

Schuchard, Ernst F. *Fresco Paintings of the Missions* (San Antonio, 1935) and *The Old Mill at Mission San José.* Two papers, of which mimeographed copies are at Mission San José.

Smith, H. P. Plan of Mission San Francisco de la Espada. A drawing at Espada Mission.

II. PRINTED SOURCES

Aguayo, Marqués de. The entire *expediente* of the expedition of Aguayo into Texas, 1721-1722, which is in *AGN, Hist.,* vol. 27, was printed in the *Boletin* of AGN, vols. 28-29. Mexico, 1957-1958.

Alarcón, Martín de. The appointment of Alarcón as governor of Texas, and the instructions issued to him for the expedition into Texas, 1718-1719, appeared in *Boletin* of AGN, vol. 6, pp. 530-540. Mexico, 1935.

Alcocer, Fr. José Antonio. *Bosquejo de la Historia del Colegio de Nuestra Señora de Guadalupe y sus Misiones. Año de 1788.* Introducción, bibliografia, acotaciones e ilustraciones del R. P. Fr. Rafael Cervantes, O.F.M. Mexico, 1958. On pp. 50-52, Fr.

Cervantes presents a list of the principal documents still preserved in the Archivo del Colegio de Zacatecas.

Arlegui, Fr. José de. *Crónica de la Provincia de Nuestro Padre San Francisco de Zacatecas.* 1st edn., Mexico, 1737. 2nd edn., Mexico, 1851.

Arricivita, Fr. Domingo. *Crónica Serafica y Apostolica del Colegio de Propaganda Fide de la Santa Cruz de Querétaro en la Nueva España.* Mexico, 1792.

Barrios y Jáuregui, Jacinto. Informe del gobernador sobre la misión de San José, May 28, 1758. *ASFG* in *BN;* Cast. Photost., vol. 12, pp. 59-62. Translation by Castañeda in Ilg, *San José, Queen of the Missions,* pp. 65-66.

Bolton, H. E. *Athanase de Méziéres and the Louisiana-Texas Frontier, 1768-1780.* 2 vols. Cleveland, 1914.

——————————. *Spanish Exploration in the Southwest, 1542-1706* (Original Narratives of Early American History). New York, 1916.

Bringas de Manzaneda y Encinas, Fr. Diego Miguel. *Sermón que en las solemnes honras celebradas . . . dixo en la iglesia de dicho Colegio* (de Querétaro) *el 19 de julio de 1794. . . .* Printed at the time; reprinted, with another sermon, under the title: *Crónica Apostolica y Seraphica del Colegio de Propaganda Fide de la Santa Cruz de Querétaro . . . Tercera Parte.* Querétaro, 1960. Besides the sermons, the work contains biographical sketches of outstanding members of the College.

Céliz, Francisco. Comienza el diario derrotero . . . Martín de Alarcón, Apr. 9, 1718-Feb. 10, 1719. This diary of the Alarcón expedition, in *AGN,* was transcribed by Vito Alessio Robles and printed in *Universidad de Mexico,* V, nos. 25-26, & 27-28 (1932-1933). It was translated by Leo Fritz Hoffman: *Diary of the Alarcón Expedition into Texas, 1718-1719* (Quivira Society Publications, V). Los Angeles, 1935.

Chabot, F. C. *Indian Excerpts: Memorias for the History of the Province of Texas.* San Antonio, 1933.

Espinosa, Fr. Isidro Félix de. *The Espinosa-Olivares-Aguirre Expedition of 1709.* Translated by Gabriel Tous, in *Tex. Cath. Hist. Soc. Preliminary Studies,* I, no. 3. Austin, 1930.

——————————. Diario derrotero. . . . Año de 1716. *AGN, Prov. Int.,* vol. 181, pt. 1, pp. 95-121. Translated by Gabriel Tous: *Romón's Expedition: Espinosa's Diary of 1716,* in *Mid-America,* XII, no. 4 (April, 1930), and *Tex. Cath. Hist. Soc. Preliminary Studies,* I, no. 4 (Austin, 1930).

_____.*Crónica de los Colegios de Propaganda Fide de la Nueva España.* Mexico, 1746-1747. New edition, with Notes and Introduction by Lino G. Canedo, Washington, 1964. The Notes and Introduction of Fr. Canedo are a valuable contribution to the history of Texas.

Fernández de Santa Ana, Fr. Benito. Descripción de las misiones del Colegio de Santa Cruz de Querétaro en el Rio de San Antonio, Feb. 20, 1740. *ASFG* in *BN;* Cast. Photost., vol. 3, pp. 35-44. Copy in *AGN, Hist.,* vol. 28. Printed in Porrua Turanzas' *Documentos* (Colección Chimalistac, XII), pp. 303-312.

García, Fr. Bartholmé. *Manual para administrar los santos sacramentos de penitencia, eucharistia, extrema-unción, y matrimonio. . . .* Mexico, 1760. This manual in the Coahuiltecan language was used by the missionaries of the San Antonio missions. Copy in U. of Tex. Libr.

Hierro, Fr. Simón de. Report on the Zacatecan missions in Texas, 1762. *ACZ.* A part of this report, not pertaining to Texas, is in Sotomayor's *Historia del Colegio de Zacatecas* (1889 edn.), I, 187. A summary of the part about Mission San José is in Bolton's *Texas in the Middle Eighteenth Century,* pp. 99-100.

Lafora, Nicolás de. *Relación del Viaje a los Presidios Internos situados en la Frontera de la America Septentrional perteneciente al Rey de España.* With bibliography and notes by Vito Alessio Robles. Mexico, 1939.

León, Alonso de. Derrotero de la jornada que hizo el general Alonso de León para el descubrimiento de la Bahía del Espíritu Santo y población de los franceses: año de 1689. Printed in the *Boletin* of *AGN,* vol. 28 (1957), pp. 33-51. Translated by H. E. Bolton in *Spanish Explorations in the Southwest,* pp. 399-423; also by Elizabeth H. West in the *Quarterly* of the Tex. State Hist. Assoc., vol. 8, pp. 199-224.

_____. Testimonio de Autos. . . . *AGI, Aud. de Mex.,* 61-6-21; Dunn Transcr., 1688-1690, in the U. of Tex. Libr. Diary of the expedition of 1690 and related documents, e.g. Fr. Damián Massanet's letter to Carlos de Siguenza y Góngora. Translated by Bolton in *Spanish Exploration in the Southwest,* pp. 366 ff. Another translation by Ben Cuellar Ximenez, in *Gallant Outcasts,* pp. 208-219.

López, Fr. José Francisco. Razón e Ynforme que el Padre Presidente de las Misiones de la Provincia de Texas o Nuevas Filipinas remite . . . May 5, 1789. Copy in the Bancroft Library at Berkeley, Calif., and photostatic copy of this in the U. of Tex. Libr. English translation by J. Autry Dabbs, *The Texas Missions in 1785* (sic), in *Tex. Cath. Hist. Soc. Preliminary Studies*, III, no. 6 (Austin, 1940).

Maas, Otto. *Las Ordenes religiosas de España y la colonización de América en la segunda parte del siglo XVIII, Estadísticas y otros documentos.* 2 vols. Barcelona, 1918-1929.

—————————. *Viajes de misioneros franciscanos a la conquista del Nuevo Mexico. Documentos del Archivo General de Indias (Sevilla).* Sevilla, 1915.

Massanet, Fr. Damián. Carta á Don Carlos de Siguenza. See Alonso de León, Testimonio de Autos, above. Another translation of this letter, by Lila M. Cassis, is in the *Quarterly* of the Tex. State Hist. Assoc., II, no. 4 (Apr., 1899). See Terán de los Ríos, Diario, below.

Maverick, Mary A. *Memoirs of Mary A. Maverick*, arranged by Mary A. Maverick and her son Geo. Madison Maverick, edited by Rena Maverick Green. San Antonio, 1921.

Morfi, Fr. Juan Agustín. Historia de la Provincia de Texas . . . años 1673-1779. English translation, with biographical introduction and annotations by Carlos E. Castañeda: *History of Texas, 1673-1779, by Fray Juan Agustín Morfi* (Quivira Society Publications, VI), 2 vols. Albuquerque, 1935.

Ortiz, Fr. Francisco Xavier. *Razón de la Visita de las Misiones de San Xavier y de las de San Antonio de Valero en la Prov. y Governación de Texas, Maio de 1756.* Printed copy in Archivo del Museo, Mexico. Reprint of 75 copies for *Biblioteca de Historiadores Mexicanos* in 3 small vols. (42, 33, and 45 pp.) Mexico, 1955. Copy in DRT Libr. at the Alamo. The author has a Xerox copy of the latter. The part about Mission San Antonio de Valero, Spanish text and English translation, is in Schuetz, *Historic Background of the Mission San Antonio de Valero*, pp. 11-19.

Odin, Bishop J. M., Diary, 1861. In J. M. Kirwin, *Diamond Jubilee of the Diocese of Galveston.*

Parras, Fr. Pedro José. *Gobierno de los Regulares en América, ajustado a la voluntad del Rey.* 2 vols. Madrid, 1783.

Peña, Juan Antonio de la. *Derrotero de la Expedición en la Provincia de los Texas.* . . . Mexico, 1722. Reprinted in Porrua Turanzas' *Documentos* (Colección Chimalistac, XII), first pages. English translation by Peter P. Forrestal, *Peña's Diary of the*

Aguayo Expedition in *Tex. Cath. Hist. Soc. Preliminary Studies*, II, no. 7 (Austin, 1933).

Pérez de Mesquía, Fr. Pedro. *Mesquía Diary of the Alarcón Expedition into Texas, 1718*, translated by Fritz Leo Hoffman, in *Southwestern Historical Quarterly*, XLI (Jan. 1938).

Porrua Turanzas, José, y Enrique Porrua Venero, eds. *Documentos para la Historia eclesiastica y civil de la provincia de Texas o Nuevas Philipinas, 1720-1779* (Colección Chimalistac de libros y documentos acerca de Nueva España, XII). Madrid, 1961.

Ramón, Domingo. Derrotero pa. las misies. . . . Feb. 17, 1716. *ASFG* in *BN;* Cast. Photost., vol. 8, pp. 63-88, in the U. of Tex. Libr. Translated by Paul J. Foik, in *Tex. Cath. Hist. Soc. Preliminary Studies*, II, no. 5 (Austin, 1933).

Reglamento e instrucción para los presidios . . . Sept. 1772. Madrid, 1772.

Rivera, Pedro de. *Diario y derrotero de la caminado, visto, y obcervado.* . . . Guathemala, 1736. Photost. copy at the U. of Tex. Libr.

Solís, Fr. Gaspar José de. Diario . . . en la visita, 1767-1768. *AGN, Hist.*, vol. 27, pt. 2, pp. 235-334. English translation by Peter P. Forrestal: *The Solís Diary of 1767*, in *Tex. Cath. Hist. Soc. Preliminary Studies*, I, no. 6 (Austin, 1931). Another translation by Margaret Kenney Kress, in *Southwestern Historical Quarterly*, vol. 35, pp. 30-76.

Sotomayor, José Francisco. *Historia del Apostolico Colegio de nuestra Señora de Guadalupe de Zacatecas desde su fundación hasta neustros dias.* 1st edn., 1 vol., Zacatecas, 1874. 2nd edn., 2 vols., Zacatecas, 1889.

Tello, Fr. Antonio. *Libro Segundo de la Crónica Miscelanea en que se trata de la conquista espiritual y temporal de la Santa Provincia de Xalisco en el nuevo reino de la Galicia y Nueva Vizcaya y descubrimiento del Nuevo Mexico.* Guadalajara, 1891.

Terán de los Ríos, Domingo. Diario . . . ano 1691. *ASFG* in *BN;* Cast. Photost., vol. 9, pp. 71-113, in the U. of Tex. Libr. Translation of this and Fr. Massanet's diary of the same expedition, by Mattie Austin Hatcher, edited by Paul J. Folk: *The Expedition of Don Domingo Terán de los Ríos into Texas, 1691-1692*, in *Tex. Cath. Hist. Soc. Preliminary Studies*, II, no. 1, (Austin, 1932). A translation of Fr. Massanet's diary also in Ben Cuellar Ximenez, *Gallant Outcasts*, pp. 188-207.

Truxillo, Fr. Manuel M. *Exhortación pastoral.* . . . Madrid, 1786.

Vetancurt, Fr. Agustín de. *Crónica de la Provincia del Santo Evangelio de Mexico*. 1st edn., Mexico, 1698. 2nd edn., as *Biblioteca Historica de la Iberia*, IX, Mexico, 1871.

———. *Menologio Franciscano*. 1st edn., Mexico, 1690. 2nd edn., as *Biblioteca Historica de la Iberia*, X, Mexico, 1871.

Viana, Fr. Mariano Francisco de los Dolores y. Relación del Estado en que se hallan todas y cada una de las Misiones, en el año de 1762, dirigido al Mui Reverendo Padre Guardian Fray Francisco Xavier Ortiz, Mar. 6, 1762. *AGN, Hist.*, vol. 28, folios 162-183; and *AGI*. Printed in Porrua Turanzas' *Documentos* (Colección Chimalistac, XII), pp. 245-275. The part pertaining to Mission San Antonio de Valero, Spanish text and English translation, in Schuetz, *Historic Background of the Mission San Antonio de Valero*, pp. 19-27.

Winkler, E. W., ed. *Manuscript Letters and Documents of Early Texians, 1821-1845, in Facsimile, Folio Collection of Original Documents*. Austin, 1937.

III. PRINTED WORKS AND STUDIES

Aguillo López de Turiso, Fr. Jeronimo. *Las Misiones Franciscanas. Breve Reseña de las Misiones de la Orden Serafica. . . .* Barcelona, 1894.

Amador, E. *Bosque Historico de Zacatecas*. 2 vols. Zacatecas, 1892.

Bolton, H. E. *Texas in the Middle Eighteenth Century* (University of California Publications in History, III). Berkeley, 1915. New printing, New York, 1962.

———. *The Spanish Borderlands*, edited with introduction by John F. Bannon. Norman, Okla., 1964.

———. "The Mission as a Frontier Institution in the Spanish-American Colonies," in *The American Historical Review*, Oct. 1917.

Brooks, Jr., C. M. *Texas Missions: Their Romance and Architecture*. Dallas, 1936.

Buckley, E. C. "The Aguayo Expedition into Texas and Louisiana, 1719-1722," in *The Quarterly* of the Tex. State. Hist. Assoc., XV (1911), pp. 1-65.

Castañeda, C. E. *Our Catholic Heritage in Texas*. 7 vols. Austin, 1936-1958.

Chabot, F. C. *San Antonio and Its Beginnings*. San Antonio, 1931.

Civezza, Fr. Marcellino da. *Storia Universale delle Missioni Francescane*. 8 vols. (vol. 7 in 4 parts). Rome, Prato, Florence, 1857-1895.

_____. *Saggio de Bibliografia geografica, storica, etnografica sanfrancescana*. Prato, 1879.

Clark, R. C. *The Beginnings of Texas, 1684-1718* (U. of Tex Bulletin, no. 98). Austin, 1907.

Corner, W. *San Antonio de Béxar: A Guide and History*. San Antonio, 1890.

Cuellar Ximenez, B. *Gallant Outcasts*. San Antonio, 1963.

Drossaerts, A. J. *The Truth about the Burial of the Remains of the Alamo Heroes*. San Antonio, 1938.

Enciclopedia Universal Ilustrada Europeo-Americana. 70 vols. Espasa-Calpe, Barcelona, 1918-1920. Often called the "Espasa Encyclopedia."

Englehart, Z. "Missionary Labors of the Franciscans among the Early Days (Texas)," in *Franciscan Herald*, vols 2 to 5 (Chicago, 1914-1917).

Forrest, E. R. *Missions and Pueblos of the Old Southwest*. Cleveland, 1929.

Friedrichs, I. H. *History of Goliad*. Victoria, Tex., 1961.

Gilbert, M. J., ed. *Archdiocese of San Antonio, 1874-1949*. San Antonio, 1949.

Grimes, R. *Goliad 130 Years After (Refugio and Guadalupe Victoria), March 1836-1966*. Victoria, Tex., 1966.

Habig, M. A. *The Franciscan Père Marquette, a Critical Biography of Father Zénobe Membré, O.F.M., La Salle's Chaplain and Missionary Companion, 1645 (ca.)-1689, with maps and original narratives* (Franciscan Studies, XIII). New York, 1934.

_____. *Heroes of the Cross. An American Martyrology*. 3rd edn. Paterson, N. J.

_____ and F. B. Steck, *Man of Greatness, Father Junípero Serra*. Chicago, 1963.

Hallenbeck, C. *Alvar Núñez Cabeza de Vaca, the Journey and Route of the First European to Cross the Continent of North America, 1534-1536*. Glendale, Calif., 1938.

_____ and J. H. Williams. *Legends of the Spanish Southwest*. Glendale, Calif., 1938.

Harris, E. W. *San José Mission, Queen of the Missions*. 13th edn. San Antonio, 1942.

Heusinger, E. W. *Early Explorations and Mission Establishments in Texas*. San Antonio, 1936.

Hodge, F. W., ed. *Handbook of American Indians North of Mexico*. (Smithsonian Institution, Bureau of American Ethnology, Bulletin 30). 2 vols. Washington, 1907-1910. Vol. I, 2nd edn., New York, 1959.

Hoermann, A. S. *The Daughter of Tehuan, or Texas of the Past Century,* translated from the German by A. Braun. San Antonio, 1932.

Ilg, J. *San José, Queen of the Missions.* 5th edn. San Antonio, 1940.

Kirwin, J. M. *Diamond Jubilee, 1847-1922, of the Diocese of Galveston and St. Mary's Cathedral.* Galveston, 1922.

Lemmens, L. *Geschichte der Franziskanermissionen* (Missionswissenschaftliche Abhandlungen und Texte, XII). Muenster i. W., Germany, 1929.

McCaleb, W. F. *The Spanish Missions of Texas.* San Antonio, 1954 & 1961.

McCloskey, M. B. *The Formative Years of the Missionary College of Santa Cruz of Querétaro, 1683-1733.* Washington, 1955.

Oberste, W. H. *History of the Refugio Mission.* Refugio, Tex., 1942.

——————. *Remember Goliad.* 2nd edn. Austin, 1949.

O'Connor, K. S. *The Presidio La Bahía del Espíritu Santo de Zúñiga, 1721 to 1846.* Austin, 1966.

O'Rourke, T. P. *The Franciscan Missions in Texas, 1685-1897.* Washington, 1927.

Parisot, P. F., and C. J. Smith. *History of the Catholic Church in the Diocese of San Antonio, Texas, 1685-1897.* San Antonio, 1897.

Portillo, E. L. *Apuntes para la Historia Antigua de Coahuila y Texas.* Saltillo, Mexico, 1886.

Ramsdell, C. *San Antonio, A Historical and Pictorial Guide.* Austin, 1959.

Ríos, E. E. *Life of Fray Antonio Margil O.F.M.,* translated and revised by B. Leutenegger. Washington, 1959. Also condensed into a brochure by B. Leutenegger: *Antonio Margil, Apostle of America.* Chicago, 1959.

Robles, V. A. *Coahuila y Texas en la época colonial.* Mexico, 1938.

——————. *Coahuila y Texas desde la Consumación de la Independencia hasta el tratado de paz de Guadalupe Hidalgo.* 2 vols. Mexico, 1945 & 1946.

Roemer, F. von. *Roemer's Texas,* translated by O. Mueller. San Antonio, 1935. Reprint, Waco, 1967.

Santos, R. "A Preliminary Survey of the San Fernando Archives," in *Texas Libraries,* vol. 28, no. 4 (Winter, 1966-1967), pp. 152-172.

Saravia, A. G. *Los misioneros Muertos en el Norte de Nueva España.* Durango, Mexico, 1920.

Schmitz, J. W. *The Beginning of the Society of Mary in Texas, 1852-1866.* Reprint of article in *Mid-America,* vol. 25 (new series, vol. 14), no. 1 (Jan., 1943).

Schuetz, M. K. *Historic Background of the Mission San Antonio de Valero.* State Building Commission Archeological Program, Report No. 1, Nov. 1966.

Shea, J. G. *The Catholic Church in Colonial Days, 1521-1763* (A History of the Catholic Church within the Limits of the United States, I). New York, 1886.

Smith, H. P. *Romantic San Antonio* (16 pp.). San Antonio, 1918.

──────────. "Old Mill of San José Mission," in *Plaza Parade,* Sept. 1935, pp. 121-123.

Streit, R. *Der Letzte Franziskaner von Texas.* Duelmen i. W., Germany, 1907.

Sturmberg, R. *History of San Antonio and of the Early Days in Texas.* San Antonio, 1920.

Torrente, C. *Old and New San Fernando.* San Antonio, 1927.

Wantland, C. *History and Guide: The Five San Antonio Missions.* San Antonio, 1962.

Weddle, R. S. *The San Sabá Mission, Spanish Pivot in Texas.* Austin, 1964.

Winfrey, J., et al. *Six Missions of Texas.* Waco, 1965.

Winsor, J. ed. *Narrative and Critical History of America.* 8 vols. Boston, 1889.

Yoakum, H. *History of Texas from its First Settlement in 1685 to Its Annexation to the United States in 1846.* 2 vols. New York, 1856. Reprint, Austin, 1935.

Zavala, A. de. *History and Legends of the Alamo and the Other Missions.* San Antonio, 1917.

ACKNOWLEDGMENTS

To the many friends who have assisted the writer by advice, suggestions, information, and encouragement, the author is deeply indebted and expresses his gratitude more than words can convey. We can not name them all, but we are particularly indebted to the following (in alphabetical order):

Roy E. Appleman, Acting Chief Historian, United States Department of the Interior, National Park Service, Washington, D.C.

Miss Nettie Lee Benson, Librarian of the University of Texas Library, Austin.

Rev. Fr. Fidel Chauvet O.F.M. of Mexico City.

Brother Franklin Cullen C.S.G., Chief Librarian of St. Edward's University, Austin.

Pierson DeVries, Superintendent of San José Mission State and National Historic Site, San Antonio.

Dr. Tuffly L. Ellis, Assistant Director of the Texas State Historical Association, Austin.

Dr. Chester Kielman, Custodian of Latin American Manuscripts, University of Texas Library, Austin.

Rev. Fr. Benedict Lentenegger O.F.M. of the Academy of American Franciscan History, Washington, D.C.

Rev. Fr. Gaspar Meyer O.F.M., Assistant of San José Mission Parish, San Antonio.

Very Rev. Joseph Nuevo C.M.F., Pastor of San Fernando Cathedral, San Antonio.

Right Rev. Msgr. William H. Oberste, Pastor of Our Lady of Refuge Parish, Refugio.

Miss Carmen Perry, Librarian-Archivist of the Daughters of the Republic of Texas Library at the Alamo, San Antonio.

Richard G. Santos, Archivist of Bexar County, San Antonio.

Ernst F. Schuchard of San Antonio.

J. Dan Scurlock, former Director of Park Interpretation, Texas Parks and Wildlife Department, Austin.

Rev. Fr. Paul Smith O.F.M., Assistant Librarian of Quincy College, Quincy, Illinois.

Rev. Fr. Raymond Solano O.F.M. of Our Lady of Guadalupe Friary, Hebbronville.

Rev. Fr. Eustace Struckhoff O.F.M., Pastor of San José Mission Parish, San Antonio.

Mrs. Don F. Tobin, President of the San Antonio Conservation Society, San Antonio.

Robert M. Utley, Chief Historian, United States Department of the Interior, National Park Service, Washington, D.C.

A topical Index is contained in the detailed Table of Contents, and an alphabetical list of the missionaries of the San Antonio missions will be found in Chapter VIII.

ADDENDA AND CORRIGENDA

Further research and the discovery of hitherto unknown documents in the archives of the former Franciscan Apostolic College of Nuestra Señora de Guadalupe in the present Franciscan friary at Guadalupe near Zacatecas, Mexico (ACZ — see p. 274) enable us (at the present time, 1975) to make some corrections and to add some new information.

Page 37, line 7: The Fr. Joseph Guerra who accompanied the Alarcón expedition into Texas in 1718 was not the Fr. Joseph Guerra who served as the guardian of the College of Zacatecas in 1713-1717 (and continued to reside there until his death in 1729 at the age of 73) but a younger Franciscan of the same name. The latter was a member of the College of Querétaro, and as such represented Fr. Olivares at the founding of San José Mission in 1720 (page 84, line 3 from the bottom). The following year he accompanied Aguayo to east Texas and was placed in charge of the restored San Francisco Mission (cf. C. E. Castañeda, *Our Catholic Heritage in Texas,* II, 149-151).

Page 44, line 15: The document which records the transfer of San Antonio Mission from its second to its third and present site in 1724, after a hurricane had destroyed its primitive structures, is the report of Fr. Miguel Sevillano de Paredes of the College of Querétaro who officially inspected the reconstructed mission in October, 1724: "Visita de las Misiones del Rio Grande," AGN (see p. 274), Historia, vol. 29, pp. 35-41. Fr. Sevillano was the "Visitor" (inspector) of the Rio Grande or San Juan Bautista missions, which at this time included San Antonio de Valero in Texas and had a Fr. President distinct from the one in east Texas. In 1724, says Fr. Sevillano, San Antonio Mission had only a primitive church but had collected stone for a new one and the number of Indians in the mission

was 273 (cf. R.S. Weddle, *San Juan Bautista* (Austin, 1968),
pp. 173-174.

Page 59, line 28, and 256, line 10: Fr. Mariano de los
Dolores y Viana died at Mission San Antonio de Valero on
March 8, 1763. The "Libro de los Muertos," fol. 32v (ACQ),
has March 8, 1762; but the year 1762 is evidently an error. The
"Libro de los Difuntos," I, 87 (ACZ) mentions the fact that
the news of Fr. Mariano's death at San Antonio Mission was
received at the College of Zacatecas on March 18, 1764 (because of the distances involved it could well have been 1764,
not 1763). As the Fr. President of the Querétaran missions in
the San Antonio area, Fr. Mariano sent an important report to
the College on March 6, 1762 (see pp. 56, 134, 168, 212). The
meeting of the governors of Coahuila and Texas with Colonel
Parilla at the Presidio of San Antonio de Béxar, to which Fr.
Mariano submitted a memorial, took place in 1759, not 1769.
The latter date is a typographical error in Castañeda, *op. cit.*,
IV, 259-260, as one can conclude from the erroneous and the
correct date appearing in footnotes 1 and 2 on page 260.

Page 67, lines 16 and 26: The church of San Antonio
Mission (the present Alamo), still incomplete in 1793 when the
mission was suppressed, had a vaulted (not domed) roof (the
present roof was added by the U.S. Army's Quartermaster
Corps in 1847 — cf. page 72). Also the sacristy, which was
used as a church in 1793, had a vaulted (not domed) roof.

Page 101, diagram: The square of San José Mission had
bastions only at two of the corners, each of which had a view
of two sides of the square. These were at the southeast and the
northwest corners, and at the latter only until the granary was
enlarged and extended to the corner. At the northeast and southwest corners there were fortifications above the gates but no
elevated bastions.

Page 129, lines 13-15: A *fanega* was not a bushel (as
Castañeda translates the term) but the equivalent of 1.6 bushels.

On the farm of Purísima Concepción Mission in 1745, 5 *fanegas* of corn seed (8 bushels) produced 1,000 *fanegas* (1,600 bushels, not 800), and 1 *fanega* of beans (1.6 or 1-3/5 bushels) yielded 30 *fanegas* (48 bushels, not 24). The irrigation canal of Purísima Concepción (same page, line 24) continued from the mission compound in a southeasterly direction for about 1,250 *varas* (not yards). A *vara* was 33 inches, i.e. 2 feet, 9 inches, or 2-3/4 feet. The *legua* or league, used in New Spain — as most historians now agree — consisted of 5,000 *varas* or 2.6 (2-3/5) miles. However, the measurements of length mentioned in reports from the frontier are in many instances merely estimates.

Page 134, line 24: The sacristy of the church of Purísima Concepción in 1762 was (and is today) a large square room, measuring 12 x 12 *varas,* i.e. about 33 feet on each side, (not ca. 61).

Page 167, lines 25-26: The church of San Juan Capistrano in 1756 (the same as today with a few alterations) was 24 *varas* long (ca. 66 feet, not 80 feet) and 5-2/3 *varas* wide. In 1762, this church is described as being 25 *varas* long (ca. 69 feet, not 83). All the reports of San Juan Capistrano agree in stating that the ruins on the east side of the square are those of a "new" church, begun after 1759 but never completed during the mission period. By 1789 the project had been given up after "about one-half of the new church" had been built. This is confirmed by the last report (discovered only recently — copy in Old Spanish Missions Historical Research Library at San José Mission, abbreviated RLSJ), the inventory of the Church of San Juan Capistrano Mission prepared by Fr. Antonio Díaz de León in 1824. This church, says Fr. Díaz de León, was still the "iglesia antigua," the old church of 1756, a long narrow hall, 25 *varas* long (as in 1762) and 6 *varas* wide (6 this time instead of the 5-2/3 in 1756 and the 5-1/2 in 1759).

Page 211, lines 12-13: The church of San Francisco Mission in 1756 was 14 *varas* (ca. 39 feet) long and 5-1/3 *varas* (ca. 14-1/2 feet, not 15-1/2) wide.

Page 270: The statistics of Indians living in the five missions of the San Antonio area given for 1786 are those found in a census report which is in the Nacogdoches Archives. They do not agree with those in another report of the same year found in ACZ: 52 — 135 — 71 — 58 — 57; and the latter seem to be more accurate, indicating as they do that there was a steady decline in the number of mission Indians during the years from December, 1783, to December, 1788.

Pages 272-273: The first three Fr. Presidents of the Querétaran missions in Texas had jurisdiction only over three of the east Texas missions founded in 1716 and restored in 1721, and they resided at Purísima Concepción Mission. After these three missions were moved to the San Antonio area in 1731, the presidents resided either at Purísima Concepción or at San Antonio de Valero. Previously the latter, founded in 1718, had belonged to the "presidency" of the Rio Grande or San Juan Bautista missions. To the list of Querétaran presidents must be added the name of Fr. Juan Joseph Sáenz Gumiel who was the Fr. President in 1772 when the Querétaran missionaries surrendered their San Antonio missions to the Zacatecan missionaries who had San José Mission from the time of its founding by Fr. Antonio Margil in 1720. Fr. Benedict Leutenegger found the inventories prepared in 1772 by Fr. Sáenz Gumiel in ACZ, and copies are in RLSJ. Other documents from ACZ (copies in RLSJ) have also made it possible to revise completely the list of Zacatecan presidents in Texas. This new list will be found in B. Leutenegger and M. A. Habig, *The Zacatecan Missionaries in Texas, 1716-1834* (Texas Historical Survey Committee, Report number 23, Austin, 1973), p. 166. The "Biographical Dictionary" in this work (pp. 107-171) contains sketches of all the Zacatecan (not Querétaran) missionaries in Texas; and these are more complete and accurate than those which were offered — as a first attempt — in *The Alamo Chain of Missions,* pp. 234-256.